IT PUTS MUSCLES ON YOUR EYEBROWS

First Published in Great Britain 2013 by Mirador Publishing

First edition: 2013

A copy of this work is available through the British Library.

ISBN : 978-1-909220-11-9

Mirador Publishing
Mirador
Wearne Lane
Langport
Somerset
TA10 9HB

It Puts Muscles On Your Eyebrows

By

Mick Power

Mirador Publishing
www.miradorpublishing.com

Chapter One

Wednesday the twenty seventh of September, 1950 was a nice bright day; this would be my last day as a civilian. Both Bill and Fanny knew I was going to join the army that day but neither of them said goodbye or wished me luck before they had gone off to work. I'd spent the morning at Jack Yates's farm; he had wished me all the best and gave me a packet of twenty fags.

It was about two o'clock in the afternoon when I set off for Lichfield to start my military career. I caught the bus at the Fullbrook down to Walsall and then the bus to Lichfield from the old St Paul's bus station. I had been on this trip a few times with Dad to Lichfield Market in the days before he had a van. There was no bus for Tamworth in the Lichfield bus station so after waiting for some time I decided to walk to Whittington Barracks; it was only about three miles out of Lichfield half way between Lichfield and Tamworth.

It was nearly four o'clock when I got to the barracks gate and stopped from entering by a soldier on guard. He directed me just behind him to a small building where I was to report to, this was the Guard Room. Inside I found a smartly dressed Sergeant with white belt and gaiters and wearing a red sash. I was to learn later that he was the Provost Sergeant. I gave him the papers that I had been issued with at Wolverhampton and he checked that I had brought my identity card and ration book with me. He then got one of his men to take me round the square to a row of Victorian two story barrack blocks. I was taken into the middle block called Wrotesley. The room had about thirty beds with a small metal locker on the wall behind them. At the entrance was a small washhouse or ablutions as the army liked to call them. It had four sinks sunk into a black slate washstand and on the opposite side of the passage was a small room for the N.C.O's (none commissioned officers).

I was pointed to an empty bed which had three blankets, a pillow and a pair of sheets neatly stacked on top. They had been folded so one blanket was on the bottom then a sheet on top of it followed by the second blanket with a sheet on top of that. The third blanket was folded length wise and wrapped round the other sheets and blankets to form an edge with the neatly folded sheets and blankets showing. I was informed this was how I was to leave my bed when I got up in the morning. I was advised by the chap who had brought me there to undo it carefully when I made my bed. I would then remember how it was done when I got-up in the morning.

I wasn't the only one there, it was the joining up day for the National Service chaps as well as the Regulars and half the beds had already been taken and lads were still coming in until late.

At six o clock a Corporal who was in charge of us lined us up and lead us all down to the cookhouse for our evening meal. We were met at the door by a Sergeant in a white jacket who was in charge of the cookhouse and he told us the times of each meal. As we were trainees we would be the first sitting in the dinning room. Breakfast would be at seven in the morning; lunch at twelve thirty and evening meal six o clock, anyone coming after these times would not be served. The Corporal then took us into the dinning room which was attached to the cookhouse; it was a large single story place with three rows of trestle tables and benches to sit on. We were sat six to a table and told to remember exactly were we sat as we would sit in the same place for each meal. The Corporal then gave us a knife, fork and spoon all clipped together plus a large white mug and told us we must keep them safe as these were eating implements, if we lost or broke the mug it would cost us one and three pence to get another one.

At the front of the cookhouse was a metal counter with the food containers or dixie as the army called them, lined up on it. At the start of the line was a stack of white platter plates, we each took one and has we moved along the line of dixie's a scoop of what ever was in them got bunged on our plates. Mashed potatoes first then a scoop of carrots then a slice of pie, some sort of braised meat with pastry on it. Next was a stack of thick platter dishes, we had to hang our mugs on one finger before we could pick one of these up. On to the end two dixie's and got given a knob of sponge pudding and a scoop of custard. When we got back in the dinning hall there was a bucket of tea on the front table, you just dipped your mug in.

One or two of the chaps did a bit of muttering, it wasn't like their Mothers cooking, but I thought it was alright and soon got it down me.

It had been cooked by the trainee cooks of the Army Catering Corps or (The Andy Clyde Commando's) as we came to call them. Whittington Barracks was a training centre for them as well as the Infantry.

2

After our meal we all went back to the barrack room to find a couple more recruits had turned up while we were having our meal and more continued to come until after lights out.

The Corporal who seemed to be in charge told us where we could find the N.A.A.F.I (Navy Army & Air Force Institutes). We could buy tea, cakes and cigarettes etc from there.

There was a barrack room full of lads and we were all about the same age except for a few who were aged twenty-one. Their call-up had been deferred until they were finishing their apprenticeships.

Recruits came from all over the west of the country, some from as far away as Liverpool, a lot from the Stoke on Trent area and a few local lads. One lad, John Rudd was from Hartlepool; he was a regular like me and had joined the Stafford's because his brother was serving with them those who had the money went down the N.A.A.F.I. but most of us just sat around talking. At about eight thirty a Sergeant wearing a red sash came in the room accompanied by the Corporal, he was the Duty Sergeant. He said lights out would be at ten o'clock and reveille would be sounded by the duty bugler in the morning at six thirty. We would hear him alright as he would sound reveille on the barracks square right outside our window. The Corporal went on to say that we must be washed, shaved, our beds made up and our breakfast had by seven thirty.

For most of us it was our first night away from home and I could see one or two of the chaps were a little upset. But this was National Service and it was the same for thousands of eighteen year olds, so those who didn't like it would just have to lump it.

I think most of us slept through the night, I know I did. We heard the Bugler but didn't need him since as soon as he had finished the last note the Corporal was in the Barrack room.

The washroom was a bit of a bottle neck as there were only four sinks for all of us. Things got better once we had the hang of things; some would go for breakfast first then have a wash and shave.

Breakfast wasn't too bad; a sausage, fried breads, a fried egg, you got a bit of bacon about the size of a bus ticket and a bowl of porridge.

The blanket folding was the difficult bit but most of us made a passable job of it; we would soon get it right with practice. The corporal made a couple of the chaps do it again, I didn't think they were that bad but it was probably just to show who was in charge.

Just after seven thirty an Officer and a Sergeant came and called us all together. The Officer informed us that we would be in B Company and he was Captain Goodchild, the second in command of the company. We were the Mercian Brigade and Whittington was their training camp. When our training had been completed we would be posted to any of the four regiments in the Brigade. The South Stafford's who were serving in Hong Kong; North Stafford's serving in Trieste, Cheshire Regiment in Egypt and the Worcestershire Regiment in Malaya. The Officer then introduced Sergeant Baker and by the look of all the medal ribbons on his battle dress, he had been in the army a few years. Along with Corporal Shaw he was to be our platoon sergeant for our ten weeks of basic training.

Sergeant Baker then said we would now get our kit and got us all lined up formed into three rows on the road outside the barrack room. He then marched us over to a large castle like building by the main gate. We were met by a large man and the Sergeant introduced him as the Q.M.S (Quarter Master Sergeant), a warrant officer who was in charge of all stores.

We were then lined up in single file at the stores door, the Sergeant and Corporal sorting us out into small first and tallest last.

We went into the store one at a time to a long counter with the store men standing behind it. The first thing we were given was a kitbag and told to put everything we got into it. Next you were asked your shoe size and that got you two pairs of boots and a pair of plimsolls. On down the counter with the men behind it handing out your kit…

Battle dress sizes were a bit more difficult as a lot of the lads didn't know what size they were. The store man behind the counter had been doing the job for years so he knew what size they needed and we got two of these and the trousers. On to four khaki shirts, a pullover, three under vests and pants, or as the army called them 'draws cellular', four pairs of socks and a pair of navy blue shorts, another vest (some got a T shirt) our P.T. kit. Two berets came next followed by a neck tie, three towels and a 'housewife;' (a little cloth bag with needles, darning wool and some cotton). The overcoat or 'greatcoat' as the store man called it was our last item of clothing, we were told not to stuff it in our kitbag but carry it over our arm. Our last call at the end of the counter was to collect two boot cleaning brushes and a button stick with a little

4

brush, (the button stick was a piece of brass plate with a slot in it). This allowed you to clean the brass buttons on your coat with the little brush without getting the polish on the cloth.

As we came out of the store the Corporal lined us up to wait for the rest of the platoon to collect their kit and come through. It didn't take long; the store men had done it many times before.

The last man to come out was the tallest, he was six foot three and they didn't have a battle dress big enough for him but he had everything else.

We were told to put our kitbags on our right shoulder and our overcoats on our left arm before being marched back to our barracks.

When we got into the barrack room we were told to put our kit on the bed and 'get fell in.' We went outside again but at the back not out the front of the barrack block.

The Sergeant informed us we were now going to B Company stores where we would collect a denim uniform and this would be our normal dress while we were in camp. The stores were directly behind our barrack block in a two story building with the stores on the ground floor and the company office above. Sergeant Baker pointed out to us the Sergeant who was in charge of B Company stores was a Colour-Sergeant and he had a little crown above the three stripes on his arm.

It was the smallest men first again and as we got our uniform and as we came out the Corporal told us to go back to the barrack room and get changed into our army denim uniforms and boots. Every one thought if they didn't have a battle dress to fit Lofty they wouldn't have a denim one either, but they found one to fit him.

The sergeant gave us half an hour to get our kit on and get fell in at the back of the block again. We were then marched down past the dinning room to a large wooden hut, the barbers shop. Sent in three at a time, there were three barbers working and they didn't mess about. They just ran the clippers up the side of your head and left you with tuft of hair on top. It gave short back and sides a new meaning. You could see some of the lads coming out were close to tears and the vainer of us waiting outside were traumatised by the shortness of the hair cut.

We were marched back to our barracks and now it was getting close to our lunch time the Corporal said he would show us how we were to fold our kit and display it in our lockers. The battle dresses together with the overcoat had to be hung up at the back of our beds on the row of hangers below the locker.

We were shown how our kit should be put in our lockers so every

5

one looked the same. Two of the towels folded, the one in use folded length wise and put over the rail at the foot of the bed with boots and plimsolls below on the floor.

The corporal marched us to the cook house, stood us in the queue and told us we had a choice for lunch (take it or leave it) and left us to it. It was mashed spuds, cabbage, a boiled onion and two slices of meat, rice pudding for afters.

The cook house Sergeant was a bit worrying; a big dangerous looking man with flat feet who spent the meal times patrolling the front of the cookhouse and the dinning room. If you had any complaints about the food you certainly wouldn't take them to him. Some of the lads moaned there wasn't enough on their plate, but this was the army and there would be no going back for seconds here.

After our lunch we all went back to the barrack to wait for our next parade at one thirty. Dead on one thirty the Sergeant and Corporal came in the room with an officer, he was Second Lieutenant Barron. He told us he would be our Platoon officer while we did our basic training.

All the lads from the room above were brought down into ground floor room and a trestle table was set up at the top of the room. The Sergeant and Corporal sat at each end of the table and called us to it two at a time in alphabetical order. We had to give them our full names, religion, next of kin, what job we did before joining the army and any criminal convictions. When it became my turn I got the Corporal and when I told him my middle name was Harry he wouldn't believe me, he reckoned it was a nickname for Harold or Henry. While I was still trying to convince him my name was Harry the officer came, as the same interviews were going on next door and he was going from room to room overseeing the proceedings. He confirmed that Harry was a proper Christian name.

After we all had our details taken we were told to get fell in out front again. The Corporal marched us over to the castle like building again; this was to collect our webbing kit. It had all been laid out ready for us to fetch. The Colour-Sergeant told us to check each item as he called them out; one large pack or as he called it 'valise', one small pack, two pouches, a gas mask two shoulder straps, one belt, a water bottle, a bayonet frog (to hold a bayonet on the belt) and a pair of gaiters. We were instructed to put it all in our large pack, place it under our right arm and we were marched back to our barracks. The webbing was in different colours depending on where the last man to have it had been serving; some was dark green and some of it a sandy colour.

When we got back to the barracks the Sergeant was waiting for us with some letter stencils, we were going to put our name on our kit bags. We were given a demonstration of how to do it by the Corporal; it had to be about a half way down the bag and across it. The letters to be done with black shoe polish and those who didn't bring any would have to borrow some. Most of the kit bags were white but a couple of us including me had been issued with an olive green one. While the Sergeant supervised the kit bag name painting the Corporal showed us how our webbing was assembled and adjusted to fit. After all the name painting and adjusting had been done the Sergeant got us all together and told us our webbing would have to be blancoed with olive green Blanco and the brass buckles polished. The webbing packs and pouches would probably need to be done once a week but our belts and gaiters must be done every night. He gave us a list of what we would have to buy from the N.A.A.F.I. black boot polish, brasso blanco and a duster to polish your brass buckles. There was still some time left before our evening meal we were told to put our belts and gaiters on and get fell in outside in columns of three, we were going to be taught how to march. With the Sergeant one side and the Corporal the other we were told when the order quick march was given we were to step forward with our right foot. When the order to halt was given we were to bring our right foot up to the left and stamp it down. We practiced this for a while but we could see the Sergeant was getting a bit aerated, what seemed to be upsetting him was some of the lads were swinging their arms with their legs. As they were stepping forward with their right or left leg they were swinging their arm with it. By the time that was sorted out it was time for tea

Marched down to the cookhouse and joined the queue for evening meal much the same as lunch. While we were eating it an Officer and a Sergeant wearing a red sash came round the dinning room, we learned later that this was the Duty Officer for the day. The cookhouse Sergeant who was stalking the front of the cookhouse and dinning room like a hawk announced that there would be a bucket of Coco placed on the table at the front of the dinning room at seven thirty to-night. Any one could come and help themselves to a mug of it.

Chapter Two

The Sergeant was the first to march into our barrack room this morning and utter the three little magic words, "Get fell in". As we got outside the Corporal was waiting for us and lined us up in a single line, tallest on the right; we were going to be taught to right dress. When the order to right dress was we were to stretch out our right arm and touch the shoulder of the man to our right with our right fist and number. Lofty was number one and I think I was sixteen and in total there were thirty-two of us in the platoon. We then marched up to Lofty forming three rows which gave the squad an even look except for Lofty, he stuck out like a sore thumb. In future this would be the position we took when the order to fall in was given. We were then marched on to the barrack square and the next hour was spent practicing our marching and halts, standing at ease and to attention; head up, shoulders back and thumbs in line with the seams of your trousers.

Falling out was also practised; you couldn't just walk off parade. When the order to fall-out was given you came to attention, did a smart right turn and then walk off.

There were three or four platoons drilling on various parts of the square, so we had to pay attention to who was giving the orders. There were still a couple of the chaps who would swing the same arm as their leg but with the Sergeant one side of the squad and the Corporal the other they soon got cured of doing it. Our last ten minutes on the square was to practise saluting, right arm parallel to the ground and forearm at thirty degrees, fingers and thumb together just above the right eyebrow. The Sergeant and corporal checked that we were doing it right and sorted out those whom they thought were doing it wrong. A stern warning was given as to the consequences of not saluting a commissioned officer and we were told that anyone with a pip or crown on their shoulder must be saluted.

When we were marched back to the barracks and before he fell the parade out, Sergeant Baker told us we were to go back to our barrack room and wait. We had to do the fall-out twice; first time was a bit ragged according to him.

All the lads who had joined with us were brought into our barrack room and the Sergeant announced we were going to get our Army Pay

Books and some of the lads would be moved to one platoon, this would be a cadre platoon. It would be made up of lads called up for their National Service who had been in the Officer Training Corps at a Grammar School and chaps who had spent time in the Army Cadet force before being called-up.

It was a bit crowded in our barracks; there must have been sixty of us in the room. The Corporal told us to sort ourselves out as we would be called in alphabetical order so A get to the front. When our names were called out we would march up to the table, stand to attention, salute, collect our pay books, salute again, about turn and march back down the room. A table was set up by the door and we were called to attention as Captain Goodchild arrived; he told us to stand at ease.

The Captain explained to us we would be collecting two pay books, part one and a part two. Part one was our main book and very important as it contained all our personal details including our army number; the smaller part two we needed to collect our pay. Our army number we must memorise as we could be asked for it at anytime.

We all collected our books without any trouble and the Sergeant told us this how we would collect our pay next Thursday all in alphabetical order. The names of the chaps who would make up the Cadre Platoon were called out and given little bands of ribbon to put on their shoulder epaulets. Blue for the potential officers and red for trainee N.C.O's (none commissioned officers). That meant about nine out of our barrack room had to move across the passage and the same number over into our room. The next hour was spent with chaps moving their kit and organising the barrack room again. By the time all the to and frowing and messing about had been completed it was nearly lunch time. Before we went to lunch the Corporal told us to get our spare pair of boots and put a label on them with our name, army number, platoon and company on it. An old fag packet was what we should use for the label. Although the boots had steel heel tips on they were going to have three rows of hobnails down the sole. When they came back from the cobblers we would send the boots we were wearing for the same. We should now tie the laces together to keep them as a pair as we would be handing them into the company store on our way to lunch. The stores were only in the block behind ours but we had to march there, boots in the right hand.

After lunch we were all paraded outside by the Corporal who told us we were going to do P.T (physical training) in the gymnasium. We were to get ourselves dressed in shorts and tee shirts with the green

9

pullover on top and our plimsolls and be back outside in ten minutes.

The Corporal marched us over to the gym and left us with the P.T.I's (physical training instructors). They wore a red and black hooped jumpers and black trousers, not khaki like everyone else round here and they were going to make us as fit as butchers dogs! They got us running on the spot to start; one of them shouting 'up' the other P.T.I. shouting 'get them legs up, they won't drop off!'. We were then trotted into the gym and began with jumping; legs apart and arms up with the P.T.I checking our arms were level with our shoulders, an inch too high or too low and you were in trouble, 'a horrible little man' according to the instructors. The platoon was now split into two groups and one group was taken over to the wall which had wooden rails all along its length. These were wall bars we were informed by the Corporal. We then had to turn our backs to the bars, reach up and grab the highest bar we could with our hands and lift our feet off the floor. The next move was to bring your legs up so that they would be at right angles to your body, keeping them straight while doing so. Of course this had to be done in military style so we all had to wait for the Corporal to say 'up' before we could start and the Corporal hooting `get um up, get um up` while we strained to achieve it. There was only about two of the group who could get their legs right up with no bending at the knees. There were a few red faces among us. While our group was busy on the wall bars the others had been taken to the horizontal bar at the bottom end of the gym. Their exercise was to jump up catch hold of the bar and hang there. When the Corporal in charge of them shouted 'up' they had to pull themselves up until their chin touched the bar and hang there until he called 'down'. A lot of the lads could do it but there were three or four who couldn't get their chin up to the bar even once. That made the Corporal`s day and he started with the 'you horrible little man, you should go to bed in boxing cloves and stop pulling your wire' and all the abusive army comments you had heard on the radio but never believed.

After half an hour of us straining and puffing and the P.T.I's hooting the groups changed round. There were a few in our group who couldn't get the chin to the bar and that started the music hall comments again. I was alright as the practice I had swinging along the goal posts in Pleck Park now paid off. I think a lot of us were starting to realise that the instructors loved the sound of their own voices. When the instructors thought we had enough the group was lined up with us running on the spot, it seemed it was a sin to stand still in the gym doing nothing. Press-ups were the next thing that got the P.T.I's in good voice again; some of us could do the required ten push-ups but some could do it only a couple of times. After a few more exercises we were lined up in the usual columns of three and trotted outside. A run around the edge of the barracks square was our next task; we had to do this twice with a P.T.I. running along side of us.

Corporal Shaw came and marched us back to our barrack block and told us to get changed back into our denims. When we had all changed he gave the order 'stand by your beds' which we did, some standing one side of the bed and some another. He then pointed out that when the order to stand by your beds was given we must stand level with the bottom right hand corner of the bed in the at-ease position. When he had us all standing in the right place he called us to attention, but of course we had to do it a couple of times to make sure we had got the message.

The next thing was him checking we had the blanco to do our webbing as we would be doing it tonight after our evening meal. Most of us had it those who didn't could borrow some. We had some time before our meal so the Corporal showed us how we were to stack our webbing on top of our locker after it had been blancoed: kit bag with our name showing, large pack with polished buckles showing, small pack and pouches on top with a mess tin, bottoms polished placed each side. We were then marched down for our evening meal and we were about ready for it after our afternoon's P.T.

The Corporal was waiting for us as we got back from our meal, he was going to show us how to blanco our webbing. He checked we had the right colour and that we had all got some. One or two who didn't would have to borrow some. You got the little brush they had issued us with, wet it and rubbed it on the blanco and then onto your webbing. It was just like whitening your tennis pumps although most of us had never owned a pair. We did the blancoing on a slate sill on the back wall of the washhouse and there was only enough room for four or five of us to do it at one time. While we were waiting our turn the Corporal told us there would be a C.O's (Commanding Officers) inspection in the morning. This would take place every Saturday morning from now on. The barrack room would have to be cleaned and the floor scrubbed with a bath brick. He showed us the stiff brushes he called bath brooms and what looked like a building brick. We had to crumble the brick up and spread it on the barrack room floor and the scrub it with the bath broom. We all took it in turns to do our bit and it did make the floor look cleaner. This together with the blancoing kept us all busy for over an hour. Fortunately it didn't take the blanco long to dry and the

Corporal kept an eye on us to see we stacked it on our locker right. Our next task was dusting; well it needed it after the dust of the bath brick and the Corporal made sure we went outside to shake the dusters. Half way down the barrack room on the right hand side was a fire grate. It hadn't been used since last winter so all it needed was a polish up and we just buffed it up with our boot brushes. After we had done all the cleaning and polishing the Corporal came with a little box with some bits of broken glass in. He then showed us how to lightly scrape the broom handles with the glass to make then look like new. When we used them to sweep up with in the morning, if we held them with our dusters we wouldn't get them dirty again. We lined them against the wall by the door before the C.O's inspection. We would have this clean-up every Friday from now on while were doing our basic training. In the morning after breakfast we would have an hour's drill, then at nine o'clock we would return to the barrack room and ensure our kit was neatly arranged in our lockers as we had been shown. Major Owen the company C.O companied by Lieutenant Barron and Sergeant, Baker would then do the inspection. After the inspection we would all change into our P.T kit again ready to join the cross country run at ten o'clock.

We were now left to ourselves for the rest of the evening, some had been for their mug of cocoa but by the time they had got there it had all gone, there was only one bucket. Most of us went down the N.A.A.F.I. where you could get food and cups of tea as well as fags, blanco and boot polish. I was having a chat to some of the chaps who joined the army with me when Ronnie Hammond tapped me on the shoulder with 'how you doing Podge?'. Ronnie had finished his training and just come back from his embarkation leave and was off to join the Worcestershire Regiment in Malaya on Monday. We had a little chat and he told me another of our school friends, Bulger Parker had been sent to Egypt to join the Cheshire Regiment a fortnight ago. I wished Ronnie luck and hoped that he would come back home in one piece.

It was seven forty five before we got on the square this morning as the Sergeant and the Corporal had checked that our lockers were up to standard for inspection. We did drill for an hour, the usual left turn, right turn, halting and a new move; about turn.

When we had finished and returned to the barrack room we practiced standing by our beds and being called to attention just to make sure we did it right. We now waited for the inspection to take place and we must have hung about for half an hour. Sergeant Baker suddenly appeared at the door and shouted `stand by your beds' and called us to attention as Major Owen entered the room. It was the first time any of us had seen him, he was an old soldier like Sergeant Baker and accompanied by him and Lieutenant Barron for the inspection. They just walked down one side of the room and back up the other and didn't seem to be looking at anything in particular.

After the inspection we all changed into our P.T kit for the run and the Sergeant told us what the course for our cross country run was; over the golf course to the Whittington Road, round the rifle ranges and back up to the barracks, a distance of three miles. An N.C.O. would be stationed at the bottom of the Whittington Road and at the back of the ranges to ensure no one took a short cut. When the run was finished the rest of the weekend was ours but we were not to leave the camp under any circumstances. One chap at the back pointed out we couldn't do the cross country run with out leaving the camp. He got short shift, Sergeant Baker asked him who the village idiot was now he had joined the army.

All the training platoons were already out on the square when we were trotted out to join them. At ten thirty sharp a whistle was blown and we were off between the war memorial monuments at the end of the square. Most of us were knackered by the time we had got over the football pitches and onto the golf course. By the time we had reached the Whittington Road most of us were half running and half walking. When we reached the road junction just out of the village we turned right and went along for half a mile before we got to the rifle ranges. We then ran towards Hopwas Wood and round the back of the ranges and back to the road. The last half mile or so back to the barracks was all uphill and through lines of Nissan huts we came to know as the Spiders.

Most of us were in a state of collapse when we got back to our barracks but we had a little rest before lunch. The Corporal had already told us that there would be no marching down to the cook house at the weekend. We were to wander down ourselves. Dining at the weekend was less formal due mainly to those in the later stages of their training being allowed to go home at the weekend. Those doing their basic training were confined to the camp for the first six weeks and then were given a forty-eight hour pass at the end of it.

If we had been thinking the camp would be a lonely place with only those doing their basic training there at the weekend, we were in for a shock. The camp was alive with men from the Territorial Army and local Cadet Forces and there were even a couple of military bands practicing on the square. The place was alive with people so you had a bit of a job to get served in the N.A.A.F.I. on Saturday evening. For most of Sunday the Cadet Companies were drilling on the square and this kept us entertained. We stood by the square to watch but were soon sent off for 'distracting the poor souls' we were told in no uncertain terms. Watching through the barrack room window was alright though.

Our first weekend in the army had gone all right for most of us but you could see some of the lads were finding it hard. For a lot it was their first time away form home and they were missing Mother's Sunday dinner. This was National Services and the same for thousands of lads our age. Volunteers like me and Rudd should have no complaints, but we did!

Chapter Three

Corporal Shaw burst into our barrack room just as the Bugler was blowing the last note of the six thirty reveille. Now we'd had three days and the weekend to get used to the army we would start our military training in earnest, so we were to make sure we all had a good breakfast. Even with us going for our breakfast, while others washed and shaved it was still a bit of a rush for us all to get through the washhouse in time for the first parade. Most of us had to have a shave and that took some time and of course we had to tidy the barrack room up as well. At seven thirty we were all ready for our first parade and Sgt. Baker appeared. He lived in the married quarters at the other side of the camp. Before our first square bashing session he explained to us the drill for reporting sick. If any one was ill they should tell the Corporal first thing in the morning, then pack all their kit in their kit bag and hand it into the company stores before seven thirty. They would then report to the Company office where they would be given a note to take to the M.O. (Medical Officer). At eight o'clock they would be escorted to the Medical Centre on the edge of the camp. Here you would be diagnosed and given one of three categories; medicine and duties, in which case you would carry on with your training; Excused duties where you would stop in the barracks and sent to Hospital if you were at death's door. It was a bit of a game just to report sick so you had to be at deaths door just to want to bother.

The next thing was that there had been complaints from some of the platoons of things being stolen from the barracks while they were out training. So, in future a man would be left in the barrack room as an orderly while we were out. If someone was on excused duties, they would do it but otherwise we took it in turns to be the barrack orderly, starting with the man in the first bed on the right hand side of the room. He would be orderly for the first day, then the man in the second bed the next day and so on round the room. Most of the morning was taken up with us on the square drilling with a quarter of and hour N.A.A.F.I. break at ten thirty then more drilling.

We were getting used to the cookhouse routine now and learnt the cookhouse sergeant was known by all as Old Squeegee. There were a couple of other sergeants with the trainee cooks but I think Squeegee must have been in charge as he was the one who seemed to police the proceedings at meal times.

After our lunch we were all marched over to a building behind the Church to what was the HQ of the A.E.C. (The Army Education Corps). Here we were going to be tested on how good our schooling had been. Sat at one at a table just so we couldn't copy, an English test was given to each of us and we were given one hour to complete. It had several sentences each with mistakes in which we had to point out what they were. There were grammar mistakes as well as spelling. I did my best and luckily you only had to point the spelling mistakes out, if they had asked me to spell I would have been in trouble. After we had put the sentences right we had to write about what we had done before joining the army. I made up a story about working on the farm, it was only about fifty words long but they seemed happy with it.

The Education corps all seemed to be Sergeants and were a lot tamer that our training Sergeant. It was good job as several of the chaps couldn't read or write very well. Although they were told not to worry about it so they didn't get the 'you horrible little man' we usually got when we did something wrong. Our next test was for maths - just a few simple adding, taking away, multiplication and division sums. The surprise was that there were also a couple of trigonometry questions. They were in there because apparently you needed to have a basic grasp of trigonometry to be able to aim mortars and guns. Most of the lads who could barely read or write managed to do most of the sums.

No results as to how we had done in our test were given to us probably so we couldn't take the piss out of the ones who didn't do very well. There was certainly no brain surgeons among us, all the clever clogs had been put in the cadre platoon. However the tests had taken us all afternoon so it was our meal time when we had finished.

The evening was passed blancoing our belt and gaiters and polishing the brass bit for tomorrow. A lot of the lads who had girlfriends were writing letters, some had written every day since we came last Wednesday. Some went down the N.A.A.F.I. but a lot of us with no money just sat around talking. It was surprising that we had only been together for five days but it was like we had known one another for years. The Sergeant came in the barrack room about seven o'clock and pinned a notice up just as we were about to make a dash for the coco bucket. It was a timetable of our training program for the next month, most of us had to have a quick look and it seemed the first couple of hours each day would be square bashing. The interesting bit was we would get paid on Thursday afternoon. Stopping to have a look at the time table was a mistake because when we got to the cookhouse all the coco had gone.

Tuesday after breakfast it was on parade for the Sergeants inspection and this would take place every morning before our square bashing. Along with the Corporal he walked up and down our ranks checking we had blancoed our belts and gaiters and polished our boots and brasses. They also checked we had shaved and those he thought hadn't would be asked. If they said they had shaved the Sergeant would tell them to stand a bit closer to the razor in the morning.

Our drilling on the square seemed to go on for ever but I think we were getting better; anyway we made it to N.A.A.F.I break. It was the Gym after break up to lunch time. Most of us had the same struggle we had on Friday with the P.T.I. telling us he would have us fit as butcher's dog by the end of our training. We had all had enough by lunch time, the expression used was `I'm on me jock straps` or `I'm three parts knacked`.

The afternoon was a lot easier and the Corporal came in the barrack room with a rifle and gathered us all round the table. The first thing he said to us was 'this is a rifle don't ever let me hear any of you call it a gun'. He proceeded to tell us it was a Lee Enfield number four and the main weapon of the British infantry. He then gave us a brief history of it and showed us how to take the bolt out and the magazine off it. The little oil bottle and a pull through to clean the barrel was stored in the butt of the weapon. Sergeant Baker arrived with another rifle and set up shop at the top end of the table and we each had a go at stripping the rifle under supervision, it was quite simple. Some of the chaps fumbled a bit but I think it was just nerves as most of them had never handled a rifle before. The thing that surprised me was how heavy it was. Another lecture on the history and the use of the weapon was given by Sgt. Baker before we were told to get `fell-in` outside and then marched over to Company stores to get issued with rifle each. These were at the back of the place; chained to the wall by a chain through the trigger guard in an area they called the armoury. Each rifle was numbered and we were told to remember it as we would draw the same rifle every time, which would be ours throughout our basic training. The rifles came with a bayonet and scabbard attached to it by lugs on the barrel. Once the store man had checked the rifle number against our name on his list we were marched back to our barrack, rifle in the right hand of course. Once we were back the Sergeant told us to take the bayonet off the rifle and put it in our locker. Most of us just couldn't resist pulling the scabbard off and having a quick look at the bayonet. It was only a round piece of metal about nine inches long and it didn't have much of a point on it - very disappointing. The bayonet was easy to take off the rifle you just pressed in the spring clip and gave it a half turn and off it came. With our bayonets off the rifle it was 'get fell-in' outside again. Corporal Shaw borrowed Lofty's rifle and proceeded to show us how to stand to attention and stand at ease with it while Sergeant Baker gave orders. The next manoeuvre was the slope arms doing each movement to the count of three. Flip it up two three, across your body two three, right back down by your side two three. Lofty who didn't have a rifle as Corporal Shaw was using his to demonstrate with was told to just go through the motions. When Lofty got his rifle back we had a few practise slope arms with the Corporal in and out of our ranks making sure our left forearm was parallel to the ground when in the slope position. Over the next month several other moves like the present arms, port arms and fix bayonets were introduced. Our rifles had to be handed back into the stores after we had finished our drill session and by the time we had done this it was time for our meal.

After our evening meal we were back to the belt and gaiter blancoing and polishing ready for the morning parade. Our spare pair of boots needed to be 'bulled' this entailed rubbing the boot polish on the heel and toe cap in little circular movements. Water had to be added and most of us used spit to harden the polish. A lot of the lads whose brothers had been in the army had several theories of the best way of doing it. But in the main spitting on the polish and rubbing it in seemed to work alright. By tomorrow we had been in the army a week and what was becoming apparent was that you didn't have christened names any more. All the N.C.O's addressed you by your surname and where you had two with the same surname your last two numbers of you army number was added to it. We had two Browns in our platoon one was Brown 64 and one Brown 92. In the barrack room we tended to do the same, well it was the name on the locker. What we were all struggling with was remembering our army number but we would have to quote it to get our pay on Thursday.

The first thing this morning after we had tidied the barrack room was to draw our rifles and after the Sergeant and Corporal's inspection we were back on the square one two threeing it. This went on until N.A.A.F.I. break and a right shower we were according to the Sgt. I think his main concern was the forth coming parade for Armistice Day which we would taking part in. Most of didn't go to the N.A.A.F.I. we went back to the barrack room. At about ten thirty Sergeant came in followed by the Corporal carrying a Bren Gun or as he called it a L.M.G. `light machine gun` we all knew what it was from seeing films about the war. Sergeant Baker then gave us a lecture on the history of the weapon, what it did and how you could set it to fire just one shot at a time or fire it automatic and how to cock it. He then proceeded to strip it down; magazine off, barrel off and pulled a pin out and the butt and trigger mechanism slid off allowing you to take the working mechanism out. The gun was assembled again with the Sergeant saying for us to watch very carefully as we would be doing it later. The next couple of hours were taken up with us stripping the gun down and assembling it. It was a bit more complicated than the rifle but we soon got into it. Over the next few months we would take it apart and stick it together again on a regular basis with us competing to see who could do it the quickest. After lunch Corporal Shaw marched us down to the twenty five yard range, rifle at the slope of course. This was on a patch of land between the spiders and the Whittington Road and Lieutenant Barron and Sergeant Baker were there waiting for us along with a couple of Bren guns and ammunition in a little truck. We were going to fire our weapons for the first time but first we were given a demonstration of how to do it by Corporal Shaw. You couldn't just collapse onto the firing point, like everything else in the army there was a drill for it. Rifle in the right hand you put your left hand on the ground then kicked your legs back to end up laying on the firing point; keeping your rifle clear off the ground and legs slightly apart with our bodies at about fifteen degrees to the line of fire. A clip of five rounds of ammunition was given to each of us with the strict instructions not to load our rifles yet. We were lined up five at a time on the little bank and ordered to take our positions. Once in the firing position we were given the order to load, sliding the clip of ammunition into the rifle and pressing it down with our thumb, closing the bolt and putting the safety catch on, as per instructions. Five rounds in your own time, `fire` was the next order and we took aim and shot at little paper targets. The recoil of the rifle didn't seem as bad as Dad's old twelve bore was. It must have gone alright as the all the platoon had a go without any mishaps. We had to make sure we picked all our empty cartridges up before leaving the firing point as we would have to hand them in later. This was a check to see all the ammunition was accounted for. After our rifle shooting we all had a go with the Bren gun firing five rounds with the single fire on and a couple of short bursts on automatic. Empty cases and clips were handed in and counted before we were marched back to clean our weapons.

When we got back to the company store the store man had a little boiler like the one Mother did her washing in and this was to clean our rifles by a process called 'boiling out the barrel'. We had to wait for the boiler or `Soya Bean cooker` as the Sergeant called it to come to the boil. Once it had boiled we took it in turns to pour four pints of boiling water through the barrel of the rifle using a tun dish specially made for the job. After we had all boiled out the Sergeant came with a roll of flannelette about four inches wide with red lines every two inches across it. This was the famous four by two for polishing out your rifle barrel. A two inch piece was issued to each of us and we were told we would get no more. It was the same all through my army service; four by two was like gold dust. You got one piece every time you used the rifle and never any more. We got the pull through and oil bottle out of the butt and cleaned our barrels ready for the Corporal's inspection. After, we oiled the four by two and lightly oiled the barrel and the rifle with it. We all helped cleaning the `light machine guns` (the Sergeant didn't like us calling them Bren guns) before handing them back to the stores along with our rifles.

Enough time was left before our evening meal to change our Denims. When we were first issued with them they had buttons on the jackets. These were held on by a washer and a split ring, bachelor buttons some said they were called. The drill was that we would draw our clean ones, take them back to the barracks change the buttons over hand our dirty one back in. That done, we could go for our tea.

Chapter Four

We had been in the army for a week now and the whole platoon seemed to be getting along fine. Some of the accents were a bit different to our Black Country talk but we understood each other alright. A lot of the lads came from places us locals had never heard of, places like Wallasey, Cheadle, Wetley Rocks, Chell and other exotic sounding places. I think some of the chaps were starting to get a bit home sick since they had never been away before but there were a few comedians among us so we had a laugh. Most of the complaining was about the food, it wasn't like Mother's cooking and a couple of them reckoned we didn't get enough; there was little or no sugar in the tea and it tasted funny but that was the bromide they put in it. The chaps who had older brothers who had done their National Service had told us about the bromide. It was put in the tea to stop us raping the Sergeant Major or something like that.

We were a smart lot in our clean denims this morning. The inspection by the Sergeant and Corporal on our first parade went off as normal with them finding something wrong with most of us.

The day went well, mostly drilling on the square and a couple of hours in the gym with a lecture on army life from Lieutenant Barron while it rained.

Thursday dawned and this was the day we had all been looking forward to- pay day. This took place in the late afternoon and we knew the drill from collecting our pay books. A table was set up at the top of the barrack room and a blanket spread over it ready for the big event. Corporal Shaw busied himself making sure we were lined up in alphabetical order and next Captain Goodchild arrived with a young squaddie like one of us, carrying a box and a ledger. He was the company pay clerk we were told later. Names were called and we marched up to the table, gave a smart salute and handed the clerk our part two pay book. Captain Goodchild paid the money out and you put it in your left hand gave another salute did a right turn and escaped.

The National Service lads were entitled to twenty four shilling but got twenty two as two bob was credited to them. John Rudd and I being regulars should have got forty eight bob but we got forty five with three bob credits. After we had all been paid Captain Goodchild explained why we didn't get all our pay. This was to cover the cost of any damage we did. When we had finished our training and left this barrack room it would be inspected for damage. And any repairs need would be paid for out of these credits, also we would be able to draw on them before we went on leave for a bit of extra cash.

The regulars like me were alright and had a bit to spend in the N.A.A.F.I. but by the time the National Service chaps had bought boot polish, Blanco razor blades etc; they didn't have much cash left. A couple of the lads were married and they did even worse as they had another ten bob stopped to send to their wives. Thursday was always pay day or pay parade day as the army liked to call it. So the N.A.A.F.I. was crowded tonight and those of us with the cash binged on tea and bacon and bean pie.

Although drilling took up a lot of our time we were now starting to do other training and a lot of this took place on a patch of land by The Spiders. As well as the twenty five yard range there was a gas chamber and assault course and some bags of straw strung between stumps for bayonet practice. We only went in the gas chamber once. The first time we were told to walk in one end and out the other without our gas masks on. The building was not that long so we could have got through it holding our breath but the Sergeant and Corporal kept the top door closed so we had to breathe some of the gas. After a couple of minutes we were let out coughing and choking, our eyes streaming with tears. When we had recovered for our ordeal we were sent into the gas chamber again, this time wearing our gasmasks. A good five minutes were spent in there and although you could smell the gas it didn't make us cough and choke. Although I don't think it was the proper gas, probably only tear gas, it gave us an idea of how our gas masks worked.

It would be about another week before we got to use the assault course and for this we had to wear our webbing and tin helmets. Not all it of just the pouches small pack and our water bottle and our rifle, of course. This rig-out was what the army called battle order. The whole course was not very long and started with a brick wall about seven feet high. This was the first obstacle and you ran at it and jumped up and grabbed the top and pulled yourself over it. The Corporal gave us a demonstration of how it should be done, you ran at the wall and stuck the right foot about two feet up the wall and sort of flicked yourself up. This manoeuvre was an acquired skill and some of us could do it and some couldn't. The trouble was if you couldn't, you just ran into the wall your tin helmet came off and your rifle barrel hit the back of your head. After a few tries the Sergeant put two of us on top of the wall, legs astride it and facing each other. Now when we ran up the lads on the wall grabbed our hands and pulled us over. The next obstacle was some pine logs on a sloping frame and the idea was to run up it and down the other side with out putting your hands on it. Most of us managed that alright although one or two of us fell off. It was only about five feet high. Running up the front of it was the easy bit. It was when you came to run down off it you tended to lose your balance. Like the wall bit this was accompanied by the Sergeant and Corporal shouting at us to get a move on and other choice comments. We got a new one today and we would hear this one whenever we were doing training exercises like assault courses and it was always the same one no matter were we where we was always being chased by a `big hairy arsed Russian`.

Our next test was some barbed wire strung on some metal pickets about eighteen inches off the ground and formed into little tunnels. This turned out to be the easy one. The main trick with this exercise was keeping your rile clean and out of the mud. After this crawl under the wire was completed it was on to the ropes. These were strung over poles; you climbed up the rope and crossed to the other side along a rope across the top and down the other side. It was not very high and probably about fifteen feet across the top. We had climbed ropes in the gym but getting up one in battle order and carrying a rifle was a bit more difficult. Another problem with it was the ropes over the top had been well used and sagged quite a bit. This meant you were crawling down hill until the last few feet then it was uphill. Most of us managed to climb up and grab the rope across the top. A few couldn't climb very far up the rope before dropping off it. They had to suffer the usual ribald comments from the N.C.O's. The next problem was if you crawled across the top rope head first this was a mistake as you needed to meet the down rope feet first. Very few of us managed to climb down the rope on the other side we just dropped off the end of the cross rope. If we had gone across feet first we would have been able to get the down rope with our legs and climb down it. As it was going head first you grabbed the down rope with one hand and as you took your legs off the cross rope you just fell off. The last bit of the assault course was on the opposite side of the road that ran down to the rifle ranges. This was a ditch that you had to jump over and due to the wear and tear over the years they had put wooden boards each side. There was about ten feet of boarding on the take off side and about the same on the landing side. The problem was it had been made with smooth planed planks and with it being autumn and damp they were like an ice rink. The first few over it some lost their footing on take off some came a cropper on landing. The N.C.O's thought it a great laugh but we soon got the hang of it. You needed to run up to the edge of the take-off and launch your self using the edge. When you landed put your right foot forward and slide down the boarding off. The Sergeant gave us another run round the course, still chased by the East European Gentleman with the hairy jotter of course, just to make sure we got the message. We were all bruised and a bit battered after our little assault course episode but it was time for lunch and we were all ready for it.

After lunch the first parade was the usual drill session and the N.C.O's were not very impressed with our performance. To liven us up they made us double round the square holding our rifles above our heads. I don't know about livening us up, it nearly killed most of us. The last hour before our evening meal was spent watching a training film, so we had a bit of a rest. We needed it as the weekly cross country run was in the morning.

With us using our webbing on the assault course this morning it had to be blancoed ready for the Commanding Officer's inspection in the morning.

It had been a fortnight now since we had joined the army and you could see some of the lads were finding it a bit hard going, the food was one of the main complaints. However we were all in it together and we all got along well. A couple of chaps were a bit quite and reserved but we all mucked in. There was a few comedians among us and one or two lads a bit slow, one a farm boy from Worcestershire was always a source of amusement if only for his deep country accent. Whenever he did something wrong his plea to the Corporal would be, 'don't charge I Corps just bollack I'.

The cross country run didn't come so hard this week, we were obviously getting fitter but we still felt the affects on Sunday morning.

The following week was just like the last, we were into the routine now; drill, P.T. and general training but mostly drill. Friday afternoon was our big event as we got our tetanus and T.A.B. injections, what ever T.AB. was. On Saturday morning the arm we had the T.AB injection in was like lead and stiff. It didn't matter how stiff it was it didn't excuse us the cross country run. It will loosen it up was the Sergeants answer. It got loosened up even more on Sunday; it was the Armistice Day parade with a drum head service held on the main square

On our sixth week we got to do some shooting again our first session was on the indoor miniature range. The riles were the old type Enfield with a two- two bore and we had to fire ten rounds each at a bull's-eye target. When we had finished we had to take our targets to Lieutenant Barron for his inspection. 'I can see you've used a rifle before Power' and I actually got a well done out of him. It all seemed a bit daft to me as I thought we should have used the point two-two rifles before the three-o-threes. However we would get to use our rifles again this afternoon.

After our lunch we were marched down to the ranges. Lieutenant Barron and the Sergeant were already there with a fifteen hundredweight lorry and boxes of ammunition. The platoon was split into to parties, one would fire and the others mark the targets in the butts. This was a concrete shelter running the width of the range and protected for the shooting by an earthen bank and cover. The targets were four feet square and mounted one behind another on a steel frame with pulleys on. This meant as you put one target up above the butts the other target was down behind it. We were given a pot of glue, books of little paper patches and a pole with a round disc on the end, one side painted white the other black. Instructions on how to use the pole were given to us. When a shot was fired at the target, if it was a bull's-eye we were to show the white disc and hold it over the bull's-eye. If it was an inner, show the black disc and hold it over the bullet hole. For an outer you showed the black and then the white. If they missed the target you waved the disc back and forwards across the target. After the whole ten shots had been fired you pulled the target down and patched the holes up with your glue and patches. The rifles were fired from two hundred yards for the first ten shots, and then we had ten shots from four hundred yards. After we had done the rifle shooting we had thirty rounds with the Brengun, ten shots on the single fire which were marked by the butt's party. Then the remainder of the magazine, another twenty shots in short bursts. One or two of us just shot the lot off in one go. That got the Sergeant and Officer going as they had given us strict instructions on how to fire short in bursts of four or five rounds. Once half had done their shooting we changed round and they went in the butts while we did our shooting. The platoon was formed up into three ranks after we had finished shooting and the Corporal had a sheet with our scores on. He didn't tell us how we had done as along with the Officer and Sergeant they were concerned that a couple of the chaps had missed the target. They were asked how they could miss a four foot target at two hundred yards. They both had the same excuse, when they had their medical they were wearing their glasses for the eye test. They hadn't brought them when they joined-up in case they got broken. You could see by the look on the N.C.O's faces all this had happened before.

The store man had got the boiler on for us to boil our weapons out when we got back to camp. A mingy little piece of four by two was issued to us to clean and oil our rifles and Bren-guns.

First parade next morning the chaps who had joined up with-out their eye glasses were sent to the company office. There were four of them two couldn't have been too bad as they must have hit the target with-out their glasses on. They joined the parade half an hour later and we found out after Captain. Goodchild had seen them and as we were to get a forty eight hour pass this next week-end they would report to the company office with their spectacles when they came back.

The last parade on Friday afternoon we all had to wear our best battle dress and great coats. Lofty had a great coat but still didn't have a battle dress to fit him so the stores found a new set of denims for him to wear. We were all lined up and inspected by the platoon commander to make sure we were all smartly turned out and had proper shoes, no suede or canvas allowed. The Sergeant the gave us a talk on how we should conduct our selves, as while we were in uniform we represented the regiment etc; We would be given our passes and travel warrants at four thirty this afternoon and strictly speaking we shouldn't leave the barracks until midnight, but after our evening meal we would tidy up the barrack room and when Corporal Shaw said it was O.K we could go. A couple of the lads were staying, one who had just come out of an orphanage when he got called up and an Irish lad who come to England to work and would sooner do his National Service than go back home to Ireland. The barrack room had never been cleaned up so quickly and by seven o'clock we were all in the bus queue for Lichfield.

Chapter Five

It was about eight thirty when I got to Alexander Road to find the house all in darkness. I sat on the doorstep until half nine when Bill rolled up on his bike with a bag of chips. He said if he had known I was coming he would had brought more chips with him. We went in the house and Bill made us a mug of coffee with his bottle of Camp Coffee and shared his chips with me. There was no food in the house only half a bottle of milk and Bills coffee. We were both still hungry. I borrowed his bike and rode to the chip shop in Spout Lane and got us some more chips. Bill told me Fanny don't come home some nights when she does it's usually around midnight. He himself was never back much before nine o'clock as he had a couple of horses at Cox's and he went there after he finished work at Carrington's. We sat around talking until half eleven Mary hadn't shown up by then so we went to bed. My bed in the back bedroom was just as Id left it the day I joined up. It felt a bit damp but I jumped in it and was asleep before my head hit the pillow.

I was woken at five thirty next morning by Fanny calling to me through the wall. She wanted to know if I had got her a music box, she had said before I joined the army if I went abroad bring her a music box back. I told her I had only been to Whittington barracks and they were not noted for making music boxes. Fanny said she didn't expect to ever get one as even if I did go abroad I was too miserable to buy her one. When I got up at about seven o clock Bill was on his way out and Fanny had already gone. Bill said she was always gone by six thirty as she called somewhere for a bit of breakfast before she went to work.

There was no food in the house as bill had most of his food out he had some sausage and stuff off Jeff Slater a couple of nights a week but kept nothing at home. Fanny only came here to sleep and that was not every night. There was no coal for the fire you had to register with a supplier as it was still rationed and I don't think any one had bothered to do so. In fact the only thing in the place was some milk and Bills Camp coffee. I warmed some water in the kettle had a wash and shave then caught the bus to Walsall and went in the Café in Bridge Street and had a mug of tea and a bacon sandwich. I bought some bread and a bottle of coffee on my way home, I would have preferred tea but it was still rationed and the coffee I bought wasn't Camp I think it was Dot or something like that. Bill didn't like it he was all Camp Coffee.

My first job was to visit my only surviving grandparent, Granny McClements so about ten o` clock I wandered down to Slaney Road. I knocked on the door of the house and it was opened by one of the relations of the old dear Granny lived with. She looked down her nose at me like I was a bad smell and asked what I wanted. She knew who I was and by her manner and tone of voice I could sense something had happened. Bertha didn't live there any more and had left several weeks ago. No she didn't know where she had gone and didn't care and with that she shut the door. I walked back to the Brown Lion and caught a bus back up to the Full Brook and went down Jack Yeats farm.

I spent a couple of hours yapping to Gogger Johnson; Jacks farm labourer, the chap who bought my old motorbike off me. On my way home I called in Jeff Slater's, there was only Jeff's wife Mini in. She tells me Jeff was out feeding Percy Haynes pigs, Percy's pig man was ill and Jeff was feeding the pigs for him. Mini gave me a mug of tea and a sausage sandwich before I left. She asked me to come back later as she knows Jeff would love to see me and find out how I had got on?

I went back home to find Fanny and her boyfriend Blondie there so I had a yap to them. The only thing Blondie was interested in was could I get him some fags. Woodbines in particular as cigarettes were still short there were only Players weights, Star and a few other odd names available, and they were in short supply. I said I would see what I could do knowing I wouldn't be back here until Christmas. Fanny was only here to get togged-up for the Saturday night out. By five thirty they were on their way and roared of up the road on Blondie's motor bike. This was the last time I saw our Fanny face to face Fanny for over ten years and when I did meet her again, I didn't know her.

They hadn't been gone for ten minuets when Bill came home he had finished work at one o'clock lunch time but had been at Cox's horse keeping since. Bill said he was going over to Jeff Slater's to see if Jeff had brought him any meat from work. I said I would go with him as I wanted to see Jeff and told Bill about my visit this afternoon. We wandered over to Jeff's house in West Bromwich Road about six-o-clock. Jeff greeted me like a long lost brother and wanted to know all about my army training, He should know all about it as he was in the army himself. Bill and I were at Jeff's talking him and his wife Mini until nearly eight o'clock. When we let Jeff gave us some sausage and four pieces of belly draught and a dab of dripping. The dripping came in handy as we had no butter or margarine and dripping was nice on toast with a bit of salt on.

Bill had brought a loaf with him when he came home so we had a feed with the sausage and belly draught and our bread dipped in the fat that came out of it, we couldn't light the fire as there was no coal. There was a small electric fire so we put that on and we were on a slot meter so it was a bit expensive. Bill and I sat talking and supping cups of coffee until we went to bed about ten thirty when the money we put in the meter electric ran out

When I got up on Sunday morning Bill had already gone off to Cox's horse jagging and Fanny had not been back. I made myself some toast and dripping with the last of the bread before I boiled the kettle to have a wash and shave. I decided to give my battle dress a press so I found an iron out and put another couple of bob in the meter to do it. By eleven o'clock I was ready to go out so I decided to visit Uncle George and Aunty Maude. They seemed glad to see me and I got a chunk of cake and a mug of tea. Aunty Maude and her mother were busy getting the Sunday lunch while Uncle George was getting ready to go down the Fullbrook Pub. I talked mainly to Uncle George until about twelve o'clock when I could see he was itching to get off down the Pub so I said goodbye to them and Aunty Maude gave me a packet of fags before I left.

I went back to Alexander Road and collected my stuff; well my towel soap and razor then caught a bus to Walsall. Being Sunday everywhere was closed except the Pubs so there was nowhere I could get anything to eat. My next plan was to walk up to the Butts and see if the lady who Granny Mac had lived with first knew where she had gone to live. When I got to the house and knocked a young man answered the door. He told me the old dear who used to live here had passed away last winter, so that was that. My thoughts now were getting back to the barracks in time for the evening meal. Back down to the St Paul's bus station and with the buses only doing a Sunday service I had to wait nearly an hour for the next bus to Lichfield. My luck was in when I got to Lichfield the Tamworth bus was waiting. I arrived back at the barracks just before five-o-clock; the Irish lad and the chap from the orphanage were stretched out on their beds taking it easy. Anyway I had made it back well in time for the meal and that was a relief. No one else was back yet the next ones to show up got back after eight-o-clock. The first jobs of anyone coming in were to blanco their belt and polish the brass ready for the morning parade. It was well after midnight when some of the lads got in. They should have been here before midnight but no one said anything. Most of the local lads had used the bus but the chaps from Chester Liverpool and Stoke had come by train. They had to walk back up to the barrack from Trent Valley station as the buses had stopped running at ten o'clock. A couple had hitch-hiked and found that the easiest way, most drivers would stop and offer a lift to lads in military uniform. However by breakfast on Monday morning we were all here, that was a surprise!

On our first parade and after the inspection Sergeant; Baker said he hoped we had all enjoyed our weekend of freedom and we hadn't used all our strength shagging girlfriends as we were about to start training proper. We had finished our basic training and would now start what he called continuation training. The Sergeant; fell us out and told us all to go back to our barrack room where we found Captain Goodchild and Lieutenant Barron waiting. Captain Goodchild told us there would now be some changes to the platoon and called out the names of six of the lads Lofty and the farm boy from Worcestershire the Corporal called the `village idiot` among them. Lofty and a couple of the other lads had volunteered for the Parachute Regiment and they would be leaving to join them this afternoon. They were told to get their kit packed hand their webbing in except for belt and gaiters and report to the company office. The farm lad was being transferred to the Pioneer Regiment and we would all be sad to see him go as he was a bit of a comic. The other lad who came from Walsall, being discharged as unfit for military service.

The emphasise would now be on more field training and weapons but we still had about an hour a day drilling on the square sloping arms and performing. After our turn on the square it was back inside for a map reading session. There wasn't enough maps to have one each we had to work in groups of three. One chap had to hold a map up; we didn't have a black board. Lieutenant Barron pointed out grid lines to us and the numbers at the end of them. To read the map you went along the bottom of the map, the longitude or the northing as he called it and remember the number at the bottom of the line. The then up the side of the map to the lines across he called the easting. Where the lines met on the map was the spot. If you were giving a map reference you read the lines from the bottom right of the square and gave it as a number. An easy way of remembering how to do it was, you go in the house, then up the stairs to the number on the side. If you had a number 2516 you would find line 25 along the bottom of the map. Then up the side of the map to sixteen and where the lines met on the map was your map reference. We were now given some practice on map reading with Lieutenant Barron shouting out reference numbers and the Sergeant and Corporal checking we had our fingers on the right square. Over the next few weeks we would have more map reading sessions and practise. Sessions out on the golf course with the compass was always a bit of a laugh. Some if the platoon comics used to get it wrong just to get Sergeant Baker going. Camouflage was another pantomime we did on the edge of the golf course. Sticking bits of twigs and bracken in out packs and helmets trying to look like bushy topped trees. Darkening our faces was also recommended, but we didn't have anything to do it with. Co-co powder was suggested but we had enough trouble getting a mug to drink at night. Old Squeegee would have our guts for garters if we have asked for some to rub on our faces.

On our second week we were Duty Company for the week this meant as well as doing our training we also had to do guard duty and the fatigues as they called it. The fatigues were doing the odd jobs like scrubbing the dinning room floors and washing up in the cookhouse. It also included the labouring like delivering coal round the married quarters and any other jobs that needed doing. Guard Duty meant you had a night with-out much sleep. Ten men would be detailed to do guard but only nine would do it, one man would be the stickman. The guard would be mounted on the square at seven o'clock and be inspected by the duty Officer and Sergeant. The smartest and best turned out would be named the stickman and excused guard duty. He would spend the next day doing company runner for the duty Officer and Sergeant. After we had been marched to the guard room we were split into three groups. This meant we would be doing two hours on and four hours off. One of the group would stand by the main gate, the other two patrolling the barracks. What happened next I could never understand and it was the same plan where ever we were serving. While it was day light we would have our rifles and bayonets and no ammunition. As soon has it got dark we would hand our rifle into the guard room and be given a pick helve five rounds of ammunition and a bicycle lamp for a torch. It was a cold night and we couldn't find anywhere to get a warm so we had to keep on the move. Anyway the Corporal came round at regular intervals just to check on what we were doing. Each group did two stags, stags being what the Corporal called our two hours on duty. The four hours off we lay on some old bunks up the far end of the guard room.

During the week I did a morning delivering coal to the married quarters and a day in the cook house. Our first job in the cookhouse was mopping the dinning room floors the getting all the water off with a squeegee. After we had done both dinning rooms we were doing washing up in the cook house. We did this until the lads doing `jankers` came on at seven o'clock.

I was one a couple of weeks later. Id had porridge at breakfast and didn't feel very hungry so I made a sandwich with my egg. I took it back to our barrack room and hid it in my mess tin, and was going to eat it during our N.A.A.F.I. break. When we got back for our break the Sergeant, was waiting for me. He had found my sandwich and told me I would be on a charge. This would be section eleven some rigmarole about prejudice to good military order and discipline or something like that. I learned later that this section eleven covered most army crimes from pinching a cook house biscuit to murdering the Commanding Officer I suddenly realised how he had found my sandwich. I had hidden it in the tin at the side of our webbing with the bottom facing the inside of the barrack room. He must have seen it through the window from outside. I didn't think it was much of crime but I was probably being used as an example being the first one in our platoon to be charged. Told to get my best uniform on by the Corporal who explained to me what would happen? I would be marched into the Company commander's office and halt one pace form his desk, salute and stand to attention. The charge would be read out and the company commander would ask if I had any thing to say. The Corporal advised me to say nothing as I was going to get `jankers` anyway and the less I said the better it would be for me. After the Company Commander had pronounced the sentence I would salute and the Sergeant would give the order to about turn and marched out. This was exactly how it happened and I got three days `janckers` for my sins. This meant I had to report to the guard room at seven o'clock and parade with the rest of the barracks criminals. We would then be given jobs to do until about nine thirty, cleaning in the cook house mainly. Then at ten o'clock it was back at the guard room in our best uniform. and stood to attention while the bugler played the last post. It was a dash back to the barrack room to get your belt and gaiters done and ready for the morning before lights out.

Chapter Six

With us doing more playing soldiers and less drill it meant we were having to Blanco our webbing more however, it was more interesting than marching up and down the square. Most of us had now got over the initial shock of being in the army and we had a few laughs. The best laugh was on Tom, a big lad in our platoon who came from Bloxwich. His father was some big noise on Walsall Council. When we had our forty eight hour leave Tom must have complained to his father about the amount of food we were given at meal times. On Wednesday we were marched down to the cook house for lunch and stopped at the door by Squeegee. He had a couple of men with him who turned out to be a reporter and photographer from the Walsall Observer. Squeegee called Tom out and took him to dining room where the C.O. duty officer and Sergeant were waiting. The cook house Sergeant took Tom along the food counter piling his plate up with food as he went and brought Tom back into the dining room and sat him at the front table. The photographer got Tom to hold his knife and fork as though he was ready to tuck in and took a couple of photos. The reporter asked Tom a few daft questions but they were quickly lured away by the C.O no doubt with the prospect of a free drink in the officer mess. As soon as they vanished through the door Squeegee grabbed the plate of food off Tom and told him to get back in the queue. We couldn't believe what had gone on but as time went by we came to realise you had to work hard to get one over Old Squeegee.

Mail was usually fetched from the company office by one of the Corporals and left on the bed of who it was addressed to. I had never got any so it was a shock when I came in one morning and found I had a letter. It was addressed to The Commanding Officer, Whittington Barracks. And had my name and number had been written over it. The letter had been opened and it was from Granny Mac enquiring as to where I was. She was now living on her own in Beacon Terrace in an old terraced house off Birmingham Road. I wasn't going to splash-out on a writing pad and some envelopes just to write one letter so I begged a sheet of paper and an envelope off one of the lads. After I had got all my polishing and blancoing done that evening I wrote back to

Granny Mac and told her I tried to find her during my forty eight hour leave. Christmas was now only a couple of weeks away and I would visit her then. I then went down the N.A.A.F.I, bought a stamp and posted my letter.

New weapons (well, new to us) were introduced like the two inch Mortar, a length of tube with a little plate on the bottom. The Stengun and a queer anti tank thing called a `Piat` (Projector Infantry Anti Tank). I think this weapon was on its way out of service as we only had one session on its use. It had a spring loaded spigot that lunched a turnip shaped grenade when you fired it. The spring was very strong so you needed to have done a Charles Atlas course just to cock it. The training on the Mortar was the same and we only had a couple of sessions on how to use it. On the Stengun we had the usual stripping and assembling sessions, it was much simpler than the Brengun. It was a cheap little thing with a tee shaped metal butt, a screw in barrel and a round metal bolt with a spring behind it; the bolt and the spring just slid out after you screwed the barrel off. A magazine which held twenty eight rounds of nine millimetre ammunition clipped onto the left had side of it. There was a little lever at the side of the trigger guard so you could set it to fire automatic or one shot at a time. Unlike the 'Piat' we did get to fire it on the twenty five yard ranges a couple of times. We fired it from the shoulder on single shot first then in short bursts from the hip. A hand grenade was another weapon we had a couple of sessions on and would get to throw a live one a few weeks later. There was a drill for throwing it - you just couldn't pull the pin out and chuck it. You held it in your right hand and put your index finger through the ring on the split pin. On the command throw you pulled the pin out while moving your right foot slightly back and lobbed the grenade in over arm at the target.

The week before Christmas we became Duty Company for the week again and I got picked for the guard duty on Saturday. I didn't get to be stickman so I did my two stags wandering round the camp. I escaped the standing on the gate one. I was lucky really as I had Sunday to recover, in the week you still had to do your normal training after your guard duty.

My next job came on Thursday; I was reading company orders on Wednesday night and saw a lad named Creer down along with mine to report to the Guard room at eight o'clock in the morning, wearing our best battle dress uniforms After our breakfast we were to report to the cook house Sergeant who would issue us with haversack rations. Neither Greer nor I had a clue what it was all about so we asked Corporal Shaw who told us we would be doing escort duty. Next morning after breakfast we got our haversack rations but nothing to drink. The rations were four rounds of thick bread with cheese on one and corned beef on the other. We put them in our small packs and went to the guard room. The Provost Sergeant told us we would be escorting two prisoners to the military prison at Colchester and Corporal Heath would be in charge of the escort. A couple of young lads were fetched out of the cells their belts and gaiters scrubbed almost white. They were national service chaps and their crime was they had been absent without leave. Greer, me and the prisoners were loaded into the back of an army lorry, the Corporal sat in the front with the driver and we went down to Trent Valley railway station. The London train was dead on time, if we had been five minutes later we would have missed it. It was a good journey down to Euston station, the two lads were very friendly and I think they were resigned to their fate. From Euston we had to go on the underground across London to Kings Cross where we had a long wait in for the train to Colchester, it was about five o'clock before we got one. When we got to Colchester a lorry picked us up and took us to the prison. The Corporal took the prisoners in while Creer and I had to wait outside. After another long wait for the train back to London we were starving as we had eaten our haversack rations on our way down from Lichfield to London. None of us had much money but we scrapped up enough for a couple of bags of chips from a shop just outside the station. Corporal Heath got his own so he must have had some cash. It was very late when we got to London and it looked like another long wait until the early hours for the train north. Corporal Heath said 'I know what we will do - stay the night' and took us to the Union Jack club not far from the station. It was half a crown for a night's bed and breakfast the Corporal said he would pay as he could claim the money back. He didn't seem willing to splash out on anything to eat so we went to bed hungry. We made up for it at breakfast the next morning, although you only got one fried egg and two rounds of toast you could help yourself to porridge. It was mid morning when we got back to Trent Valley station and the Corporal had to phone the barracks for a lorry to come and pick us up. It had been the first visit to London for both Creer and I but we hadn't seen much of it, but we had been on the underground. Every one in the barrack room wanted to know where we had been and what we had

35

done. They must have thought we had spent the evening in a Soho night club.

Before we knew it Christmas was on us. Rumours of what leave we would be getting were everywhere and we only had confirmation of what we would be having a couple of days before it. There would be no travel warrants issued; those who went would have to make their own way home. I think the main idea was just to get as many people as they could out of the camp over Christmas to save on the cooking. We would be having a thirty six hour leave and with Christmas Day being on the Monday we would return Boxing Day afternoon. In the event, after we had done our usual Saturday morning cross country run the Sergeant came and told us to clean up the barrack room as he would be back to inspect it at one o'clock. We all moaned a bit about tarting the place up for Saturday afternoon but we did it. When he came back with Corporal Shaw at dead on one o'clock he walked into the top of the room and shouted 'Merry Christmas and you can all clear off home until Tuesday'. We all packed our washing and shaving tackle in our small packs and drifted off. Even the Irish lad and the one from the orphanage went off. I think a few of the chaps must have told their mothers about them when we had the forty eight hour pass and they had been told to bring them home with them on their next leave.

When I got off the bus at Walsall I thought I would go home prepared by taking some food. With most of the things still being on ration, bread and cake was about all I was going to get. That turned out to be a bit of a job in the end. With Christmas day coming on the Monday, Saturday would be the last day the shops would be open so people would stock up with what they could get hold of to eat. As I walked out of St Paul's and on to the Bridge, Pattisons was the first cake shop and they had been stripped bare. I walked over to Robinsons in Bradford Street and they had a few cakes but they were only for people who had ordered them and all the bread had gone. There were no buses in for the Delves so I decided to walk up to Alexander Road. As I walked through Caldmore the little shop that used to be Ellis's bakery was open and they had a couple of loaves and a ring of scones so I bought a loaf and the ring of scones.

When I got to the house I didn't have the key as I must have left it the last time I came. However when I tried the back door it wasn't locked but all was in darkness - the lights wouldn't work as the meter was empty as usual. After investing a couple of bob and putting the lights on I got my first surprise; Our piano, Mother's pride and joy had gone and in it's place was an old peddle organ. When Bill came home he told me Mary had swapped the piano for the organ with Alice, a woman from the house next door but one to us.

I hid the scones before going over to Jeff Slater's in the hope that he may have bought a bit of sausage from work. My luck was in - not only did I get some sausage to cook but Mini gave me a mug of tea and a chunk of cake! It was about nine thirty when I got back home and Bill was there. We had a cup of coffee and a scone each before we went to bed.

Bill had gone of to Cox's when I got up on Sunday morning and he would be there all day. My first job was to go and visit Granny Mac but not too early as she would probably be at the God Shop, so I went and got a Sunday paper from the shop on the corner and got another bottle of coffee and chicory while I was there.

The place where Granny was living was not far, just along the Broadway and up the Birmingham Road a bit. At about eleven I strolled up to Beacon Terrace to see her. She was over the moon to see me and said I looked better than I had been for some time. She gave me some lunch (which was what I'd been counting on) and we spent the afternoon talking. She told me the church was putting a Christmas dinner and a bit of a do on for all the old folks and asked where I was having my Christmas dinner. I told her I was going to Jeff's, I wasn't but if I had told her the truth she would have put her plans off just to cook for me and that was not on, I wanted her to go and have a great day out.

We had a bit of tea and as I left promising to write to her she shoved a large piece of cake in my hand. The weather had gone colder and as I walked back home wished I had brought my greatcoat with me. There was nothing to make a fire with so I made myself a hot drink and sat in my greatcoat until Bill came home. He had brought a bag of wood with him, bits of old carts but it burned well. I asked him about tomorrow, Christmas Day and he told me he was having his dinner at Cox's. There was no sign of Mary again and Bill said we wouldn't see her until after Christmas. We sat by the fire talking then made some toast for supper before going to bed. It was gone ten o'clock Christmas day before Bill went off to Cox's so we had a bit of breakfast together, toast with dripping on. The rest of the day was mine to do as I liked and the weather didn't look too bad so I had a walk down to Pleck Park. There were a couple of morning football matches being played so I had a bit of entertainment. Being on my own didn't bother me, I suppose I could have gone round to Jeff's or Aunty Maudes, but they would probably think I was on the scrounge, which of course, I was! Anyway, I had saved four links of sausage Jeff had given me for my Christmas dinner and with the bread dipped in the fat out of them and scones for afters, a good feed was had. A fire was lit with the rest of the wood Bill brought in the hope that he would come back with some more tonight. He came back early, at about seven thirty and with more fire wood. We had a talk and messed about on the old treadle organ until next door started knocking on the wall; neither of us could play it.

The next morning, Bill came and said goodbye to me before he went to do his horses but there was still no sign of Mary. I stopped in bed until after twelve o'clock as it was warmer in there. I had to put more money in the meter to make myself a drink and some toast and I managed to scrape a bit of fat out of the frying pan to put on it. By the time I had washed and shaved and got my kit together it was two o'clock and I wandered back down to Walsall. The wait was long and cold for a bus to Lichfield as they were only running a Bank holiday service. From Lichfield I had to walk back to the barracks but I was in plenty of time for the evening meal. That was Christmas 1950 over - to be endured more than enjoyed, I suppose.

Chapter Seven

By the first parade on Tuesday morning every one was back; some a bit blurry eyed as they didn't get back until the small hours. An hour drilling on the square soon woke us all up, followed by playing soldiers down the Spiders; bayonet practice and of course the bags of straw were the hairy arsed Russians. Corporal Shaw decided to do a bit of showing off by challenging us to try and stick him with our bayonets. Pitt (one of the lads from Liverpool was the first to try, he was game for anything and he ran at Corporal Shaw with his rifle and bayonet. Just as we thought the Corporal was going to get it in his stomach he caught the muzzle of the rifle with one hand, put the other hand under the magazine and sent poor old Pitt flying through the air. It was a good laugh but no one else wanted to try it after. Pitt picked himself up but no one bothered to ask him if he had hurt himself - they never did. We took some right knocks during training but as long as you could stand up and walk you were deemed to be fit. The Corporal had taken us on a couple of training exercises of how to fall down the main thing being once you are falling relaxes your body completely. If you are falling face first try and flip yourself on to your back. But most of all relaxes as you only damaged yourself if you hit the ground stiff. It seemed to work none of us got any broken bones. Most of us were happy when the training finished for the day it as had been a hard day for some. In the evening there seemed to be a competition of who could tell the tallest tale about how they managed to get back to barracks last night and their exploits over Christmas. I'd still got a few bob left so I went down the N.A.A.F.I. As I walked out of the barrack block I bumped into a lad from Wolverhampton who was in our platoon. He was just standing there looking sad and gazing at the sky. When I asked him if he was alright he said 'I'm going home' and just stood there. I left him and carried on to the N.A.A.F.I. had a mug of tea and got some fags. By lights out it seems the star gazer was as good as his word although he'd done his belt and gaiter ready for the morning parade. It would be the last we ever saw of him.

Early in the New Year we were told to get ready for a week of battle training at a place called Trawsfynydd in mid Wales. Sergeant Baker gave us a list of what kit to take with us which we must pack in our large valise or pack in English. A couple of army lorries with little wooden seats down the middle and sides picked us up on Saturday morning. It was a cold trip in the back of the lorry most of us were perished and by the time we reached Shrewsbury it was snowing. The journey took about four hours to Trawsfynydd and it snowed on and off all the way there. The camp which was along the main road was an A.O.C. Army Ordinance Corps Depot. The lorry took us through the camp up to a collection of Nissen huts on a hill overlooking the main camp. Sergeant Baker got us out of the trucks lined us up in about six inches of snow. A new platoon commander was introduced to us as Second Lieutenant Williams who would over see our battle training. As soon as he opened his mouth to speak to us you could tell he was a bit of a Hooray Henry from some public school. He explained that he would only be taking over while Second Lieutenant Barron was on leave. Sergeant Baker pointed out the two huts we would sleep in and where we would go for our meals and said our first parade would be eight o'clock in the morning. Corporal Shaw supervised who was going in which hut by calling the names in alphabetical order. He had already picked his bed out in the first hut. When we got into them there was a row of little iron cots down each side and three blankets and a pillow stacked on a bare mattress. Much to our delight there was a stove in the middle of the hut, but that soon turned to disappointment when we found there was nothing to burn in it. Lunch was at twelve thirty and in was quite a good feed. There were a lot of men in the other huts they looked quite old compared to us young lads. They were territorials of the Royal Artillery regiment here for weekend training. That's probably why the food was better than we got at Lichfield plus the fact the cooks were two experienced Catering Corps men. After lunch most of us went down to the N.A.A.F.I. in the main camp for even if you had no money it was warm in there. Outside the camp was a row of little bungalows with corrugated iron roofs each side of the road that run down to Trawsfynydd village. Anyway it was quieter down there as the artillery had their guns just off the road and was firing up over our huts so we got the full benefit of the blast off them. They went on until tea time when we thought that was the end if it, but we thought wrong. At about eight thirty the night firing started; I think they were different guns as they sounded different, more of a dull thud that a sharp bang. The racket went on until well after midnight.

Sunday morning we stayed in bed late and it was seven thirty before got the Corporal got us out. If we were not fully awake when we got up we soon were. The wash house, 'the ablutions' where in the middle of the huts. It was a corrugated sheet construction with gap of about a foot at the bottom and the same at the top. The taps were on a board that ran down the length of the place and a metal trough under them. There were no basins so you had to wash and shave under the running cold tap. If you weren't fully awake when you went in you certainly was when you came out. Sergeant Baker rolled up and announced breakfast would be at eight and first parade at eight thirty outside hut one and we should be dressed in battle order and with our rifles. The covering of snow we had yesterday had melted in the night and it was just a cold damp miserable day as we did our first parade. Sergeant Baker inspected us just to make sure we had shaven and had a wash I think. After the parade we were taken into an empty hut where Lt Williams was waiting. By now it was daylight and the guns had started firing again. The huts were shaking but Lieutenant Williams gave us a talk on the uses of the Mills Bomb or the hand grenade as we called it. He explained that it had a seven second fuse and a three second one. Depending on what and where you were using it determined the fuse you used. We were given a demonstration of how to prime the grenade and how it must be held. Sergeant Baker and Corporal Shaw had taken us all through this at Lichfield on a couple of occasions before but I think Lt Williams was just making sure we had the message as we would be throwing a live one later. At the end of the lecture we were issued with a grenade each and instructed to put it in our right pouch. The Corporal lined us up outside before we set off for the hills in single file. A brisk pace was set as we only had our denims on and it was a bit chilly. After half an hour's marching we reached the grenade throwing range; a circle of sand bags stacked about seven feet high. There was a smaller circle a few yards away and this was where you threw the grenade from. If you had a accident you were only going to blow yourself up. The drill was that we would all wait in the large circle and go one at a time to do our throwing. The Sergeant said that just to be on the safe side only seven second fuses would be used and you would only prime your grenade when you were in the throwing area. Corporal Shaw was supervising in the throwing bunker while the Sergeant gave us a fuse each as we left the waiting bunker. We all knew the drill of the army's way of chucking a grenade and the Sergeant had already said he didn't want to see any John Wayne antics off us.

It was a bit long winded and we were all frozen but we all managed to do it right. Lieutenant Williams and the Sergeant went back to camp in the jeep while Corporal Shaw jogged us back to camp to warm us up a bit.

It was lovely when we got in the dinning room for our lunch since the cook house was on the end of it and made the place nice and warm. There weren't many of the Territorials having lunch as they were only weekend training and a lot had gone home. By about two o'clock there were only us left in the Nissen huts. While we were having lunch Sergeant Baker came and told us that we wouldn't be doing anymore training today. We stayed in the dinning room as long as we could until we were chucked out at about one thirty for the floor to be cleaned. The N.A.A.F.I. was closed between two o'clock and five so most of us got into bed to keep warm.

Our evening meal was another good feed, I think it was food the territorials hadn't used so we all filled our bellies. A lot of us went down the N.A.A.F.I. after tea just to keep warm. There were a lot of civilians in the bar, local men from Trawsfynydd. All the pubs in Wales closed on Sundays and it seemed the locals came here for a drink. The usual piano recitals were given by some of the R.A.O.C. during the evening. Playing by ear most of them, it sounded like that's what they were using to play the piano. However we had a good night until closing time at nine o'clock.

Next morning was back to normal with parade at seven. There had been a little snow in the night but it only just covered the ground. After our inspection Sergeant Baker told us to go and put our great coats on and then report to the lecture hut. Lieutenant Williams was waiting in there when we arrived with an ordnance survey map pinned on the black board. Today we were going to put our map reading skills to good use. The platoon was split into groups of three and each given a map and a compass. We were taken out in a lorry and dropped at various locations around the area and left to find our way back to camp. The distance wouldn't be more than ten miles away so we should be back in time for lunch. The platoon was loaded into fifteen hundred weight lorries and we set off. Our truck drove down through the village and along the lake before turning into the hills and dropped us off in a wooded valley. We studied our map to figure out where we were when Stan had a brain wave. The brief was to find our way back to camp; no one said we had to go across country. Why don't we just go back down the road we came? The three of us walked back up to the end of the valley where there was a little town and a café. We all had a few coppers in our pocket, so decided on a cup of tea. Talking to the lady who ran the café we discovered it was about eight miles back to Trawsfynydd. An hour was spent in the café and we suddenly realised we could get back in time for our lunch. The lady pointed out to us that at eleven o'clock the bus would be stopping just up the road and if we were quick we could catch it. A dash was made to the bus stop but we still had to wait for it to come. A conference was held while we were waiting and it was decided to get off the bus at the stop before the town of Trawsfynydd and walk back to camp from there, it would only be a couple of miles. This was exactly what we did and nobody even asked or checked as to what we had done. Most of the platoon made it back in time for lunch. Corporal Shaw came while we were having our lunch and shouted parade outside the stores in battle order with our rifles at two o'clock.

The Corporal lined us up outside the stores at just before two and the Officer and Sergeant came and announced we would be practicing a platoon attack. A Bren gun and blank ammunition would be required for this exercise and detailed the lad on the end of the row as the Bren gunner. He would leave his rifle in the store when we drew the Bren gun and blank ammo. A couple of magazines were loaded and a little thing put on the muzzle of the Bren gun so the blank ammo would work when it was fired and five rounds issued to each of us. We had practised Platoon attacks before on the golf course at Whittington but not using blank ammo. The practise area was only just outside off camp and in the hills. The attack was the same as we had done before; rifles firing to cover the Bren gun moving into position then charging the enemy while the Bren covered us. With the grass being long and the ground wet we got soaked crawling into the firing position didn't we. Anyway Lieutenant Williams seemed chuffed by the way we had performed so we only did it once. When we got back to camp Sergeant Baker and the Corporal checked in our empty cartridges in and counted them just to make sure they were all accounted for. He then told us all to change into our battle dress uniforms and made arrangement for us to hang our denims and wet boots in the warm dinning room. Our last task was to give our rifles and the Bren gun a good clean and they would be inspected before we handed them into the stores.

We collected our dry denims and boots at breakfast ready for our first parade at seven thirty. We were happy as we didn't need to use our best bulled boots. Battle order was the dress again as we were training up in the hills live firing. The snow had gone by now, it was just damp and miserable as Corporal Shaw marched us off up into the hills. After about an hour we stopped in a little wooded valley with a rock face at the one end. The Officer and Sergeant were already there with boxes of ammo and two Sten guns in the back of their jeep. Sergeant Baker explained we would be firing live ammo and like the hand grenade throwing we would do it one at a time. There were ten targets hidden in the trees at the end of the valley. They were old ammo tins painted with red and yellow stripes, some with vertical lines some horizontal. As you walked through the trees and saw one you must fire your rifle at it. The one with the vertical lines you would fire from the shoulder. The ones with horizontal lines we should fire from the hip. The Sergeant or the Corporal walked behind as we did it and when my turn came I thought it great fun; the Corporal even picked up my empty bullet cases up as we went along. After we had all had a go with our rifles we moved to another little range at the side of the valley. Here we were going to do the same sort of firing with the Sten gun. Twenty eight rounds of nine millimetre ammo were issued to each of us and the first to go told to load his magazine and not to put it on the gun. As he was taken off to shoot the next was given his magazine to load and told not to put it on the gun until he got to the firing area. I don't think there was any way of scoring, well no one said anything you just did it. I didn't enjoy the Sten firing as much as the rifle but it was good all the same. It was well past lunch time by the time we had finished and our empties had be accounted for Lieutenant Williams said he had arranged a late lunch for us so we should be alright.

The afternoon was spent cleaning our weapons and the Sten guns. It was the inspection that the fun started; the Sgt couldn't see down the barrel of one lad's rifle. He explained that Woodall had told him you could fire a nine millimetre round in a three-o-three rifle so he had tried it. The empty case had ejected from the rifle alright but the bullet had stuck in the barrel. We all thought the Sergeant was going to have a heart attack by the look on his face and then he sent the Corporal to fetch Lieutenant Williams. When he came they all went into a huddle and we realised as they were in charge they would be in trouble as well as someone would want to know how we came to have a spare round of ammo to play with. Nothing was said to us but nothing could be done until we got back to Whittington. The rifle would be kept in the stores until we went home on Saturday. After our evening meal one lad had a bright idea, the tables in the dinning room were folding tables and holding the legs out was a piece of thick wire. If we could pinch a length off one of the tables we may be able to knock the bullet out of the barrel with it. A couple of days went by before the opportunity came to pinch the table stay and the hook at the end straightened out using the door key hole. The rifle was drawn from the store along with the others on the excuse of cleaning and oiling. It only needed a slight tap to get the nine millimetre round out of the barrel and nothing was said to any of the N.C.O's we just handed it back in the store with the others. We still got the dire forecast of doom from the Corporal, courts of inquiry, court marshals and lives in jail that was due to the culprits of this crime. The dinning room was not locked up at night and it was easy to put the stay back on the table. However when we got back to Whittington and they found nothing in the barrel of the rifle I think the N.C.O's were probably more relieved than us lads. Being the army some one had to carry the can of course, so the chap got seven days `jankers` for his troubles.

By Wednesday we were coping with the cold and damp a bit better; one of the tricks was to
save half your breakfast mug of warm tea to shave with.
At our first parade the Sergeant said that we would be firing the two inch mortars today as this was one of the training requirements. The weapon was only used to lay smoke screens these days. For our practise so we would be using H.E.`high explosive` and as the weapon had a history of being unreliable we would have a session on how to safely unload it if it misfired. The next half an hour was spent practising with the mortar and a dummy round. If it misfired the person using it picked the weapon up gently and held it in the horizontal position. His number two put his hand at the muzzle end making sure it would not touch the end of the mortar bomb as it came out. The base plate was slowly raised until the bomb gently slid out on to the palm of his hand. He would the grip the bomb round the centre of it, carry it to safety and gently lay it on the ground some distance away.

After our safety lesson we were marched single file up into the hills with the Corporal checking we kept a fair space between us as we went. The Lieutenant Williams the Sergeant along with a Sergeant and Lance Corporal from the R.O.A.C, I think they were there just to take care of any misfires; in the event we didn't have any.
As our turn came to fire we were each given a bomb and the Sergeant supervised the priming of it. There were no sights on the mortar, you set the range by the angle you fired it at. The maximum

range of it was said to be five hundred yards, held at a forty five degree angle. This was what we were instructed to do and it all went off with no problems and with out hitting any of the sheep. I think firing the mortar was just something we had to do because it was in the training schedule.

After lunch the Sergeant said we would be doing another required training element; we would be doing a march in battle order with our weapons. Most of it would be at the double as we had to complete the distance of two miles within eighteen minutes. Our small packs must contain our washing gear mess tins, socks, boot brushes and all things laid down in army regulations. The Corporal checked some of our packs just to see we weren't cheating before we set off.

We went down to the main road and set off using what the Corporal called Scout pace, march twenty paces, run twenty paces. It was hard going and after a while seemed like we had done five miles before we reached Lieutenant Williams and the Sergeant sitting in a jeep by the roadside. Here we turned round and started back towards Trawsfynydd to find Lieutenant Williams waiting at the camp gate when we got there. It had taken us a little over the time to do it and we were all knackered. Nothing was said to us about it but I think our efforts were marked as a pass or we would probably have had to do it again.

By now we had all had to wear our best bulled boots to train in. We got our boots soaking wet most days and the huts were never warm enough to dry our boots overnight.

Most of Thursday was spent practicing platoon attacks using blanks with the Officer and Sergeant chucking thunder flashes among us while we did them. The sheep must have been used to it all as it didn't seem to bother them at all. It was dark before we got back to camp and arrangements had to be made with the cook house for us to dry our clothes again.

At our fire parade on Friday morning the Sergeant told us we would be doing what he called a battle inoculation. Off we went up into the hills in single file. After an hour's walking we reached a stream that ran down into a little valley. What we were going to do was advance down the stream keeping our distance apart with our rifle at the port position. While we were doing this a Bren gun mounted on a tripod would be firing tracers over our heads. The stream was only shallow, probably a foot at its deepest and we were too buoyed up with anticipation to feel the cold. We set off and the Bren gun only fired a few short bursts as we went underneath it and there were some explosions that had been set on the bank. I had just got under the Bren fire when an explosion on the bank sent a piece of rock whizzing past me. It hit the lad in front of me, Dixon on his pack and knocked him over. He picked himself up and as we carried on further along Pitt was sitting on the ground holding his face in his hands. All the while the Sergeant was on top of the bank shouting 'carry on don't stop!'

At the end of the valley the Sergeant got back up the bank and lined us up. Lieutenant Williams and Corporal Shaw came out with Pitt who was bleeding from the ears and nose. Pitt was taken off in the jeep to see the Medical Officer and the rest of us taken back to camp. Pitt was already in the hut when we got back, a bit red in the face but fine. The injury was only a bit of blast damage and not serious, he may have been looking down at a thunder flash when it went off. I think that with the way the chunk of rock whizzed past me and knocked Perry over, they were using something a bit stronger than thunder flashes. However we were let off for the rest of the day with the Sergeant telling us he would inspect our huts before we left tomorrow. With the cleaning up and doing our kit it kept us busy for the day.

We were all glad to be leaving Trawsfynydd; it may be nice in the summer but was a bit rough in January. We had our lunch before the lorry came to take us back to Lichfield and the weekend soldiers had started moving in by the time we left.

Chapter Eight

We were all relieved to be back at the barracks if only for a warm. We didn't have hot water in the mornings but at least we got a small bucket of coal for a fire in the evenings. It was dark when we got back and were all a bit tired, so after our meal we just lay about talking of the events at Trawsfynydd. Sunday it was all go blancoing and polishing our kit ready for Monday.

On our first parade on Monday morning The Sergeant told us we would finish our sixteen week's training at the end of the month. There would probably be a passing out parade and the best recruit, in the opinion of the N.C.O's, would be presented with a small walking out cane.

It wasn't going to be me getting it so I didn't bother much.

The next couple of weeks were spent practicing things we had done many times before and the P.T.I's had been right; we were a lot fitter than when we joined the army. During this period we had more training films including how to avoid catching V.D. (venereal disease) and the affects of it if you did. There were some graphic details of the damage caused by gonorrhoea (the clap) and syphilis and the general advice was to keep it in your trousers. It was pointed out that it was very prevalent in some foreign countries and in these countries the army took precautions. They had a prophylactic hut in most camps where V.D. was a problem in that area for the low life that couldn't control themselves. Before indulging you must draw a condom and a tube of cream and when finished squirt the cream down the pipe of your chopper. All this would be very confidential in the usual army way. You signed your name and number when you collected it. Most of us thought it all hilarious but afterwards any one who came with a pimple somewhere on them, it was always a `syph` pimple - they had got a dose.

On the Friday just after lunch and just as we were getting ready for afternoon parade Captain Goodchild came rushing into our barrack room all breathless. Along with Corporal Shaw he checked all the platoon were present and told us to pack all our kit and any personal belongings in our kit bags. Our webbing equipment we would wear and parade outside the company office at three o'clock. Everyone was wondering what it was all about but we packed up and paraded at B company office as instructed. Major Owen came out and explained that the Gloustershire Regiment was going to Korea and were under strength. So together with some other infantry units we were being sent to reinforce them. Major Owen then asked if any of us was under eighteen years of age. Both Rudd and I put our hands up and was then told to fall out. There were no goodbyes and the rest of the platoon was then marched to the waiting lorries. Rudd and I were taken to a barrack block at the end of the square and told to find ourselves two beds in it. We found a couple of beds then unpacked our kit, placed our webbing on the locker as per regulations and made our beds up. The room was about half full and seemed it was just for passing soldiers. Most of the others were chaps who had come back to Lichfield for various reasons and were waiting to be sent back to their regiment. Corporal Shaw came back later to tell Rudd and I we were to report to the company office at seven thirty in the morning.

Both Rudd and I were waiting outside the office by seven thirty with our boots blacked.

The Company Sergeant Major came and said we would do fatigues while it was decided what to do with us. With today being Saturday we would go and get ready for the cross country run then report back here at one thirty. When we got back after lunch there was a Sergeant waiting for us, he took us down the Spiders. The T.A. was using some of the huts this afternoon and our job was to guard them and see that no unauthorised person went in them while the territorials were out training. There wasn't a lot do and by about three thirty some one was in all the huts. The Sergeant who brought us down rolled up looking all officious and holding a clip board. He said we may as well fall out as it didn't seem we were needed anymore. No one had told him what we were supposed to do next, 'just turn up at the company office on Monday morning' he told us.

Monday morning we were there at seven thirty sharp, all polished up. Rudd got the job of company runner for the day. I was told to report to the Sergeant Adcock of camp pioneers in a little building by the main stores. I got over there to find a nice little warm workshop with a Corporal and a couple of squaddies in there. The Corporal told me the Sergeant would be along about eight o'clock and to sit down and have a fag until he came. This was the camp maintenance shop where they repaired door hinges, broken windows and did other little jobs. The Corporal said he lived in the married quarters but the Sergeant who came from Walsall lived at home and so did one of the squaddies; in Alexander Road would you believe?

The Sergeant had been to the Sergeant's mess to scrounge a mug of tea before he started. The Corporal told him that B Company had sent me for him to find me a job. 'You're just the chap I'm looking for' said the Sergeant and handed me a large cross cut saw. He took me outside into a little alcove between the buildings and showed me a pile of tree branches. 'Saw these up into logs of about six inches long for the fire in the Officers Mess' he said, and take your time. The work shop seemed to be run on a 'don't over do it' basis, no one worked up a sweat and you took a break when you felt like it. At four thirty the Sergeant and the sqaddie went home.

Before the Sergeant left he told me he had seen the B company office and I would be working here again tomorrow.

After parading at the company office with the rest of the chaps I went to the log sawing again and by midmorning I had sawn them all up. I sat in the workshop yapping to the chaps who worked in there until the Sergeant came in at about twelve o'clock. He asked me if I could climb ladders and when I said yes, 'I've got a nice little job for you after lunch' he said.

At two o'clock the Sergeant came back from the Sergeant mess and told me I would be repairing broken windows. There were three broken panes in a barrack block on the far side of the square by the Church. The Corporal rigged me up with an old wood chisel, a mallet and a bucket. He said there were a pair of leather gloves somewhere but the lad who usually did the glazing must have hidden them and he was on leave. He then told me how to do the job; I was to chip the old putty and glass out of the frame and put them in the bucket making sure none was left on the floor. I was to then come back to the workshop for the glass putty and sprigs. I collected the old wooden extension ladder and set off round the square, it would have been a lot shorter if I could have walked across it. Apparently it was sacrilege to go on there unless you were drilling. The ladders were heavy so I had to stop for a rest on the way.

It was a two storey block like most of the others with casement windows and small panes of glass in them. One pane in the upstairs room and two in the ground floor were broken. It had warmed me up carrying the ladders but I soon got perished up the ladders only wearing denims in January. However I got all the old glass and putty out of the frames and put all the bits in the bucket and made sure the sills were clean. Back to the workshop and get warmed up a bit. I could see how I had got this job now but it would have been nice in the summer. The Corporal gave me the glass putty and six sprigs two for each pane of glass, they must have been solid silver and strict instructions on how to put them in. I was to make sure that each pane had a sprig in both sides. If I didn't when the residents cleaned it ready for the Saturday inspection they would probably push it out of the frame. He handed me a mangy little bit of cotton waste saying 'make sure to clean the out side of the windows before you leave it'.

The job was finished by about three thirty and I took all the tackle back to the workshop. Most of the others in the shop seemed to have finished for the day so I joined them. No one in the place knocked themselves about over working; it was like a semi retirement home for old soldiers. When Sergeant, Adcock called in on his way home he told me I would be here for the rest of the week. The Lance Corporal who usually worked here was on leave and he would keep me until he came back on Monday. I had a good week working in there although I didn't do a lot, just ran errands mostly.

We still got rounded up for the cross country run on Saturday and I needed the weekend to recover from that.

Monday morning at seven thirty Rudd and I were lined up with the rest of the odds and sods outside B company office. The Sergeant Major. gave us a quick inspection just to check we had washed behind our ears. Both Rudd and I were sent to work in the camp cook house over by the education hut. This was where the camp staffs had their meals and was not an A.C.C. training cookhouse like the other one. Cook house cleaners seemed destined to be our army career for both of us. However relief came with company orders on Wednesday evening - we were both to pack our kit and report to the company office in the morning.

Thursday morning we were there dressed in our best unifrorms and standing in the rain with our kit bags. We were called into the office where Captain. Goodchild told us we would be joining three platoon. This was the training draft that had joined a fortnight after we had and were now to be posted. The company clerk took us down to some barrack blocks by the Tamworth Road and handed us over to a Corporal Adams. The rest of the platoon was out training so the

Corporal said 'find yourselves a couple of beds and un-pack your kit'. Facilities were a lot better down here as the wash house had a row of proper sinks and there was a row of toilets, they were a bit more modern than the blocks by the square. By mid morning the platoon was back and Rudd and I joined them for a film on sniping after N.A.A.F.I. break. It seems we had come a day late as we had missed last night's fun; well I didn't think it very funny - it seems some poor chap had hung himself in the wash house with a rifle pull-through last night. The police had been and asked a few questions and the army would be having an enquiry. But all in all it had all been cleaned up and things were back to normal now.

At the afternoon parade the platoon Sergeant Bradley told us or posting had now come through and it looked like we would be going to Hong Kong to join the South Stafford's. This afternoon we would be issued with our tropical kit. The platoon was marched to the main stores where the B Company Colour Sergeant was waiting for us. He sorted us out into sizes and ushered us into the stores one at a time. First thing we got was a little white kit bag and a jack knife with a spike on for poking Boy Scouts out of horse's hooves. Four cotton jackets, two pairs of shorts, two pairs cotton trousers, one bush hat along with a pair of hose tops and pair of putty's. All in fashionable olive green of course. The next items had been left until the end probably because of the shock they would give when we got them thrown across the counter at us; two pair of pale blue cotton pyjamas. We were overwhelmed as most of us had never owned any before and they looked more like women's wear than Squaddie kit. It brought to my mind one of Pitt's little jokes. (It was only a soft little thing that stopped me joining the A.T.S.).

Kit bags were placed on the right shoulder and we marched back to the barrack room to try the jackets and trousers on. The Colour Sergeant came round inspecting us; if the jacket was a bit loose our belts would pull it in. The only thing that might need altering was the length of the trousers. Most of them were alright but a few us including me need them shortening so the Colour Sergeant marked them with chalk. We put a label with our name and number on them and handed them into the stores and they would be sent to the camp tailor or we could take them home and get our mother's to do them during our embarkation leave. As soon as we got our tropical kit sorted and packed in the little kit bags as per army regulations it was time to collect our pay. Before the pay parade started the pay clerk announced we would be drawing our pay for embarkation leave next week. If any one wanted to draw any of their credits they must let him know by tomorrow lunchtime.

By the following morning we were fully integrated into three platoon. After morning parade we had a map reading session. Then after the break we were down by the ranges chasing that East European man with the hairy arse again. It was P.T. for an hour after lunch and the Corporal announced we would be getting our inoculations this afternoon; he then doubled us over to the Gym. After the P.T.I's had finished with us we needed a monkey gland injection not an inoculation. By three thirty we were lined up at the medical hut, right sleeves rolled up. A couple of the orderly's came along the line one wiping your arm with iodine the other giving the injection. Next we were filed past a table where one orderly dabbed some stuff on the top of our arm while his mate stabbed it with a needle a in a cork a few times. With this one we had to come back next week to see if it turned into a scab. If it didn't we had to have it done again. That was it for the week; we only had C.O's inspection and the cross country run to look forward to now.

Things were easier now we had finished our training and after lunch on Saturday most of the chaps went home for the weekend. Some went to Tamworth, some to Lichfield, Rudd and I went playing darts at the Church Army place on the main road.

Monday morning we were on the rifle ranges at Kingsbury for the day. They must have had a round up for this event as there were four lorry loads of us and the butts wasn't long enough to accommodate everyone so we were split into two parties. We hadn't seen the officer in charge before but he was obviously a sporting man. He suggested we all back ourselves with a tanner each and the one with the highest score collects the cash. This produced some rumbling in the crowd as we thought he was to pull a fast one but the officer sensed the problem and he said he wouldn't shoot. With the amount of chaps to fire we only had twenty rounds each, ten at two hundred yards and ten at four hundred yards. When it was all totted up the officer said 'it's a man named Power with the highest score'. Some of the old soldiers with us were not very happy at me beating them and wouldn't hand over their tanners. I wasn't bothered as I made seventeen and a tanner out of it.

It was a bit late when we got back to barracks and we had to dash to get our lunch. The afternoon was spent cleaning our rifles and drying our denims as it had been a wet morning on the ranges.

Thursday was the day we were all waiting for and for the next couple of days we just had our scabs inspected and went through the motions. The big day arrived and we had drill on the square for most of the morning just to let us know we were still in the army.

Then we packed our kit we didn't need for our leave and put it in the stores. The officer and pay clerk came after lunch and set up a table for him and Captain. Goodchild and we got two weeks pay. Travel warrants were given to those who had asked for them and we also got some food ration coupons. Everyone changed into their best uniforms and the Sergeant inspected us just to make sure we were smart enough to go on embarkation leave. Most had gone by five o'clock but I had the evening meal before I went.

I took my uniform off when I got home and put on the suit I had before I joined the army. I had no idea what to do with the food coupons - the next fortnight would be all toast, chips and what we could scrounge off Jeff Slater. It turned out to be a good fortnight as I spent some time with some of my friends from school. I did some visiting and I even went to see Jack and Rose who lived at the farm with us. One thing about visiting was you nearly always got offered something to eat, so I did alright. I never saw Mary once during the leave although we talked through the bedroom wall on a couple of mornings. She would be gone by the time I got up. Bill was there every night but he only slept there and he spent most of his time at Cox's. I visited Granny Mac a few times and I took her out. She liked to go in Patterson's Café on the Bridge for a pot of tea and a cake. Every time I saw her she would tell me, as we parted, that I must not marry a foreign girl when I went abroad. I'd had a good fortnight - said my goodbyes and vanished back to barracks, looking forward to Hong Kong.

Chapter Nine

We were only back from our embarkation leave for one day before we were off. The company orders on Thursday night informed us we would collect haversack rations after breakfast on Friday morning. The evening was spent packing our kit bags after we had blancoed our belts and gaiters, well you could bet we would be inspected before the off.

After packing I strolled off down to the N.A.A.F.I. and who should I meet but Twiggy Arms a lad who had been in my class at school. I learnt form him that he had joined last Thursday along with Gordon Poppit, another lad from our class at Hilary Street School but `Poppie` as everyone called him had not come down the N.A.A.F.I. with Twiggy. We would all meet up again later.

Friday was a bright sunny day as we lined up waiting for the transport to the station and it was warm for the end of January so it's always stuck in my memory. The Lorries came and took us to the station in Lichfield; usually if we were going south we went from Trent Valley station. We were lined up on the car park and marched onto the platform by the Sergeant in charge of us. He then split us into groups of eight to fill one compartment in the carriage and supervised our getting on the train. It wasn't a corridor coach and with our kit bags the compartment was a bit cramped. It was about twelve thirty when we got off the train in to London and lined up on the platform. A young National Service second lieutenant arrived and announced we would have to cross London to Kings Cross station. The Sgt marched us to the station entrance where some army Lorries where waiting. All the kit bags should be put in the first lorry shouted the young officer, but it soon became obvious that we were not doing it quickly enough. He was poking some of the lads along with his cane and you could tell by his accent and attitude he had been fully trained on how to keep the peasantry in their proper place from an early age. By the way he was carrying on some one was going to have him by the throat sooner or later. On our journey across London we could see a large silver cigar shaped object sticking up into the sky. This was the Festival of Britain site and that was as much of it as any of us was going to see. The lorry with our kit bags had got to Kings Cross first and dumped our kit in a pile at the side of the entrance. We collected them and marched on to the platform which was full of squaddies like us all bound for foreign parts. The train got to Southampton at about four o'clock and went right on to the dockside. We were lined up on the key side the Sergeant checked we all had our kit bags. The ship we were to embark on was called the Empire Fowey and was dwarfed by the Queen Mary in the dock behind it. Each draft was called on to the ship separately and we must have stood for an hour and a half before our turn came to board the ship. As we boarded we were each given a small blue plastic disc - this was or meal ticket and we were the last sitting. There were to be three meal sittings; red first followed by white then blue. One of the crew took us down to C deck which must have been below or very near the water line as the port holes were screwed up and blacked out. The deck was all rows of what the Corporal called standees. These were fold up bunks with a tubular frame and canvas stretched across them and one above the other. The first job was to sort our plimsolls out of our kit bags. We would wear these for the rest of the journey, no boots allowed on the deck. Once all the troops were loaded on board and had their pumps on we were called back up on deck. This was for life boat drill and instruction on fastening out life belts. The ship tannoy gave us our instructions with the Sergeant making sure we got it right. If we ever heard short shape blasts on the ships siren we were to assemble at this point with our life jackets on. This we would do several times during our voyage just to keep us on our toes. The Sergeant said that when the ship was made the first rivet in the keel was solid gold. If any of the ships crew offered to take us down to see the golden rivet we should decline the offer. That fetched a groan from us we had all heard the golden rivet joke before.

There were post cards of the ship for sale in the shop and a notice the last post from the ship would be at eight o'clock tonight. I bought one and sent it to granny Mac. There were fags and things for sale as well but we would wait until we were out at sea then they would be duty free. A Corporal Stone from the South Stafford's who was returning to Hong Kong was in charge of us down on C deck The Sergeant and Officers had cabins up on the top deck. There was plenty of advice for us new lads as there were several old soldiers on the draft with us. After we had finished the life boat drill it was time for our meal. It was about the same as we got at Lichfield; meat pie, mashed spuds, cabbage and carrots followed by some sort of sponge covered in lumpy custard.

By the time we had eaten our meal which we were ready for as we hadn't eaten since our haversack rations in the morning, it was seven o'clock. Some of us went up on deck just to have a look but it had turned bitter cold. Down on C deck it was warm and most of the nozzles blowing cold air had been turned off. We were informed by the old soldiers these were called `punkers` and we would be glad of them when we reached the tropics. Corporal Stone who was in charge told us he would parade us each morning after breakfast. One of the Lance Corporals pointed out that we were the last meal sitting and our breakfast would be eight o'clock until eight thirty. So it was decided we would parade at our lifeboat station at nine o'clock. No one saw the point as we wouldn't be wearing our boots gaiters but some one said it was just to check none of us had jumped overboard.

When we woke next morning we could feel the ship moving so we couldn't resist sneaking on deck to have a look but we were only just leaving Southampton port. Our breakfast was got down us in double quick time so we could see what was happening before our parade. The Corporal inspected us just to make sure we'd shaved and looked smart. He was about to fall us out when the Sergeant arrived. He announced we would be doing some P.T. while on board probably two sessions a week. The details would be published later as he needed to book a time and the space on deck to hold it. He went on to explain that the front of the ship was called the bow and the back the stern. The right-hand side looking towards the bow was starboard the left side port and would we please use these terms. Not the sharp end and the blunt end as he had heard some of us refer to the front and back of the ship.

As soon as the inspection was over it was a rush to the ships rail for a grandstand view as most of us had never been on a ship before. The ship was now passing the Isle of White and we could see a large flying boat on the shore, this was the Princess flying boat we were told. By mid morning the ship was passing a line of pointed white rocks. These were the needles off the Isles of Wight the ships tannoy informed us. The ship was fully loaded with troops bound for the Middle East and the Far East. There were also a few girls from the W.R.A.C. (Woman Royal Army Corps) and two or three from the (Queen Alexander Royal Army Nursing Corps) who wore grey uniforms. Some army families were onboard but they where in cabins and had a deck on their own along with the officers and Sergeants.

By lunch time the event we had all been waiting for happened, the duty free shop opened. Cigarettes were the main item on most of our lists. Most were in boxes of fifty and cost half a crown a box, there were some twenties in flat tins but these were either Pall Mall or Markonvitch Black and White. Woodbines Senior Service and Players were the main fags on sale, the Players being in round tins. All the fags were the same size, there weren't smaller cheaper ones like we were used to. The shop sold other things as well but they were a bit dear as they had a captive market. During the afternoon a school of Dolphins came swimming along side the ship. Every one wanted to have a look and it was a bit of a scramble to get a place by the rail. They swam in the ships bow wave for some time so most of us did get to see them. The ship had a recreation room on the main deck and it was quite a nice place with comfortable chairs, a bar and a piano on a little stage. This was where we would spend most of our evenings during the journey to Hong Kong. By tomorrow we would be entering the Bay of Biscay and this got some of the old soldiers telling tales of previous trips. One had stories of waves ninety feet high and the ship had to back up them; and even the ships cat had been seasick. No one took much notice of their tall stories, we were used to old soldiers' tales by now and we had a smooth crossing anyway. Once we were out of sight of land and the Dolphins had gone there was only the occasional passing ship to see.

After dark it was very cold up on deck and after our evening meal a lot of us went up the recreation room. The bar was open from seven until nine o'clock but you were only allowed two pints of beer. You had to go to the ships shop to pay for it and they gave you a voucher to give the barman. Like most things for sale it was a bit pricey so only the hardened drinkers bought it. A squaddie was doing his best on the piano and as one stopped playing there always seemed someone ready to take over. A couple of card schools playing pontoon with fags as currency were in operation and an old soldier had a crown and anchor board going. It was strictly against the rules to gamble but no one seemed to bother about stopping it. With it being Sunday the ships Chaplin arrived on the scene about seven thirty. The crown and anchor board and the pontoon schools miraculously vanished as if by magic. The Chaplin held a bit of a service and got us to sing a couple of hymns accompanied by a squaddie on the piano. He hadn't got two paces out of the door before the pontoon schools and the crown and anchor were back on.

At our Monday morning parade the Sergeant announced he had booked two slots for our P.T. sessions, Tuesday morning's eleven until twelve and Thursday afternoon's three until four o'clock. These would be held on the forecastle, a little raised deck at the front of the ship. Those of us expecting a stormy time going through the Bay of Biscay were in for a disappointment as the sea was calm. The next time we saw land we were passing a light house with a building that looked like a fort near it. We were informed this was Cape St Vincent at the tip of Portugal and the fort has been sacked by Sir Francis Drake in sixteen fish and chips or something like that. The ship must have gone through the Straits of Gibraltar in the night and the weather was a lot warmer now. We could see land on the starboard side of the ship. It looked nice with little white buildings nestling on green hillsides with the sun glinting on them. This was Algeria in North Africa and the last land we would see until we reached Port Said in Egypt. On Tuesday evening a couple of middle aged ladies appeared in the recreation room and announced there would be bingo sessions or 'Housey Housey' as they called it. These would be between seven o'clock and eight on Tuesday evening and on Thursday evening. The prizes would be what now seemed to be the common currency on board this ship, Cigarettes. We learnt later that these two old dears were (W.V.S. Women's Voluntary Service) Ladies. There was always something going on in the room of an evening; besides piano playing most nights someone would get up and sing and occasionally some body would fancy they were a bit of a comedian and do a turn.

On the Thursday afternoon after our P.T. session we saw the officer who came with us for the first time since we had been onboard. He had rolled up for our pay parade and once he had doled out the cash he vanished again. We passed a few ships as we sailed down the Mediterranean and some of them signalled to the ship with a flashing lamp in Morse code. None of us could tell what it was about but there were chaps form the Royal Signals on board who probably could. When we awoke on Saturday morning the ship was in Port Said harbour so our first thing was to go up for a look. There was not a lot going on as we must have just docked. By the time we had our breakfast and the Corporal; had paraded us, things were beginning to happen. Several little boats were by the ship with the locals shouting their wares for sale up to us on deck. Embossed leather wallets, belts, dirty photos and other junk. If you wanted anything they threw a string line with a little basket on up for you to put the money in first. Some of the old soldiers who had seen it all before would get them to throw the string up then tie it to the ships rail. However there was always some kind soul who would untie it for them. The best show was the kids diving for coins - if you chucked a penny in they would dive and retrieve it. We tried throwing as far out as we could but they would still get them. They must have made more money this way than they did selling things.

Later in the morning the tannoy announced there would be shore leave this afternoon. This to be fourteen hundred hours until seventeen hundred hours. Only those with shoes would be allowed to go, no boots or plimsolls permitted. Most of us had our shoes in our kit bags as we had been forewarned before we came that we might need them. A large raft was brought along side the ship or what they called 'a lighter' and it took two or three trips to get us all ashore. There were an army of peddlers waiting for us with all sorts of bargains; fruit and bottles of pop which we had been warned to avoid at all costs as they got their water from the Nile; offers of come and see my sister jiggy jiggy Johnny, 'very cheap' were declined.

The gang of us Stafford's walked down into the middle of the town but it was a bit of a tatty place. There were quite a few army people about as it was one of the main posts in the Middle East. We had to run the gauntlet of peddlers all afternoon and they got on your wick after a while. All in all it was an experience never to be forgotten and we all had tales to tell later. After our evening meal there was a film on The Third Man. A screen had been set up on the stern of the ship and it was a lovely warm starry night and sat there watching that film, we were now a million miles from cold, wet, rationed England.

On Sunday morning the ship was in a convoy with other ships going up the Suez Canal and we spent most of the day on the ships rail watching our progress. There was a lot going on along the bank; people on donkeys, a camel train all wandered along going somewhere. There didn't seem to be any bridges so they probably had to go long distances if they wanted to cross the canal. By lunch time we reached a little lake and the tannoy told us we were at Ismalilia. We could see what looked like an R.A.F station there and an Army camp as well. By late afternoon we had moved on up to a large lake, these were the Bitter lakes we were told. There were lots of ships in the lake as it was the crossing point for ships going up the canal and those coming down. The ship dropped anchor here as there was probably ships still coming down from the Red Sea. The boat was not at anchor long and by bed time we were passing Port Suez and into the Red Sea. It took us about fifteen hours to get through the canal, we had all been taught about it at school but journeying through it was something else.

Chapter Ten

Although it was only early in February the weather was very hot and sunny. The Red Sea seemed much warmer than it was sailing down the Mediterranean. The punkers down on deck were going flat out but it was still hot and smelly down there. We spent most of our time up on deck on what seemed the favourite pass time, playing cards. Two lots of cigarettes were needed - a box for smoking and a box for card playing. Using them as currency and being in the hot sun the tobacco dried up and gradually fell out of them. Long before our journey's end most were only paper tubes.

Our half hour P.T. sessions were now hard going but the Corporal kept us at it and we were often on our knees when he finished with us. The Sergeant didn't knock himself about much as he was only there in a supervisory role. He gave us advice about sun bathing- don't do it. Any one getting sunburnt who needed medical attention would be deemed a self inflicted injury and this was a chargeable offence. The army didn't issue sun tan lotion so it was up to individuals themselves to acclimatise a bit at a time. The only good thing was the ablutions on C deck, these were good by army standards and had a row of showers although they were only salt water so you couldn't get the soap to lather. You could buy sea water soap from the shop but you didn't get very much lather with that either. Everyone seemed to be enjoying the cruise except for the morning clean-up. The Corporal always inspected to see we had swept up, cleaned the ablutions and folded our blanket as regulations before morning parade.

After a few days we reached the Port of Aden and it was announced there would be shore leave again. Once again we were warned on how to behave ourselves and of the perils that awaited us if we didn't. A notice was put up in the recreation room that anyone with a bathing costume could go for a swim. This was at some forces club in Aden but as most of us didn't have a costume there weren't many takers.

After the Sergentt had inspected us to make sure we were smart enough to face the Arab world, off we went. Just like in Port Said, the ship had the crowd of `Bum` boats around it again, all selling some junk and we were accosted with all sorts of bargains on our way into Aden town, one even had a Leopard skin he was trying to sell us.

There were lots of Camels and we hadn't seen any in Port Said. Len William tried to stroke one and the Camel spit on him. Len didn't have anything to wipe it off with so we tried rubbing a hand full of sand on it and that did it. If we thought Egypt was a rough place, Aden beat it however it was all new to us young squaddies and we were fascinated by the people and their antics. All who went ashore had tales to tell when they got back on the ship. Several had bought handkerchiefs with pictures of forty different ways to have sex on them; these seemed to be the prize possession. The couple of lads who had been for a swim at the club told us it had been in the sea. It was a small bay and there was a steel net across the end to stop the sharks getting in.

If we were expecting to get another film while we were in port we were in for a disappointment -The Third Man in Port Said was the only one we ever got.

Things started to get a bit out of hand on C deck when a couple of the old soldiers thought they shouldn't help in the morning fatigues. The Corporal had put us in groups of four when we had sailed from Southampton. Each group had taken it in turns to clean the wash house toilets and sweep the floor. This was always done before our nine o'clock parade in the morning. It had all gone well while the Corporal was directing it all. But now he had lost interest and just left us to do it, and the old un's thought it their duty to skive off. One of the skivers, a chap in his thirty's, had been complaining to the Corporal that some one had been creeping up on him while he was sleeping. No body took any notice of him as if you spoke to him he didn't seem very bright. He would probably spend all his life in the army until they threw him out. Things got better when the Corporal took charge of the proceedings again and made sure the one on his list did it when their turn came.

The Indian Ocean was very calm and we had a new thing to amuse us, Flying fish. They would shoot out of the water as the ship passed and glide on their long fins. Some would go a fair old distance.

It took about a couple of weeks to sail from Southampton to Colombo in what was then called Ceylon which was our next stop. There was shore leave again and we dropped off a couple of R.A.F. chaps there. Unlike the last two ports Colombo was a city, but we were still surrounded with bum boats selling everything. It was the same on shore with the beggars and all the offers we couldn't refuse. A group of us had a walk up into the city. It would have been an interesting place if we had the time to explore it, we even saw a chap on an Elephant!

Sid Walters bought a little violin made out of a coconut shell for half a crown. He could play a tune on it when he bought it but by the time we got back to the ship it had fallen apart. We were all happy it had been another adventure. As we sailed out of Colombo the weather turned rougher with wind and rain. This made the boat rock a bit and chaps who hadn't been seasick now were. However after a couple of days we sailed out of it.

Some of the squaddies who had been doing the recreation room entertainments decided to have a concert party. This was planed for next Saturday and auditions for anyone wishing to take part would be held. This resulted in the recreation room being closed on the following Thursday and Friday afternoons. A selection committee was set up, lead by some old Major from the Service Corps along with the W.V.S. ladies and the squaddie who had suggested it in the first place. The recreation room closure didn't make much difference as we spent most of the time on deck anyway. The Saturday night concert went well, there were several singers but the best turn was a snake charmer. He dressed as an Indian and had a snake made out of a length of old rope. He and the comedian got the best cheer of the night. The singers were good but we had them every night.

As we sailed towards Singapore we sailed close to some island in the Malacca straits and we saw our first Shark. It wasn't very clear, you could just see his outline under the water but with the ship moving we only got a quick glance of it but it made our day.

As the ship approached Singapore harbour there was a flurry of activity on the boat. There were a lot of the squaddies going to Korea on board. It seemed things were going badly in the war there and they needed reinforcements. They would now disembark at Singapore and be flown to Pusan in Korea from Changi Airport. There would also be some more troops not originally bound for Korea who would join them. With us being infantry we thought we would be a racing certainty to be going and were mightily relieved when our names were not called out.

We were given half a day's shore leave but that didn't get us very far - only around the shanty town by the docks. However it was the first time we had got ashore without being surrounded by hawkers. There was still a lot of damage for the last war evident around the dock area. The walk round let us stretch our legs a bit but our P.T. sessions had kept us fairly fit in the last three weeks. A day after we had left Singapore one of the old soldiers, Onion as every one called him, was taken ill. He just lay on his bunk and couldn't get up and after threats from the Corporal failed to shift him the Medical Officer. was sent for. Heat exhaustion was the cause. Two squaddies were detailed to get one each side of him and take him to the sick bay. At the morning parade the next day we were given a lecture by the Sergeant every one must ensure that we drink at least six pints of water a day and put plenty of salt on our food. The main cause of heat exhaustion according to him was not drinking enough. Of course it was the usual self inflicted injury and a chargeable offence. Old Onions was only in the sickbay for a day and a half before they chucked him out. It seems the cure for heat exhaustion was salt tablets and to drink gallons of water.

The ship encountered a couple of day's rough weather in the South China Sea but I don't remember anyone being sea sick. We had been on the voyage for a month now and were becoming seasoned sailors. When we awoke on Wednesday morning (our last day at sea) the weather had turned nice and sunny. At our morning parade the Sergeant gave us a list of what we needed for our embarkation O.G. jacket and trousers, beret along with boots, belt and gaiters would be worn and we would go for our breakfast in Plimsoll's. Boots would not be worn until after breakfast when we were ready to disembark. Kit bags would all be packed the night before we docked and only our washing and shaving stuff left to pack.

All of us young squaddies were excited as to what would happen tomorrow although the old sweats had seen it all before. They were full of legendary stories of Hong Kong and we learnt from them that Chinese women's fannies were horizontal not vertical like European women. One thing most us new recruits had leant in our short time in the army was old soldiers could tell some likely stories.

By the time it got dark we could see the lights of Hong Kong as we passed between some islands just off the mainland. When we woke on Thursday morning we could feel the ship was not moving and when we got up on deck we could see the ship was tied up to the dockside and they had already started unloading from the hold.

After breakfast the Sergeant came down on to our deck, which was unusual for him as most of the trip he had only met us on the top deck (well it did smell a bit down on C deck). We were to parade in our usual place at eight thirty with our kit bags and accoutrements. Once we were out on the deck we must stand in rank as they didn't want us clopping all over the deck in our boots. There were not that many troops left on the ship so we wouldn't have to wait long. Although there was still a few for Korea they would go to the army transit camp at Kure in Japan. The British army staging post for Korea was there.

We were all on parade by eight thirty and the Sergeant gave us an inspection to make sure we were fit for Hong Kong to receive us. There was now a bit of a hold up while the ships Purser inspected C deck for damage. How we were ever going to do any damage to it without an acetylene burner or a hacksaw is any one's guess. The order to disembark was given along with 'pick your feet up and don't scrape them on the deck'. We were met on the dock side by a Captain and a Sergeant from the South Staffordshire Regt. All Our kit bags were loaded on to a lorry but we were going up to Fanling by train. The Sergeant lined us up in the usual columns of three and marched us over to Kowloon station which was a Victorian structure with a clock tower and a life sized stuffed Tiger in a cage advertising the Siberian Fur Store by the entrance. The Captain came, looked us over and told us it was only about thirty miles to Fanling and a lorry would meet us there and take us to Bird's Hill Camp. As soon as the Captain had vanished one chap asked the Sergeant how far it was to China. Measure it and when we have done thirty two miles jump off the train or else that's where you'll be. However in your case just stop on the train it would be a relief to us all.

The Sgt organised our getting onto the train, well he couldn't leave a rabble like us to board a train by our selves could he? We hadn't been going for long when the train went into a tunnel - this was through a line of hills that separated Kowloon from the New Territories. As we emerged form the tunnel there was a hill on the right hand side. I was taken aback when I saw it as I was utterly convinced that I had been on that hill before. It frightened me for a while but by the time we reached Fanling I had got over it.

A couple of lorries were at the station to take us up to Bird's Hill camp about a mile up the road past Fanling village along the Sha Tau Kok Road. The camp was off the road across a causeway over the rice paddies and spread along a range of low hills. The first thing we saw as we went in the gate was two large funny looking Tigers made of wood standing on a lawn in front of a Nissen hut. The Nissen hut turned out to be the guard room and the funny Tigers Chints captured in some battle in India or Burma long ago. The Lorries pulled up just behind the guard room in front of a large Romany hut, the camp head quarters. The old soldiers who had returned to the regiment were told to go back to their companies and us new one's were lined up. We were called to attention when a Major came out and announced he was second in command of the Battalion. He said that the battalion commander was Lieutenant Colonel Martin normally liked to welcome new additions to the regiment but was in hospital at the moment. He gave us a talk on what was expected of us as members of the first and second battalion of the South Staffordshire Regiment and how things would be different now we were serving and not training. While he had been yapping to us a Full lieutenant had shown up. The Major introduced him as our Medical Officer and he would now brief us on how to stay healthy. The first thing was what we had on the ship, drink plenty of water and take salt with your food. In his words we were to make sure we had at least two good pisses a day - dribble and a puff of steam were not good enough. He came to the V.D. topic using the same simple English; he pointed across the road to a little Nissen hut that was the prophylactic hut and went through the 'what to do with the little tube of ointment' again. He then went on to explain what to do if you do catch a dose or a Blobby Knob as he put it. Like sunburn, it was a self inflicted injury in the army's book.

Rashes were next on the agenda, namely something called Tinea and ringworm. Tinea was very common and most of us would get it between our legs and under our arms at sometime. Ringworm was more common in the rainy season due next month and mainly occurred around the stomach where your belt fitted. Prickly heat was another common ailment and standing naked in the rain was the best cure for it - so don't bother him with it. Snake bite was last and if we got bitten we must seek help immediately as the longer the poison had to circulate the more difficult the cure. If possible, we should kill the snake and bring it to the M.O as this would tell him which antidote to use. Last but not least Mosquitoes or mozzies as he called them. It was inevitable we were going to get bitten so we must take a Pladrin tablet every day as a precaution against malaria. There were tins of these tablets in each barrack room and the Corporal was charged with seeing everyone took one. As the evening was their most active time we must wear long trousers and shirts with the sleeves rolled down after six o'clock in the evening.

The Major came back and said we would now join our company's and divided us up into four groups A, B,C & D and handed us over to an assortment of Corporal's who had been waiting patiently in the shade of the Romney hut. Once more I was in B Company.

Chapter Eleven

We were handed over to the waiting Corporal who would take us to our new company's. Before we were marched off the Corporal in charge of our group, Corporal Fellows explained where all the main offices were; the large Romany hut we were standing out side was the H/Q, which we knew. The Nissen hut was opposite the Medical room and we'd already located the guard room. The Romney hut by the paddies with the lorries parked out side was the M.T. Motor Transport Platoon; a collection of little bungalows on the hill overlooking the M.T was the Officers mess.

The road through the camp ran round in a semi circle with a road off it going over a steep little hill and meeting it again later. We took the circular path past the main battalion stores and round past D Company and on to B Company. A Company was further on. All the companies were set up the same with four little bungalow type barrack blocks standing on a hill with a veranda along the front.

The company H/Qs and stores was a Nissen hut by the road with steps leading up to the barrack blocks. Here Corporal Fellows lined us up on the road and called us to attention. A thick set older man came out of the Nissen hut and announced he was Company Sergeant Major Packer who looked a jolly sort of a chap. He went on to tell us a Major White was our company commander with a Captain Wells as his second in command. He then explained that now the weather was warming up again the normal dress while in camp was boots, socks, shorts and bush hats, or hats `pisspotical` as he called them, and 'don't let me catch anyone out in the sun with out one on!'

With it only being late February the sun was not too strong here yet and as we had been in the sun on the ship for about three weeks most of us were used it by now.

However, shorts, boots and hat only applied while we were in camp. Anyone going out of camp should of course be smartly dressed.

The Major now handed us over to Colour Sergeant Heal who issued us some bedding and a rifle and told us which platoon we would be in. We were each given the normal pair of sheets, a U.S. blanket, a green lightweight blanket and to our surprise a tin of foot powder. This was in a beautiful olive drab tin with the Government crow's foot stamped on it. The Colour Sergeant said this was to stop us sending it home for our girlfriends to use as face powder. I was put in one platoon and would be in the first hut at the top of the steps. We would go and find a bed, settle in and then come back to be issued with a rifle. There were plenty of empty beds as the company was way below strength.

The barrack blocks were a big improvement on Lichfield; nice and airy with a door leading on to a veranda at each end. There was a row of ten beds along the back wall and along the front wall were two beds, then a door, four beds another door and two more beds. A built in wooden cupboard along the end wall were only to be used for jackets and coats as we had foot lockers for our personal kit.

Corporal Fellows who had brought us up to the barracks was the only platoon Corporal and he soon sorted us out with a bed and locker and said all the chaps were out in the hills and would be back by six thirty. He pointed out the cookhouse which was on the other side of the road by the perimeter fence. The toilets and washhouse where also down there with earth closets, a row of taps along a board and some showers. There was also a hut made of bamboo mats on poles about six foot off the ground; this was the local builders hut as the camp was still in the process of being built. In fact C Company still lived in tents.

The Corporal said we had left it a bit late for our midday meal but if we got down to the cookhouse sharpish we may get served. He came down with us and explained to the Sergeant why we were late. They were packing up when we reached the cookhouse but the cooks found us some food. It was the usual exotic meal; Pom transmogrified carrot and something meaty in pastry followed by custard with bits of banana in it. We were informed that our midday meal was not called lunch out here but 'Tiffin.'

After Tiffin we went back down to the stores for our rifle which we were told to draw clean and then take back. We would need to keep the sling off it to Blanco as there was a Regimental Sergeant Major parade in the morning.

The rest of the company was up in the hills digging defences and we were told we would spend a lot of our time doing that. They wouldn't be back until about half six so in the meantime just got ourselves settled in, put our mozzie nets up and packed our kit in the foot lockers. As there was a Battalion parade in the morning we had to make sure we had a decent jacket and shorts however, with them being in our kit bags for the last month they were rather creased. Corporal Fellows suggested we damp the jacket and shorts and hang them on the wire that held the mozzie net up above our beds over night. Although we had or nets up the Corporal said we wouldn't need them at night until the rainy season started. The mosquito that carried the malaria bug was seasonal and it hatched out in warm wet weather. After a long period of dry it gradually died out except for places that were permanently damp.

The company came back dead on six thirty and handed their picks and shovels into the stores where the store man checked they were all returned. They were the same mix of chaps we had trained with - Black Country lad's, Scousers and from all points in between. There were a couple of lads in our platoon who only joined last week. They had been in Korea with the Middlesex regiment who were in camp on the other side of the Sha Tau Kok Road. It seems that when things were going pear shaped in Korea last year, the Middlesex had been sent in a hurry and had borrowed some of the Stafford's to make a side up. The company should have four platoons of eighteen men each but only had four platoons of twelve.

We introduced ourselves, although we didn't need to, as they were a friendly bunch and off we went for our evening meal. That was down on the list as dinner and I hadn't brought my dinner jacket. Our stomachs were not going to be upset by a change of diet since the food was the normal army stuff served on the usual bullet proof platter plates. The only change was that most of the vegetables were dried although we did get some fresh vegetables sometimes.

I had just got mine and was about to find somewhere to sit when I heard 'Worro Podge'. I turned round and there was Johnny Giles a lad from Hilary Street School who lived in the Pleck, so I sat with him and had a natter.

It was all go after our evening meal with polishing and blancoing ready for tomorrow's parade. Before the parade there would be an inspection of the barrack rooms by Major White, so we had to tidy up for that as well. I decided to go down to the N.A.A.F.I afterwards; this was on a patch of flat land between the battalion H/Q and the paddies. There was also a large tent down there which we were told was the Contractors. Most of these were Indian and they did the boot repairs, tailoring and barbering for the camp. They also sold civilian clothes and shoes. Another of their services was coming round the barrack rooms at night and early morning selling biscuits and mugs of tea from large brass urns.

The first person I met in the N.A.A.F.I was Ronnie Hammond who

I thought had gone to the Worcester Regiment in Malaya. It seems there had been a change of plan while they were on the ship and he ended up in the Stafford's. Well, we had to have a drink didn't we? I only had two little bottles of Sam Miguel but it was more than enough for me not being used to it. It was in the morning I felt the effects of it

The Company Commanders inspection past off alright and it was the first time we new chaps had seen him. He was a tall dark man with a Clarke Gable moustache and a superior air about him. The togging up for parade didn't take long but the difficult bit was putting your putties on. They had to be wound round where your boots and hose tops met. This had to be with two steps of the puttee showing and the tape fastened on the out side in the middle of your leg.

This took some practise but with the help of all the other squaddies we did it. All the rest of the company had pressed starched shorts and jackets. They told us we could hand our laundry in once a week but it took a week to get back. Most of them gave it the Chinese from the village at the back of the camp. They came every night collecting washing and would bring it back the next night washed and pressed for a few cents.

At nine thirty we got the call 'get fell in B' so we clambered down the steps and on to the road for the usual right dress and number. Sergeant Major Packer gave us a quick inspection before marching us down to the main gate to join the rest of the battalion assembled on the causeway over the paddies. Regimental Sergeant Major Threatle a little Banty cock of a man was standing outside the guard room watching proceedings as we marched passed. Bird's Hill camp didn't have a parade ground so we had to march over the road to the one at the Middlesex camp. I was in a bit of a whirl as we marched over to the square and all I remember about it is The Regimental Sergeant Major tapping his sick on the ground and looking at his watch as we marched on to the square to check we were marching at the right speed. Things went alright until it came to fix bayonets and I fumbled mine and dropped it. I didn't get 'you horrible little man' this time, it was just 'Sergeant Major I want that man after this parade'.

We spent about an hour drilling during which time the Regimental Sergeant Major had collected another couple of candidates to see after this parade before the march back to our camp.

When we fell out at B company lines the Sergeant Major told me I would have to report to the guard room after lunch (sorry, Tiffin)

Saturday afternoon was free time except for those on duty, so a lot of the chaps didn't wait for their midday meal; they togged themselves up in civilian shirt and trousers and took off down town. I reported to the guard room with the other parade criminals and the Provost Sergeant stood us to attention out side.

We must have stood to attention in the hot sun for nearly half an hour before the Provost Sergeant said we were to report to the Sergeants Mess. The Mess flunky, a Lance Corporal was waiting for us and our punishment would be to clean the Mess windows. He gave us some rags and told us what windows to clean. The mess was only a couple of Romney huts and only had windows in the ends of them so it didn't take too long. I think the idea of it was that it buggered your Saturday afternoon up as by the time you had finished it was to late to go out. That was more of a punishment than cleaning the windows. We had nearly finished when the Lance Corporal came out with a bottle of orangeade for each for us. He was like most of the senior N.C.O's - savage on parade but softies off duty, well they had all been squaddies themselves once. I was to have another little run in with him a few weeks later.

This occurred when B Company was Duty Company for the week. A platoon of us was sent down to do guard duty in Kowloon and was stationed at a camp in Chatham Road. We guarded two places, the gate at Sham Shui Po Depot and the Security motor park on a patch of ground in front of the Peninsula Hotel. I never understood why we had to only guard the gate at Sham Shui Po as the rest of the depot was patrolled by Military Police with dogs.

Before we started our platoon, Sergeant got us all together to make sure we all got the message although most of the lads had heard it many times before; 'while on duty, if any one approached you in civilian dress, check their identity card carefully'. The army field security operated in the colony and they usually turned up at guard posts just to test them. They would have a proper identity card or pay book to show when challenged. It was the details you needed to check carefully as it would have some anomaly like his height would be down as ten foot or some other deliberate mistake. If you let him pass you were in dead trouble.

I was on the Sham Shui Po gate one evening about six o'clock and it was very busy as there were married quarters within the depot and the way to Stone Cutters (a little island in the bay) was through the depot.

A car rolled up with four men in it and I asked for the drivers pass. He was just handing me his army pay book when a little voice in the back of the car shouted 'don't you know your own bloody R.S.M?' The man driving was .Sergeant Major Price of D Company, and with him was the A Company .Sergeant Major and his Colour Sergeant, and of course Mr. Threatle our beloved Regimental Sergeant Major. They were all in civilian dress disguised as gentlemen; I had only ever seen them in uniform. However I got a 'well done Power' off Corporal Whitehouse who was in charge of the guard.

The security car park was the best place to do guard as it was mainly Service Corps squaddies driving motors in and out. You didn't have to miss a night's sleep on that guard as the park had to be cleared of vehicles and locked up at midnight and it wasn't opened again until six o'clock next morning. Why they needed a security car park there I could never figure out as Chatham Road camp was only fifty yards down the road.

Spending time down in Kowloon was a bit of a shock to the system after austerity Britain. The whole place was open twenty four hours a day. You could go and buy yourself a new suit at two in the morning. The shops had for sale all the things that were still rationed at home. I made my first trip over to Hong Kong as the Star Ferry was just down the road and only ten cents to cross the harbour.

I was to return back to Chatham Road camp sooner than I expected. We had been back at Birds Hill camp about a fortnight when along with Sid Pugh I was marched in to see Maj White our company commander. There was to be a course run by the army on field cooking and Sid and I had been volunteered for it. It was to be run by the A.C.C. at the Chatham Road camp in Kowloon and would start next Monday.

We packed our kit bags on Sunday night and together with another eight volunteers were taken down to Kowloon in a lorry. We were put in a Nissen hut at the far end of the camp and told to report to the stores. A Staff Sergeant who was obviously in charge just stood watching while the store man issued us with a white jacket and trousers and a chef's hat. After we had signed for our rig outs the Staff Sergeant took us to a large hut with two rows of coal fired ovens and an area with some chairs and a black board at the side. Another Staff Sergeant joined us and they introduced them selves as Staff Sergeants Domit and Staff Sergeant Walters and they would teach a week's course in basic cookery. We all had a good week as the two old Catering Corps buffers Domit and Walters both had their families living out here in married quarters, so their main concerns was what they were going to do after they have finished for the day.

During the week we made allsorts; pies, buns, soups, stew and fancy potato dishes. What I couldn't figure out was what this had to do with field cooking and if we were out in the wilds cooking, where were we getting the coal fired oven from? However I wasn't going to point that out as the course was a good skive anyway and by the end of the week we had all passed with flying colours. Another good point of being away from the battalion was we had missed all the parading and bull involved practising for the Queens Birthday parade.

It had been a good week all round as we had been out most nights. I even meet another lad I knew from school, Norman Higgins in the Y.M.C.A. He was in the Royal Artillery out here.

There were several forces clubs in the colony but our trouble was that the money didn't last too long. We were paid in Hong Kong Dollars at the rate of sixteen to the pound which sounded a lot but didn't go very far. For a lot of the lads, acquiring a camera was their main aim. There were Japanese cameras on sale here far superior to the Ilford's and Kodak's available back home and cheap too.

A lorry came on Saturday morning and took us back to Birds Hill - all good things come to an end.

We got back to camp to find we had a new Commanding Officer the old one had been invalided out of the army. The new one Major Degg who had been Company Commander of A Company had now been made up to Lieutenant Colonel in command of the battalion.

Chapter Twelve

I had been in Hong Kong for over three months now and was just about getting the swing of serving with an infantry battalion. I'd even got through several Saturday morning parades without getting into trouble. All the lads who had come out with me were starting to look the same brown colour as the rest of the regiment.

I decided it was time I sent Granny a letter as you could get stamped envelopes or the airmail sheets with the stamps already on them from the N.A.A.F.I. A lot of the lads preferred to use the envelopes as you could put a pair of nylons in them. They must have been the camp contractor's best sales line because every time most of the lads wrote to their girlfriends they would put a pair of nylons in the letter. It was what they put on the backs of the envelopes that used to amuse me. B.O.L.T.O.P (better on lips than on paper); B.U.R.M.A and one or two other coded messages. I wrote a letter to Granny Mac and one to Jeff Slater while I was at it. I knew I would get a reply off Granny but it was a surprise when I got one back of Jeff.

I had my first flour label at breakfast and held it up for the cheer. All the bread for the army was baked down in Kowloon and when they were making the dough they just cut the string on top of the sacks of flour. When they tipped the bag up string and label went into the mix so occasionally you would get a round of bread with a label in or a bit of string. When this happened you would hold it up and shout got one! This would bring a droll cheer from the rest of the diners. The N.A.A.F.I didn't do much in the way of food Char Fan. Fried rice with bits of vegetables in was their best offer at a dollar a plate. In the main the food wasn't too bad as the cooks were experienced A.C.C men.

We still got paid on a Thursday and by Monday most of us were skint. Ali the Char Wallah who came round night and morning selling tea and bickies was your only hope as he ran a strap book. and the Watson's ice-cream man on his bike wearing his pith helmet. He sold milky ice lollies called popsicles at ten cents a time from a box on the back of the bike. He was a bit cautious of whom he gave credit to, and you had to show him your pay book to get on his strap book. He was still looking for M. Mouse, D. Duck and a few others to settle their bills. After pay parade on Thursday these pair would be the first to show up and half the pay some of the lads had drawn would be paid out to these two.

The rainy season was just starting and we had a few showers which brought the mozzies and snakes out.

The company had spent most of the week digging defensive bunkers up in the hills along a ridge that straddled between Bird's hill and the next range of hills. This covered the way we came up from our camp along the Jeelan valley. 'Dig them deep as they will be your graves if the Chinese come' Sergeant Philpot would tell us. It was common knowledge that if the Chinese did launch an attack the plan was just to hold out while the people who mattered escaped Hong Kong with their loot.

We had been digging all morning and were now having our lunch which had been bought up in a jeep and trailer when Maj White's driver come flying up in his Jeep. The whole company was to return to camp immediately. Sergeant Philpot told us to finish our lunch. It would take us a good hour and a half to march back down the valley so ten minuets here or there weren't going to make much difference. Lieutenant Broadbent was supposed to be in charge but he always fell in with anything the Sergeant said, so after a leisurely meal we wandered back to camp and entered through hole in the wire at the back of B Company lines where any Tom Dick or Harry could come and go. The Locals always came that way to collect our washing. This was always a source of amusement with the guard post and barbed wire with trip wires at the front of the camp.

When we got back and handed our tools into the stores the Sergeant Major paraded us on the road in front of company office. Major White came out and said we would be doing a night patrol and we needed to draw haversack rations after our evening meal. We would parade again at eight thirty in full battle order making sure our water bottles were full and we had our water sterilizing tablets. Those who didn't have any should see the store man and draw some water tablets as soon as this parade finished.

The rest of the afternoon was spent resting on our beds until the seven o'clock meal. Most of us took our washing kit down and had our shower. The ablutions were down by the cookhouse. Our haversack ration was the usual two rounds of cheese and two rounds of corned beef or prairie chicken as the lads called it. The lucky ones got a flour ticket or a bit of string with theirs.

It was just gone eight when the 'get fell in B' call came up from the road. Drawing our rifle was the first move, and then the Colour Sergeant issued us with a bandolier of ammo each. The Sergeant Major then told us to put the ammo in our pouches and on no account were any weapons to be loaded. I later learnt the reason for this caution as there had been an accident a few months ago just where we were standing now; patrols had returned and were jumping down from the lorry that had brought them back. A Corporal still had the magazine on his Stengun and the inertia of him jumping down for the lorry had caused the Sten bolt to move back. It hadn't been enough to lock onto the trigger but enough to load a round and fire it. It hit a squaddie and killed him.

Major White (named 'Chalky' behind his back) along with Lieutenant Broadbent came up from the Officers Mess dressed in their combat gear. He told us we would be doing a penetration patrol along Starling inlet and out to Wong Chuk. This was all we needed to know at this time. Information would be given out on a need to know basis. A couple of three ton lorries rolled up and we clambered on to them.

Now I never knew why, but if more than four or five squaddies got on the back of an army lorry they had to sing. We had not left the camp before the cabaret started with all the songs your mother never taught you, like Mary in the garden, Nuts in May, Queen Farida and one or two others not suitable for singing at christening parties. Sha Tau Kok was only five miles up the road so our choir practice was short lived. We got off the Lorries at the boarder post which was a shed on the side of the road and a couple of the Hong Kong police joined us to be our interpreters. The company set off in single file, Chalky leading with Johnny Giles his wireless operator close behind. Once you left the main roads there were only paths that connected the out lying villages and most of them ran along the paddy field walls. It was a warm damp night that brought the mozzies out in full force along with the fireflies, little points of bright light just floating in the air. Chalky set a steady pace and we stopped for a five minute fag break every hour on the hour. It wasn't far and by about midnight we were on a hill just above a village on the coast. Looking out to sea we could just make out one or two islands just off the coast in the South China Sea.

The company was organised into a line covering the approaches to the village and the sea shore. The platoon Sergeant organised a guard roster and told the rest of us to get our heads down for a kip. Stand to would be at dawn and if anything happened in the meantime a red flare would be fired. I was doing my hour's guard at dawn when the whistle for stand to went. As it got lighter we could see the Navy had been out on the little islands and were now coming ashore. By now the villagers were out and Chalky, Lieutenant Broadbent and the Sergeant Major along with the two policemen went down to them. The four naval chaps joined the party and you could see they were questioning mainly one man who, we learnt later was the village head man. We settled down to eat our sandwiches while the conference was going on and Corporal Fellows found a little stream for us to replenish our water bottles. The trouble was, were ever it came from it would be paddy water so we had to put our sterilising tablets in it and wait an hour before we could drink it. The stream water certainly wasn't fit to drink but later we all had a wash and shave in it.

Conference over, the navy launch went back to the little warship we could see out in the bay. The two big junks with the muzzle loading cannons on the deck were given the all clear to go and a couple of the navy 'Special Forces' chaps came back with Chalky's party to join us. We set off over land and by about ten o'clock we stopped on the beach near a village on the far side of Taipo Bay. The Sergeant Major informed us we now to wait for a navy frigate to show up, so while we were waiting we got our kit off and had a swim. We didn't need a second telling, we were soon all in our birthday suits and in the water.

About half an hour later the frigate McBride's Bay came round the head land which was probably the ship we saw out at sea this morning. We got our kit on again all except our boots. The ship was going to take us over to Taipo and they were not going to have us clomping over their nice scrubbed deck in our hobnailed boots. The ship was not very big and we waded out to it rifles above or heads. All of us squaddies and N.C.O's sat in line at the back of the ship with Chalky, Lieutenant Broadbent and the Sergeant Major up creeping round the Captain.

The ship had just pulled up anchor when the cook came with two buckets of tea for us and it made our day. It only took about half an hour to reach the little jetty at Taipo where we disembarked and put our boots on. The Sergeant Major lined us up on the jetty and made sure no one had a loaded weapon and all ammo was accounted for. He had just finished his inspection when the Colour Sergeant showed up in a fifteen hundred weight truck with some food for us. We soon got our mess tins out and got lined up then sat on the rocks on Taipo beach and stuffed ourselves. Just when we thought we were going to get another swim the lorries came to take us back to camp. The rest of the day was spent blancoing our webbing and cleaning and oiling our rifles.

One or two of us had a bit of ring worm round the stomach were our belts had been. We rubbed a bit of MacLean's tooth paste on it as that usually cleared it up. There was nothing for the mozzie bites and one chap had had a centipede bite in the night. The centipedes out here were the size of your finger and when they bit you a lump came up like a duck egg. There was no cure and it itched like mad for a couple of hours then it would go.

Over the next few weeks we got into the rainy season proper and when it rained it rained, it came down in sheets. Our Ponchos kept the worst off but it was terribly sweaty wearing them and your boots and bush hat still got soggy.

The Chinese working in the paddies always amused us as they wore bamboo capes. First they ploughed the paddy with a water buffalo pulling what looked like a big rake. Then the women would come, line up across the paddy and plant the rice. Maintaining the water levels was then their main problem after the planting. They had a series of dams to control the water off the hills but sometimes they needed to lift it up to the fields. They did this with little water wheels made of bamboo which they peddled for hours on end.

It had been done this way for thousands of years. They must have disturbed the beetles as we would get them flying in to the rooms at night. Great big black things, we would hear them fly into the fans and splat, we would brush the debris up in the morning. What with them and the mozzies we were well blessed and most of the bites we got were at night when we would roll against our mozzie nets and they would bite us through the net. I suppose that was what our `ponsie` blue pyjamas were supposed to prevent; every time some one fetched a jacket out it would be greeted by a chorus of wolf whistles so nobody had the guts to wear one.

Things carried on much the same, rain or no rain and on our next duty company I was sent with the detachment to guard the ammo dump on Bird's Hill; me to do the cooking, of course and I still had to do guard duty as well. The ammo was stacked just off the jeep track with our tents on a patch of flat ground just above it. What the army called a 'hundred and eighty pounder' tent stood between the ammo and the jeep track. This was the guard room and the cook house. About fifty yards back down the jeep track was a little waterfall which was our shower room.

Our week up there proved to be very eventful with Juggy Jones, the company's V.D expert from experience who had suffered a couple of doses, first. A Chinese woman came up the track with her baskets on a pole selling bottles of pop, chocolate, beer and fags. We could see Juggy was in earnest conversation with her and got her up into one of the tents. Juggy then got her laid out on the first bed and folded the tent flaps back so she was in full view. He then announced to us that he was going to give us a demonstration 'shag'. It all turned into a bit of an anti climax with Juggy not being able to get him self in the necessary condition but trying his best anyway. The only thing I learnt from it was the tale we had been told about the make up of Chinese women was not true. After the event the lady got a bit agitated, I think she thought she was worth more money. However when the rations had come up a couple of days ago they contained a small tin of sardines for each of us. Only half the guard had eaten theirs so the remaining tins were still in the guard room come cookhouse. There were three tins left so we gave them to her and she toddled off down the track happy.

While all this had been going on Sergeant Woodall who was our guard commander had been having his afternoon nap. When he found out what had been going on he blew his top but there was little he could do about it. If he charged Juggy, Chalky would want to know what he was doing while it was going on.

The next bit of entertainment happened on the Friday before we were due to change guard. One of our jobs while we were up here was to keep an eye on the defences we were digging. The trenches had to be shawn up in places with timber and the Chinese would come and steal the wood. Corporal Fellows and four squaddies were sent up to the D company positions higher up the track so they couldn't be seen from the guard camp. Sure enough, the Locals were up there helping themselves to the timbers and as soon as they saw Corporal Fellow's squad they bolted. Ben Brown, a lad from Wednesbury and one of life's comedians fired a shot at them and fortunately he missed. When they came back the problem was not that Ben had fired a shot at them but we were now a round short on the ammo inventory. However they had a bit of luck as where our tents were must have been one of the British armies defensive positions during the Japanese invasion in nineteen forty one. When they were clearing the ground to pitch the tents they found a few rounds of three o three ammo in the ground. These had been left in old ammo tins in the guard tent along with a few other bits and pieces. Ben was given one to clean up but told not to use Brasso on it in case the Colour Sergeant smelt it when we handed it in. Everyone was happy as there would have been an enquiry and reams of paperwork over it.

The rainy season petered out at the end of May and it was getting really hot now. At the start of June it was announced that we would move to summer schedule so this meant reveille would be at six in the morning. Our first parade would be six thirty then break fast at seven thirty. We would then do our normal duties until thirteen hundred hours when we would finish for the day.

A mug of tea called gun fire would be available in the cookhouse at six each morning. Sergeant Major Packer soon put the odd hour before breakfast to good use and would have us drilling and some mornings we would doing pokey drill. Of course, if you were Duty Company the one o'clock finish didn't affect you, you did the full day.

Chapter Thirteen

Our company C.O, Chalky decided we should use Wednesday afternoon for recreation. So when he could scrounge a couple of three ton lorries he would take us down to Castle Peak Beach at Ty Lam for a swim. Very keen on the company all being able to swim he was, in fact if you could swim one hundred yards it counted towards your star grading. The salt water was also good for the mozzie bites. This was always a good afternoon and we would sing our way there and back. The company's swimming competence would be tested on our rest and relaxation week down in the old camp at Taipo. It was during this week that I found out that I had made a grave mistake doing that cookery course. While all B Company was swimming and lying on the beach sipping their bucks fizz, Pughie and I were doing all the cooking using the old derelict house as a cookhouse. On Thursday afternoon I was summoned to the beach to do my one hundred yards swim. Chalky had set up two little buoys in water deep enough to stop you putting one foot on the bottom. Corporal Fellows was before me and he was always a funny sort of a bloke. He was supposed to be a black belt in bongo playing or some thing like that. He gets out to the starting buoy and vanishes. Well, no one seemed concerned - it was the army and one dead body here and there didn't matter was the attitude. They would give him a few minutes and then send the rescue team in. It wasn't long before Corporal Fellow's head popped up just past the hundred yard marker. Chalky and Broadbent went into a huddle to decide if Fellow's effort counted - it did. I was rushed out to do my swim as it was getting late now. I could see what was going through their minds, the longer I was down here the later the dinner would be. I don't know about a rest and relaxation week me and Pughie needed a rest care by the time Saturday arrived! The only bit of recreation we got was a couple of hours down Taipo after we had cleaned up form the evening meal.

Being one of the company cooks meant I always knew what I would be doing when we were Duty Company. I would be on the ammo dump up Birds Hill; they never seemed to pick Pughie as his cooking was never very popular. I would have liked to have gone on the Observation Post at Lo Wu where the railway crossed the Shenzhen River that formed the border in that area. You sat in a bunker on the hill watching the Chinese soldiers on the other side through binoculars and writing down every thing they did in a book. We used to get up the border on patrol in the Sha Tau Kok area and the border with China was only marked by a line of pickets painted yellow along here. Two or three of the villages in this area straddled the border with China and was a favourite place for smugglers and refugees to cross into Hong Kong. We did night patrols with the Hong Kong Police a couple of times looking for smugglers, Smuggling petrol from the new territories into China was their main game. If we caught any refugees the police along with the Field Security man would search them and take them off for interrogating down Kowloon. After obtaining all the information they could about things in China they were allowed to go free. However the Birds Hill ammo guard wasn't so bad, it was lovely up there in the late summer the little Chinkie women used to come up cutting the ground scrub for fuel or animal bedding. They would make this up into bales about three feet square and stick one each end of their carrying poles. The Chinese women were tough little buggers, they were all well under five feet tall and would put one on their shoulder and off down the track at a steady lope, some with kids on their backs. I tried to pick one up once to move it off the track and it was as much as I could do to shift it. Some nights we would hear a kind of barking on the hills, we were told it was little Chinese Muntjac, deer but we never saw any.

I was used to the heat by now and all the Chinese folk had started to look different, they didn't all look the same to me any more. Most weekends we would get down to Kowloon on the train or at least down the road to Fanling. There were two or three films a week in the Romney hut proudly called The Globe Theatre down by the main gate.

It was in the summer on our morning parade that we were told the South Stafford's had been chosen to make a training film. This was planned to take a week and would be done in the afternoon so finishing at one o'clock would be suspended for this week. This film would be a company attack across a river at a defended position. Due to the battalion only being at half strength both B Company and D Company together would just about make up a full infantry company. The spot chosen for this little caper was about a mile up from Fanling towards the Chinese boarder near Tsung Yuen village on the Ng Tung River. Canvas boats would be used for the river crossing and these had a wooden bottom and plywood rim or gunwales as it was called. They were flat and when you wanted to use them you snapped the folding stays around the inside of the boat upright and this held it rigid.

The plan was that we would carry the boats up to the river under cover of a smoke screen laid by two inch mortars, cross the river in the boats and attack a low hill. The boats must have held about twenty or so of us because we used four or them and ninety chaps made a full infantry company.

After our practice run, instead of putting the boats back on the Lorries we decided to paddle them back down the river towards Fanling. This soon developed into a race in the usual winner takes all army style. It was a distance of twelve hundred yards from were we started to where the road came near the river again and this is where the finishing line was. We couldn't have gone much further as at this point the river widened and was shallow and full of water buffalo's having their afternoon nap. This little boat race would go on every afternoon until Thursday when they made the final film. There was always some one getting bashed on the head with a paddle and an argument at the end of the race but Sergeant Major Price of D Company was the senior N.C.O in charge and soon sorted it out. He was chief mediator of the punch-up that always ensued at the finishing line. It had been an interesting experience.

The Saturday morning parade was still one of the highlights of the week especially when the band was on parade. The colours would be marched on, accompanied by the fife and drum. The officers would be on parade as well and they got the same treatment as the rest of us. The only difference being, they were called mister, not that man. Regimental Sergeant Major. Threatle was king on that parade ground.

In the late summer it all took on a new meaning when it was announced that the battalion was to be presented with a set of silver bugles. These had been paid for by local businesses from around Walsall and Wolverhampton. They would be presented to the battalion by an old boy of the South Staffordshire regiment, a General who lived in Walsall - and there was me thinking Troop Sergeant Major Purchase of the charge of the light brigade fame was Walsall's top military man.

It was during one of these Saturday parades when it happened. Threatle was going through his usual South Stafford's thirty eighth of foot rigmarole when a dog barked in one of the near by villages and half the battalion came to attention. There was a deathly silence and we could see old Threatle turning purple. After what seemed like minutes but could only have been seconds Threatle composed himself and gave the 'as you were' order. The rest of the parade went off all right in spite of most of us having the titters.

The actual presentation parade took place in August and went off without a hitch with all the names of the donors being read out as the General handed them out to the buglers of the Core of Drums. The battalion gave the general a final 'present arms', the band struck up the regimental march, Come Lasses and Lads and we all marched back to Birds Hill.

Now the weather was cooling off a bit we did all the things for our star ratings like the assault course, marches and the firing range. This was a new eight hundred yard range that had been built over by the village of Shek Wo Hui. The march over there was an education as the trees by the village were full of spider's webs with the biggest spiders you ever saw in them. They must have been harmless or else the Locals would have shifted them. Grazing on the range was a horse with a number stamped on his hind quarters. He had been left here by the Japanese army when they left in nineteen forty five. He was in good condition so he must have looked after himself in the last six years. The only surprise was the Chinese hadn't eaten him by now. The range itself was alive with snakes, probably due to disturbance while building the place.

To finish our tests off we had a week of live firing at the battle school down Sai Kung. It was while we were here that I would fire a two inch mortar for the last time ever. I think the army scrapped the weapon about this time.

As we got into the autumn, rumours abounded about the regiment going back to England. This was confirmed a few days later on the daily Battalion orders. The battalion would leave Hong Kong in the middle of November and return to the U.K.

Brownie had to have his final do with the Locals didn't he? It was their practice to bury their dead in a communal grave on the hill side. After several years they dug them up again and placed their remains in large earthenware pots, we called chatty pots. These were placed on terraces dug into the hill side. As we were coming back from working on the defensive positions one day when Brownie decided he was going to have a look inside of one. The Chinese working in the paddies saw him and within a couple of minutes we were surrounded by an angry mob. The officer in charge of us, a Lieutenant Barton who had only joined B Company in the summer, could speak the local lingo. He assured the village head man who had turned up that Brownie would be punished for it. That seemed to placate them and Brownie got seven days jankers, under the armies catch all section eleven 'Conduct prejudicial to good order and military discipline', for his endeavours.

All the talk now was of our move back to the U.K. A Scottish regiment who had been camped in the west of the New Territories would be moving into our camp. When this took place we would move out and spend a night at the Chatham Road camp in Kowloon. This was to allow the Jocks to move into Bird's Hill camp and the regiment replacing the Stafford's to move from the ship into the Jock's old camp. When the great day arrived we were marched down to Fanling station to board a train to Kowloon. It was just our luck that B Company arrived at the same time as the Quarter Master Sergeant with a couple of Lorries. The Quarter Master comes and asks our Sergeant Major if he can borrow some men so Packer volunteers us to unload the trucks. Most of the stuff was marked the Band and the boxes were made of right thick planks of wood. The platform was about ten foot above the car park so we had to get the boxes up there first and then onto the train with the Quarter Master shouting 'hurry up the trains due to leave in five minutes'. We were soaking wet with sweat when we finally got on the train. We made sure to get well down the train in case we got volunteered to do the unloading.

When we got to the Chatham Road camp tents had been put up on the football pitch to accommodate us. The camp itself was a long camp running from the little park by the army post office to well up the road. It was bordered by the Chatham Road on one side and the railway line to the New Territories on the other. For about half its length it followed the road but at the top end it veered away and there was a bit of scrub land between the camp and the road. As the evening fell the local 'Night Cavalry' moved their head quarters from the little park behind the station to this patch of scrub land. They were offering their services through the fence from ten cents up to a couple of dollars a time. Things were going well as this was the last chance for mommies little heroes, while mommy was still ten thousand miles away and couldn't see what the apple of their eye was up to. Then it happened, one soul must have indulged and he being one side of the fence and she the other, decided he wasn't going to pay up. The greedy sod went back for second helpings later in the evening but they were waiting for him and you can only imagine what a set of strong young Chinese teeth chomping down on his pride and joy must have felt like. The Medical

Officer was called and it was a trip to the military hospital for him. That brought the evening's fun to an end and a guard was posted along the fence.

We were marched down to the docks the following morning to embark on the Empire Clyde. The married quarters were already on board and the Hanna's, the Chinese women who had been their domestic servants were seeing them off. Some of them were letting off strings of fire crackers to ward off the evil spirits and ensure a safe journey.

B Company quarters were down in the bowls of the ship on a triangular shaped deck with the double deck standees. The facilities were not as good as the ship we came out on but this boat was much older. We must have been below the water line as there were no port holes on our deck. It was mid day when the ship pulled out into the main harbour and we had our last look at Hong Kong with The Hong Kong and Shanghai Bank sticking up like a sore thumb. No one was allowed to trade with the wicked Communists of China but it was obvious what this bank was here for, money talks its own language. I thought it would be the last time I would ever see Hong Kong but I would be back four years later.

The ship called at all the ports we called at on our way there and I did the shore leave on all of them. Being with the battalion meant we would parade for inspection each morning. We also did some training while on board and an officer from the Educational Corps decided those who did not yet have their third class army certificate of education would make a start on getting it. This resulted in me and a load of other squaddies spending Tuesday and Thursday afternoons in the recreation room learning the finer points of maths and English. We were supposed to take the exam before the ship docked at Liverpool but for some reason it never happened. Our spare time was spent playing cards for fags and the W.V.S still ran the bingo in the recreation room a couple of nights a week. There were impromptu concerts some afternoons when someone would get up on cover of the hold and do a song. This would encourage the crowd to shout for more. Most of the singers in the regiment were well known and the call would be from the crowd; we call on Fred Smith to sing us a song. 'Sing sing or show us your ring', they usually sang.

As we went through the Suez Canal and reached Port Said the weather had turned cold and we all changed into our battle dress uniforms. We didn't get shore leave as the ship only stopped for a few hours before moving onto Malta. Shore leave there was for the whole day and most of us went ashore. I went up the hill to Valetta and did the main area. At the far end of the town was the palace and the armoury and a lady standing by the door invited some of us in for a free tour of the place. On my way back to the ship I passed a tobacconists shop that had skeins of twist hanging in the window. I thought old Harry Bagnel would love some of that, so I bought him ten bobs worth.

It was only another six days sailing to Liverpool and we got there during the night as we were docked when we woke that morning. There were a party of Stafford's on the dock side who had been sent up from Lichfield as a working party. They had been working on the docks unloading most of the night. We had to go through customs as we disembarked and if you said you had cigarettes you had to show them. Smithy, who had more than his two hundred allowances, had rolled tins of fifty fags in his socks to hide them. When the custom man asked to see his fags and he started rolling them out of his socks they wanted to see what else he had in his kit bag. Smithy ended up with a bill for twenty eight quid in duty and fines. I don't know how he paid it I think the company paid and took it out of his credits, it was always the same when we came through customs they didn't let us get away with anything. I don't know what they thought we were bringing into the country, never a lot on army pay that's for sure.

It was near lunch time when we were loaded onto coaches and taken to an old Fleet Air Arm camp at Burscough near Ormskick in Lancashire.

Chapter Fourteen

The camp at Burscough was all Nissen huts with the usual central heating - a coke stove in the middle and things being normal for the army, we had no coke to burn in them. It was a bit of a shock to the system after Hong Kong and we all slept with our great coats on the bed but we were still frozen.

It was announced on company orders that we would be paid for our disembarkation leave tomorrow. Our food ration coupons to cover our leave period together with some sweet coupons would also be issued. The sweet coupons could be used in the N.A.A.F.I who had made up bundles of five shilling worth of sweets, which is what our back sweet ration amounted to.

All travel passes would be made out to the recipients nearest home railway station. If anyone wanted it different they must inform company office before nine o clock in the morning. Our first parade tomorrow morning would be at eight o'clock on the road outside the company office wearing our best battle dress and we were to wear the shoes we would be going on leave in. The company commander would inspect us just to check them, no brothel creepers (crepe soles) allowed. The place was all excitement now with what we were going to do on our leave and we all had cases packed ready. Well some had bought cases in Hong Kong but for most of us it was our large valise.

Chalkies parade next morning went off all right, a couple wore their best boots but we all got the OK. Pay parade was at ten o'clock and we drew our pay in the normal way, a separate table manned by the Colour Sergeant and his store man was there to issue the ration coupons including coupons for our sweet ration. It was announced that the N.A.A.F.I would be open for anyone who wanted to buy their sweets. They had three different combinations of sweets made up for us in five bob lots. A small box of chocolates and some bars, a mixture of chocolate bars and bags of toffee and just bags of toffees. I had the bags of toffees.

Travel passes were given out when the coaches came at twelve o'clock. Most of us were going from Lime Street Station and some from Liverpool Central. Quite a few of the lads were scousers and only wanted a lift to Liverpool and would get a bus home.

It was about one thirty when we got on the train and our first stop would be Stoke as a lot of lads came from that area. Our stop would be Wolverhampton then for the Burton and Lichfield chaps Trent Valley, Lichfield. As we walked out of the station Chalky was waiting for us B company lads and shook our hands and wished us luck and a good leave. He was leaving the South Stafford's to take command of a T.A battalion. Why he couldn't have told us that on our morning parade I don't know.

I caught the bus to Walsall, then one up to the Fullbrook. When I got to the house the door was unlocked but no one was at home and the first thing I had to do was put some money in the electric meter. The house itself was in a bit of a state, you could see some one was living there.

There wasn't anything to make a fire with and no food at all in the place. I checked my old bedroom and it looked like nobody had been in there since I last left it. The bed felt a bit damp but I would have to put up with that as there was nowhere else to sleep. I went to Jones's paper shop on the corner of our road and bought some milk and a bottle of Camp coffee to make myself a drink. Later I went up to Caldmore and got myself some chips and a pie for tea.

I left it until after eight o'clock before going round to Jeff Slater's as I knew he would be home by then. Jeff welcomed me but I think he was happy I was in the army and out of his way. It seems both Bill and Fanny had played him up a bit over the last twelve months. An hour and a half was spent talking and I got a mug of tea with sugar in it as well.

Bill was home when I got back and he had brought some bread and a pot of dripping someone had given him. We feasted on toast and dripping while Bill filled me in with what had happened in the last year; things were about the same as when I had left, Fanny was sleeping here only occasionally. I gave Bill the shirt and tie with horses on I bought in Hong Kong but I hadn't got Fanny a music box so I was going to give her the toffees.

Bill had gone off to work when I got up next morning but he had left me a couple of rounds of bread for my breakfast. I decided to clean the place up a bit before I did anything else when there was a knock on the door. It was the woman from the top house who introduced herself as Alice Fletcher. She came in and gave me a hand to help clean the house up a bit. We got talking and she asked what I was doing for food. I explained that ate what I could get hold of - chips and toast plus a bit of sausage we scrounged of Jeff. She said that she could do me a bit of dinner when she did her husband Jim's. We agreed that I would pay her and two quid a week seemed fair so I gave her the ration coupons as well.

She had Jim's dinner ready for about five thirty most days. Jim worked on the buses so he did shifts and wasn't always home so Alice kept it warm for him. Pat her youngest daughter who was still at school had her dinner at that time so I would dine with Alice and Pat if Jim was at work.

It was now December the twenty third and I was thinking about a Christmas dinner. Alice must have read my thoughts as she said the arrangement we had just made included my Christmas dinner as well, my first one for two years.

I set off to visit Granny Mac who had moved from the little house in the terrace to a Council home. She had told me all about it in her last letter and it was only two minutes walk from where she had lived. The Walsall Council had set up a home in a large house on the Birmingham Road that was for men and women who were elderly but still fairly active. If you were sick or needed nursing you still ended up in the old workhouse which was part of the Manor Hospital. This was a new venture in social care being tried out. There was a large common room, a dining room and kitchens on the ground floor. Upstairs they each had their own little bedroom.

Granny was surprised to see me as she thought I was still in Hong Kong and I didn't mention I was coming home in my last letter. I spent an hour there in the common room with all the rest of the inmates as they had no separate rooms for visitors. This was the time allowed for a visit, I was informed by the Matron. However Granny seemed happy that she had managed to get a place. I wished her a merry Christmas and assured her I hadn't married a foreign girl and left.

I walked down into town and had a look round, the decorations were up but nothing else had changed in the twelve months I had been away. It was past one o'clock by now and I was feeling hungry. So I went in Dancers Dinning Rooms and had a couple of rounds of dripping and a mug of tea.

I caught a bus to Shelfield after my feast to visit my Aunty Sarah. She was very welcoming as I'd not seen her or Busty her husband since we were at the farm. She wanted to feed me, so it was a pity I hadn't gone there before going to Dancers. I only had a mug of tea; well I didn't want to spoil my dinner at Alice's tonight did I? Aunty Sarah told me Gordon her youngest son was now in Greece doing his national service. Ken her next son who used to help my Dad on the farm was still in the army. He had singed on and was a regular like me. Her other three sons Bill, Ron and Doug had all been in the last war. Aunt Sarah gave me a packet of twenty fags before I left to catch the bus back to Walsall.

I got back home just after five o'clock and changed out of my uniform and into my old suit to go up to Alice's. The Shepherds pie was almost ready and it smelt good. Jim, Alice's husband was missing as he was doing a shift on the buses called splits. This entailed working in the morning rush hour then having the middle of the day off, and then working the second half of his shift during the evening rush hour.

The pie went down very well and I had been given a good plate full. I stopped at Alice's talking to her and I learnt she had another daughter named Doreen and a son John who didn't live at home because they had fallen out. Doreen was married to Paul, a lad I had known at school. It was warm in there so I was in no hurry to leave so I stayed until Jim came home at seven thirty. If I went back home I knew it would be freezing cold so I went over to the Fullbrook Pub, bought myself a pint of mild and made it last me until after nine o'clock when I knew Bill would be home.

When I got home Bill already had a fire going with some wood he had brought from work.

There was still some bread left from last night so we had toast and dripping again for supper.

I told Bill that Alice had been down and I was fixed up for my dinners and for my Christmas dinner. Bill said Alice was alright and had been a friend of our Fanny until they had fallen out. Knowing our Fanny, that wouldn't have been very hard to do.

We had just gone to bed when we heard Fanny come home and go straight up to bed. Our usual conversation through the wall started. The first words were 'have you got my music box?' Well I hadn't, so I got told what a miserable old sod I'd always been. My excuse was that they didn't have music boxes in China but she could have the bags of sweets instead. They were in the cupboard drawer and she could help herself in the morning. I didn't get an answer and that would be the last time I would speak to her for years.

Next morning Bill and Mary had both gone to work when I got up. To my surprise Fanny hadn't had any of the bags of sweets. It was very unlike our Fanny to miss an opportunity like that. I didn't mind, I could use them for Christmas presents at Alice's tomorrow when I went for my Dinner.

It was now Christmas Eve and I decided to make sure we had some food in to last us over the holiday. Bread would be the main thing and although a lot of things like bread were now off ration they were still in short supply. With the Christmas holiday coming up people would buy extra to cover it. My first try was the Co-Op over on the corner and they said I could have one in the afternoon if they had any left but they must make sure that all who had registered with them for rationing got theirs first. However I did get a big box of cornflakes, a bottle of milk and a large bottle of Camp coffee off them. I had a walk up to Caldmore and tried the shop I had a loaf from last year and I got one and took it back home. From there I caught the bus down to Walsall and got another large loaf and a couple of cakes out of Robinsons shop on the Bridge. I called in the café next door and treated myself to beans on toast for lunch. Hopefully we were now fixed up with something to eat over the holiday - stale bread was better than no bread at all.

There were still a few people to visit like Aunty Maud and Harry Bagnal but I thought I would leave it now until after Christmas so I had a walk round the town an hanged about in the stores like Woolworths and Henrys; well it was warm in places like that.

I was back at Alice's for my dinner just after five o'clock, I knew I was a bit early but I got a mug of tea. Stew was tonight's dinner and we all had a good feed although there wasn't much meat in it. Bill would probably be home a bit earlier tonight so I left Alice's at seven o` clock after wishing them all a Merry Christmas. He had been to Jeff's who had given him enough sausage and bacon for the both of us and a knob of lard as well. We were now fixed up for breakfast and our suppers; Bill was having his dinner at Cox's, me at Alice's; nice doings!

Bill had bought a sack of logs home with him from Cox's so we had now gone from destitute to living in the lap of luxury.

Bill was up late on Christmas day as he didn't have to go to work and he was already togged up for his dinner. I fried some of the bacon and sausage along with a couple of rounds of bread. It was a pity we didn't have a few mushrooms and tomatoes to go with it but we didn't want to over do ourselves as we were looking forward to our lunch.

Bill went off about eleven o'clock and I found an iron out and pressed my uniform and my suit to wear at the lunch. Alice had said the Christmas dinner would be ready about one so I made my way up there just after twelve thirty. I took the bags of toffees with me and gave them out as presents. I think they were a bit embarrassed as they had nothing to give me. Jim gave me a glass of beer but neither him nor Alice were drinkers so we only got one glass each been as it was Christmas.

The dinner was good; we had duck from the butchers Christmas club, a little bit of pork followed by the pudding. It was a good blow out and we were all `podged`. I helped with the washing up after, well I felt it was the least I could do and it proved to be a good move because I got invited to stop for tea. The wireless was put on to hear the King's speech but most of us were half asleep and only Alice seemed interested in it. No one really wanted any tea since we were still full from our lunch but Alice did a few sandwiches and there was jelly and a Christmas cake. I had a piece of cake and some jelly. I left for home at seven thirty after thanking them for a great time; I had stuffed myself all day.

Bill had been home a while when I got back and he had got a fire going. He had had his dinner but no tea so he was cooking the last of the stuff Jeff gave us for his supper.

Boxing Day, Bill was off down Cox's and spent the day there and I didn't get up until after ten o'clock. I did myself some toast for breakfast and there was still some fat in the frying pan from last night so I warmed it up and dipped my toast in it. It was no use going out as everywhere was closed. I still had a few relations to visit but if I went during the holiday they would think I was on the scrounge. With it being holiday, dinner at Alice's would be the normal lunch time of one o'clock so I strolled up there at twelve thirty and had my dinner.

Bill was home early again and he had won a cabbage and a pot of strawberry jam from somewhere. We only had bread and dripping so we tried some of the cabbage with it. The heart of it was nice so we put some strawberry jam on it and it was alright with bread and dripping.

With the Christmas holiday now over I went and paid a visit to Aunty Maud's. Her son my cousin Ronnie had been called up and was now doing is training with the Army Catering Corps at Catterick. Uncle George her husband was at work so I didn't see him but I said I would go and have a drink with them on Saturday night in the Fullbrook.

On the Saturday afternoon I went and took Granny Mac out to her favourite port of call, tea and a cake in Patterson's Café on the Bridge.

I left it until Monday before I paid Harry Bagnal a visit, his eyes popped out of his head when he saw the ring of twist I had for him. Harry was still gardening although he had to give up his allotment. It was the last time I would see him as he died a few weeks later. I hope it wasn't the twist that caused his death.

The New Year for nineteen fifty two was let in at Alice's by our Bill; he had black hair like our mother had. There was a bit of a party and Doreen the elder daughter had bought some of her friends. I got quite friendly with one named Joyce and by the end of the party I had arranged to take her to the pictures on Thursday night. I took her out a couple of times during my leave and we got on well. She was not a drinker so it was either the pictures or a cup of coffee and a yap.

At the end of my leave I had done alright - I had wormed my way in at Alice's and got a girl friend as well. The only fly in the ointment was that I'd got that nasty dry cough back I had as a kid.

Chapter Fifteen

I wasn't sorry when my leave came to an end, except for my dinners as I was living hand to mouth and I had run out of things to do.

My travel warrant was from Walsall station so I caught a train to Wolverhampton then had to wait for one to Liverpool. The train to Liverpool was very smoky and I coughed my way there. There was no transport laid on to take me back to camp- it was make your own way so I caught a bus to Burscough town then one on to the camp. There were quite a few back when I got to our hut, all moaning about how cold it was; we had to wait until six thirty for the evening meal to get a warm in the cookhouse and after that we could sit in the N.A.A.F.I. until it closed.

Next morning I had my breakfast and it was a lot better than the toast and dripping I had been having for the last couple of weeks. First parade and roll call was at eight and everyone had made it back. The Sergeant Major announced that we would be moving to Ballykinler in Northern Ireland at the end of the week. He then gave us an hour's drilling just in case we had forgotten how to do it. After the drill we were all detailed to do different jobs round the camp. Dillon and I were sent to the Officer's mess where we got the breakfast washing-up to do first job. Next we were sent on an errand to fetch a gallon of paraffin, so one of the officers must have brought a heater back with him. We walked to a village call Rufford about two miles up the road to get the paraffin. It didn't need two of us but we both went and made it last so it was lunch time when we got back. We had been hoping that we might get some lunch in the mess kitchen as it would be better than the cookhouse swill. No chance - we were sent to the cookhouse with instructions to report back to the mess at two o'clock. The Corporal. in charge of the mess was a right little slave driver and kept us busy all afternoon sorting out boxes of stuff ready for our move to Ireland. We finished our officers mess fatigues just in time to catch the last sitting for our evening meal. It wasn't very good and it was cold by now, the meat like old rubber shoe soles. Most of us left a lot of it and just eat our sponge pudding and custard and planned to go out for some fish and chips later.

All washed and brushed up we caught the bus down to Burscough at seven o'clock. None of us had a lot of money so we looked for somewhere cheap to eat. After a stroll around the town centre we found a little chip shop with tables and chairs along one side, the ideal place for us to have our supper. A large cod and chips for each of us plus two rounds of bread and butter and a pot of tea was ordered. The whole lot came to five shillings and four pence, one and four pence each. The piece of cod was big and a load of chips so we had a job to get it all down us but we did. A check on our finances was taken and we found we had enough for a couple of pints. We caught the bus back up to camp and went in the little pub opposite the camp gates. The place was packed with squaddie from the camp and it rounded off a good night.

My cough seemed to be getting worse particularly at night and when I went into the cold air. On the morning I decided to report sick and go through the usual pantomime just to see the Medical Officer I needn't have bothered seeing the Medical Officer as all I got was told was to stop smoking, no cough mixture or anything. However I had missed the morning parade so hadn't been found a job for the day. That didn't last for long as I was getting my kit back from the stores Sergeant Major Packer grabbed me and told me to report to the company office. I was made company runner for the day so I spent the day carrying bits of paper around the camp site. A sort of company clerks postman.

Thursday night's company orders confirmed that we would be moving to Ballykinler on Friday. We would be on the overnight ferry from Liverpool to Belfast. The evening meal would be half an hour earlier on Friday to allow for the move. Each company would parade at seven o'clock wearing full marching order with their packed kit bags outside their company offices. Coaches would then take down to Liverpool dock for the night ferry to Belfast. Friday morning Sergeant Major Packer gave us an hour's drill just to warm us up I think. The rest of the day was spent packing our kit ready for the move. Most of our kit bags had been packed anyway as there were no lockers in the huts and we had been living out of them since we came back off our disembarkation leave. We were all lined up by seven o'clock on a damp cold misty night. The coaches arrived but how were we going to get on them in full marching order was a problem. Kit bags had been stowed in the luggage bay at the side of the coach. We had to hook our large packs and Sgt Philpot directed us on to the coach two at a time and told us to keep or pack on our laps. The whole battalion was paraded on the dock side with the Liver Building just over the road. Word went round we would be boarding when all the civilian passengers were loaded and we would be on as deck cargo. It must have been over an hour we stood there before we boarded and we were 'monkey frozen'. Our main concern once we were on board was to find somewhere we could get out of the wind. By the time we were out in the Irish Sea I was coughing for England and had to have a fag for comfort. After midnight things seemed to go very quite so some of us crept down into the passages below deck as it was warm down there. One of the cabin passengers must have heard us and called a steward. He turfed us out on to the deck again on the grounds we were disturbing the passengers. It was still dark when we got to Belfast and luckily no one had died from exposure. The battalion was disembarked a company at a time and lined up on the dock side. A count was taken just to make sure no one had jumped into the Irish Sea on the way there. The whole lot of us were perished to the bone and shivering as we stood there. It was a relief when we started to march off the dock side and down to some large huts at the end of the terminal. There was food laid on for us to have some breakfast. It was a relief to be inside although there was no heating it was warmer than on the dock side. We soon got our mess tins out and lined up for the standard army fare. Half a rasher of bacon, a cackle berry (egg) and a piece of fried bread in one mess tin and a dollop of porridge in the other. With a couple of rounds of bread and a scrap of margarine it was a feast to behold. It was most welcome, after our sea trip most of us could have eaten a horse between two bread carts. The mug of hot tea was the best of all it went down a treat and warmed us up a bit and it even stopped me coughing for a while.

It was a leisurely breakfast, we must have been in there for over an hour. All the civilian baggage had to be unloaded before our kit bags, probably in case we contaminated their dainty Park Lane luggage. We all had to collect our bags as they came off the ship and check they were O.K. before putting them on the lorries. Coaches arrived and we boarded them for the trip to Ballykinler about thirty miles away in County Down. Ballykinler camp was fairly modern and most of the accommodation was in one large two story block. The barrack rooms were smaller than we had been used to. They held ten beds and were heated. The toilets or ablutions as the army liked to call them were just down the passage and had baths and showers. After the Burscough camp this was luxury living for us. The platoon Sergeants sorted out who was going in each room making sure there was and N.C.O. among them just to keep us in order. We had the weekend to settle in but all most of us wanted to do was have a sleep. However by Sunday most of us had recovered and were on the mooch around the camp. Just out side the camp was a large building built of corrugated sheets, this was the Sandes Home. It had a café and a little cinema and was run on Christian and Evangelical principals. If you went and listened to a sermon and sang a couple of hymns on Sunday night you got a free film show. About half a mile over the sand dunes was Dundrum Bay with a nice sandy beach which ran up to the inlet into the town of Dundrum. From the shore there was a large area of sand dunes our training ground to be. Looking across the bay you could see the town of Newcastle and the mountains of Mourne.

Monday morning saw our first parade and roll call at eight o'clock. The rest of the morning was taken up with issuing us with rifles and a trip to the main stores to be kitted out in some new underwear. We couldn't believe our eyes when we got two woolly vests with long sleeves and two pair of woolly long johns. We may have laughed when they were issued and remarked our Granddads had some but we were soon all wearing them. It couldn't have been a normal army issue because when I came to get demobbed the Quarter Master at Lichfield wouldn't believe the British army had ever had such garments.

On company orders on Wednesday night I was down for a visit to the dentist. This was a surprise for me as I didn't know I had anything wrong with my teeth. Certainly no one had looked at them since my medical to join the army. That was eighteen months ago at Wolverhampton. After our first parade at eight o'clock was over on Thursday morning I reported to the company office as per last night's orders. The company clerk gave me a chitty to take to the dentist. No one seemed to know where the dentist's surgery was as they had never been in a camp with a dentist in it before. The clerk suggested I ask at the guard room. So I marched up to the guard room where I was immediately pounced on by the Regimental Sergeant Major's. henchman, the Provost Sergeant. 'Where do you think you're off to private?' he shouted in my ear. I explained I was looking for the dental surgery. He knew where it was, well he should, he was the camp chief of police after all. He pointed me to a row of huts just outside the camp and the dentist was the end one. I wandered down there and knocked on the door and was let in by a private from the Medical Corps. I was soon in to see the dentist and it seems I was their only customer. The dentist himself was a big man with a strong Irish accent and hands the size of legs of ham. He gave my teeth a good inspection and announced I needed two fillings. This would be done this morning and his orderly brought up a treadle driller. The dentist set to work on the teeth at the back of my mouth on the left side. I must have been in the chair for a good two hours while he drilled and hammered stuff into the holes in my teeth. It was a relief when he had finished. But I must say he must have made a good job of them because they lasted until I had all my teeth out forty years later.

The barracks had a square and it wasn't long before we were on it with mister Threatle directing proceedings. We hadn't had a full parade since last November back in Hong Kong and it was a bit cooler here in January. We would soon get used to it, we had no choice. It was announced that we would be getting a visit from the Officer Commanding Northern Ireland, some Lieutenant General. On the parade for his visit the drill of the 1st South Staffordshire Regiment would be exemplary. The Battalion were hoping to be chosen to do the parade for the opening of the Northern Ireland Parliament. After a few parades we were back up to scratch on our drill. The parade for the General Officer Commanding was on a cold bright morning and the General looked quite old to me. The normal bigwig's inspection usually meant they just walked up and down the ranks only talking to our commanding officer while the band played The Grand March form Iida as they went but this character stopped every now and again and had a word with a squaddie. As he moved along the ranks towards me I was dreading he would ask me some daft question. He stopped by Birdie who was next to me and asked what he did before joining the army. 'I worked in a shop Sir' barked Birdie. 'And what do you think the army's done for you private?' asked the General. 'I think its put mussels on my eyebrows, Sir' Birdie replied. Both the General and our Commanding Officer had to smile but all us squaddies were biting our lip to stop us giggling. However we must have made a good impression as the battalion did get to do the Parliament opening.

There was another little spit and polish do coming up in the summer. The Battalion were going to get presented with new colours.

Things were back to normal now and it wasn't long before we were Duty Company again. I got picked for guard duty and was on the main gate on Wednesday morning when the news came that King George had died. There was a bit of a scuffle around the guard room while the

Provost Sergeant decided what to do. In the end the camp flag was put at half mast while the duty bugler played the last post.

The best stag on the guard was guarding the armoury from the I.R.A (Irish Republican Army). This was in the middle of the barrack block and nice and warm. When you did your stag you were marched over there by the guard Corporal and locked inside it for your two hours. Although you were guarding it from the I.R.A we still had the usual weapons when on guard duty. Our rifles and no ammo during the day, after dark no rifle but a pick helve, five rounds of ammo, a torch and a whistle. I think we were supposed to blow the whistle, dazzle them with torch then hit them on the head with the pick helve.

With all the sand dunes to train in we were soon back to fighting the east European gentleman with the hairy jotter.

The battalion was getting regular drafts in from Whittington so we were being bought up to full strength. We had a couple of new lads in our room the one in the bed next to mine one of the new three year regulars. The government had started a new scheme. When you got called up to do your two year's national service, if you agreed to do an extra year making it three years you got the regulars pay rate. Forty eight bob instead of the national service twenty four bob.

Dave was one of them and we soon became great friends. His parents lived in Whittington by the barracks. It was a couple of weeks later that we found out why they lived near the barracks.

On the following Sunday morning a gang of us were walking along the road between the sand dunes and the camp which lead down to the camps married quarters. Who should come marching towards us but our C.O, Lieutenant Colonel Degg. We all give the smart salute, Degg stops and walks up to Dave and made enquires after his parents health etc; well after Degg had gone we called Dave traitor, C.O's spy and other disparaging names. He took it all in good part and gave us the whole tale; his father was a Major and was stationed at Lichfield. Both his father and Degg had been Sergeants in the South Stafford's before the last war. When the war broke out a lot of senior N.C.O's who were literate were sent for officer training. Many of the now company commanders in the county infantry regiments had been commissioned this way. They stayed in the army after the war because they were never going to get jobs like it in Civy Street and a pension as well.

Dave said his dad had married the battalion Regimental Sergeant Major's daughter. That counted against poor old Dave as well to have an R.S.M for a grandfather.

Chapter Sixteen

Since we had been in Ireland my cough had got better, it must be the sea air.

My nineteenth birthday came and went and I got a card off Granny, it was something I suppose. I decided to give myself a birthday present of some new socks. Most of my army issue socks had got no heals left in them, well you know how it is. You are always going to do some darning but never manage to get round to it. On the following Saturday afternoon I caught the bus to Downpatrick with a view to buying some new ones. After a search around the town centre shops I couldn't find any thick woolly ones like the army issued. I had to settle for thinner ones but in the same grey colour as the army socks. The old socks I had to keep for kit inspection purposes and folded regulation style they didn't show the holes in them, so I now had a set of socks for inspection and a set to wear.

The following week we had our efficiency tests on the assault course to do, although the rope climbing was missing off the course here. The two miles in eighteen minutes one made me cough a bit. I managed the nine miles in two hours alright but the route march turned out to be a bit of a laugh. The company had been marching through the countryside for a couple of hours and we had just stopped for our second five minute break. While we were having our smoke we could see the platoon Sergeant's and the company Sergeant. Major having a conference about the map. It was clear to most of us that they were lost. Brownie, always the comic, shouts out 'I know where we are Sir, were lost'. That got him the usual' report to me when we get back to camp' from the Sergeant Major. When we started marching again we just went back the way we came. We had only done four hours marching when we should have done five. Nothing was ever said and we all past for our star grades.

On the Monday morning parade we were told some of us would be moving to Support Company. This was part of the battalion being bought up to strength for a move to Western Germany in the autumn. Names were called out, mine along with mostly lads who had recently joined us. We were told to pack our kit and report back to the Company Office before being marched down to Support Company.

They were billeted in a row of large wooden huts down by the sand dunes. There were a lot of squaddies from other rifle companies down there and chaps from Support company with not much time left to serve going to join the rifle companies. There were four platoons in Support company; The Assault pioneers - their job mine laying and clearing, setting up barbed wire entanglement and bridging; The Anti Tank platoon, they had three seventeen pounder guns; The M.M.G. (Medium Machine Gun) platoon they had Vickers machine guns and the three inch Mortar platoon.

Dave and I got detailed for the M.M.G. platoon and were directed to their hut. There was still a lot of the old platoon still in the hut they were the Bren Carrier drivers, most of them regulars like me. Our new platoon officer a Lieutenant Ball gave us a talk on what he expected of us and introduced the N.C.O's; Sergeant Chapel, Sergeant Meek, Sergeant Burrows and Corporal Wallbanks. Unlike the rifle companies where you had one platoon Sergeant the M.M.G. platoon had three sections each with a Sergeant in charge. By the time it was all sorted out it was lunch time and Sergeant Chapel who seemed to be the senior Sgt said he would give us the afternoon to settle and to unpack our kit.

Tuesday morning, after fist parade, roll call and inspection to see that we had stood close enough to our razors when we shaved, we were taken to an empty hut. Three lads were detailed to go with Sergeant Meek to the stores and fetch the weapon we were going to train to use, a Vickers Medium Machine Gun. What they came back with we have all seen before on the pictures. John Wayne used one to mow the Japanese hoards down with. There was even one in the Three White Feathers film mowing the Fuzzy Wuzzy's down at the battle of Omdurman. The gun itself was water cooled and mounted on a tripod; the tripod was the heaviest part of the whole set up. Sergeant Chapel went on to tell us to forget all the nonsense we had seen at the pictures since the weapon was not used like that. For starters if you fired at a target a few hundred yards away all the bullets didn't go through the same hole. The shot fell in an oval pattern known as the beaten zone and used for covering fire like artillery. Sergeant Chappell rambled on about its history and other things about it until N.A.A.F.I break. After the break Sergeant Burrows took over, he got us round a table and proceeded to strip the gun down holding the parts up and naming them as he went. By the time he had finished explaining the parts and their function and got the gun back in one piece it was lunchtime. At the afternoon parade we were marched to the stores to draw the gun's tripods and a two gallon water can. There were three guns so we were split into three groups. Lieutenant Ball told us that each gun had a crew of three - a number one, a number two and number three. The number one was in charge and aimed and fired the weapon. Number two lay at the side of it and made sure the ammo was fed into the gun smoothly. Number three stationed himself about ten yards to the rear of them and was responsible for bringing up the ammo, water and anything else they needed. While we were training we would all take turns at the various jobs. The positions of who would be number one two and three would be decided in six weeks. When the platoon was functional and up to strength it would consist of three sections of tow guns to a section. This afternoon we would learn how to put the tripod up and mount the gun on it.

For the next few weeks it was all go, learning how to use a dial sight, working out ranges using a map, and using a little slide rule. We all had to have a go at it but I think only the senior N.C.O's would use it in practise. It was used to work out the range of a target when firing at something up a hill as the range would be the hypotenuse not the distance measured on a map. All this plus our normal parades, so we were kept busy.

The weekends were spent chasing rabbits in the sand dunes or we would go down the beach if the T.A were not firing their guns. It was about half a mile from the camp to the beach and across the middle was a firing range with a moving target. Some weekends the local T.A would bring Bofors anti aircraft guns and practice shooting at the moving target. We reckoned Irish planes must fly along the ground. However with the weather now getting a little warmer we enjoyed being down in the huts.

Another lad from Hilary Street School joined our platoon, a Peter Partridge. I had been in the infant and junior school with him but he being clever clogs had gone to the grammar school. They would be the last draft to join the M.M.G. platoon as we were now at full strength.

After six weeks Lt Ball got us on parade and told us he would now sort us out into who does what in the platoon. There would be six gun crews, four radio operators and three range finder operators. He then asked if anyone had owned a motorcycle before and they were called up. I was the only one to put my hand up so I got the motorcycle orderly job. The platoon was split into the three groups, guns, wireless operators and range finders under a Sergeant each to supervise the training. I was handed over to Corporal Wallbanks who was in charge of the Bren carrier drivers. He took me over to the large Romney hut that was the Motor Transport Platoon and handed me over to the M.T

Sergeant. He took me over to the area where the carriers were parked and showed me a old three fifty C.C. Matchless motorbike. By the look of the dust on it, it had not been used since the last war. He then took me back to the office and I had to sign for it. Like everything else in the army if you hadn't got a chitty you couldn't have it. I was then given a small hand full of cotton waste and told to go and clean it. There wasn't enough of the cotton waste but I was told that's all you can have, it seems it's like the four by two for cleaning your rifle, strictly rationed. I cleaned it, blew the tyres up and gave the spark plug a polish. To my surprise it started after a couple of kicks with clouds of smoke coming out of the exhaust. The M.T Sergeant came running over shouting 'get the bloody thing outside'. After the smoke had died down Corporal Wallbanks took me to the office and got the M.T clerk to give me a chitty for two gallons of petrol. I was allowed to ride it along the road by the dunes and down to the beach and told under no circumstances was I to go outside the camp area on it until I had been tested.

We still spent a lot of our training on the guns and this seemed the main focus as ieutenant Ball was always telling us we needed to be capable of operating the weapon in an emergency.

We had now started to have battalion drill parades to polish us up for the presentation of new Regimental Colours on the twenty second of May.

We now had a bit of luck as Leiutenant Ball announced on our morning parade that the South Stafford's M.M.G. platoon had been chosen to enter a competition. While the platoon were training for it we would be excused the colours presentation parade. The platoon should be fully trained by the second week in May and we would be what he called a scheme. Most of had done schemes before with the rifle companies and it usually meant running round the countryside playing soldiers. About a week before the scheme was due to start the evening company orders had me down to report to the M.T officer at ten o'clock in the morning. I was there with my boots blacked and badge and buckles shining. The M.T officer said that he was going to take me for a test on the motorbike as when the platoon did the scheme I would be riding outside the camp. He said I was to ride off towards Downpatrick and he would follow after me. I set off, being careful not to exceed the speed limit and when we had got halfway there and I had stopped at a halt sign, he pulled along side of me. 'Turn back to camp' he shouted and so we rode back to Ballykinler.

'I can see you've ridden a motor bike before, Power' and took me in the office. He got the clerk to make out a war office driving permit and put my name and the colour of my eyes and hair on it and the officer signed it. I was now legal to ride anywhere the army was stationed.

The twenty second of May was the day for the battalion to be presented with their new battle colours. They were going to be presented to the battalion by The Duke of Gloucester at a camp at Lisburn in County Antrim. The day itself was a nice sunny one, which was a surprise because it seemed to rain most days. The whole battalion was transported to the parade ground at the camp. The M.M.G platoon dressed in our best B.Ds were taken there after lunch in three Lorries. We were lined up at the back of all the other invited guests to watch the proceedings. At three o'clock the battalion was marched onto the square and when they had gone through the normal drill the battle colours march on with the usual fife and drum. The old Duke rolls up; he looked like he would be better in a wheel chair, however he managed a quick inspection of the ranks. The old colours were then marched off and they would be laid up in Lichfield Cathedral. The new colours were brought on and handed to the colour party; The Duke just held his hand on the poles while they were given to the two Colour Sergeant's who normally carried them. The new battle colours were now marched back on while the battalion presented arms. The band strikes up with maypole high and off they went on the march past while the Duke took the salute.

A few of us wondered why all this couldn't have been done at Ballykinler, security reasons we were told but it was an afternoon out anyway.

With things being back to normal the scheme to put all we had learnt into practice was put into motion. The platoon would camp out in the sand dunes for two days and practice communications and setting up and laying the guns. The whole operation would end with a live firing session using dial sights. Before we set off, Lieutenant Ball gave a talk on what he expected of us and not to harm the old Billy Goat that ran wild in the dunes.

Thursday morning we all set off into the dunes with the guns loaded on the Brengun carriers and me on my motor bike. The weather was nice but of course it was pissing down by lunch time and stayed for the rest of the day. The three sections of the platoon were given different areas to move it to and H.Q set up in a little hollow further back. This included Lieutenant Ball, his driver, Fred Willets his wireless operator and me. All I was doing was errands most of the time from one section to the other. That was a bit difficult at times as the bike tended to sink in the sand.

At about seven in the evening Lieutenant Ball called all the sections together for the night and with the tarpaulins off the carriers and our ponchos we made some covers to eat and sleep under. The ration we had been issued with was the standard five man crew boxes. They had the normal tins of meat, tins of vegetables, a small tin of tea, sugar, a tin of boiled sweets, bacon and sausage and some porridge oats and hard tack plus some toilet paper. Some of the tins of meat were stewed steak and some Lancashire hot pot so we tipped the lot in a dixie along with the vegetables and made a stew. Next morning after breakfast and inspection by Sergeant Chapel to make sure we had all had a wash and shave, it was back to practicing the manoeuvres until lunch time. During the afternoon the platoon pulled back towards the camp as we would be firing at a range of over a thousand yards. It was about half a mile out of the camp where Lieutenant Ball set up the firing positions. The guns were mounted and aiming markers put out and the gun zeroed on them. The maps were consulted by the section Sergeants and the gun number ones to work out the ranges and angles. Then the order given to load and two taps right and left fire. Things were going well and Lieutenant Ball reckoned with the weather being wet he would be able to check the fall of shot in the sand later. We could hear the little coastal steamer going into Dundrum blowing his hooter although we couldn't see him.

Lieutenant Ball and the Sergeants went to check the target later and could just see the marks on the beach where bullets fell. They had fallen on the inlet to the bay. We had been back in camp for an hour and was all go cleaning the guns when our company commander Major Dillon came flying down all breathless. It seems the Captain of the steamer had complained his ship had been fired at although the ship had not been hit. The Captain must have seen the bullets kicking up the sand on the dunes and thought we were firing at him. However we heard no more of it since the area had been a live firing range since the First World War.

The Anti Tank platoon was the next to get complaints while firing their seventeen pounder shells at the moving target in the dunes. Some of the shot must have skimmed off the sea and were ending up at Newcastle. This was later explained away as due to adverse weather conditions. Normally the sea would be rough and the shell would just dive into the waves. The day the Anti Tank platoon were firing it was dead calm so some of the shot skimmed off the sea and over to Newcastle. But I don't think this was the first time something like this had happened. It seemed to be treated as just one of those things and nothing was going to be done about it. I suppose the army had to pretend to treat it seriously just to keep everyone happy.

Chapter Seventeen

I had written to my Girlfriend Joyce every week and some weeks I had even splashed out my sweet coupons in the N.A.A.F.I. and sent her a box of chocolates. I thought it was about time I paid her a visit so I applied for a seventy two hour pass. I got it but forgot put in for a travel warrant so I had to pay the fare myself. On the Friday evening after our evening meal I caught the bus to Belfast. I got to the ferry terminal just before the night ferry to Liverpool was due to sail. I bought a return ticket to Wolverhampton forty eight and a tanner, (£2.42). When the boat docked at Liverpool the next morning I walked over to Lime Street station and caught the eight thirty train to Wolverhampton. From there it was on the trolley bus to Walsall. I called in the café on the bridge and had five rounds of toast couldn't afford much else; I only had a couple of quid after paying my travel fare and was hoping to take Joyce out this evening. I got a up to Alexander Road just after one o'clock there was no one in but the door was unlocked. It's a good job I had stopped in town for something to eat there was only a stale crust of bread in the house. The house its self was in a bit of a state there didn't seem to have been any cleaning done since I was last here. I went up stairs and my bedroom was just has I had left it so I had a lay down and I nodded off. It was nearly six o'clock when I woke and made myself a drink with Bills Camp coffee. I then made a dash to the paper shop on the corner of Alexander road before they closed to see if they had anything to eat. The only thing they had left was a large loaf and that felt stale to me. However beggars can't be choosers so I bought, it would be alright for making toast. After a wash and shave I was off to see Joyce who lived in Caldmore and pay her a surprise visit. I thought I would make a quick call in Alice's as I went passed; just let her know I was here. To my surprise Joyce was at Alice's and just about to go off to the picture with Alice's son John. It seems John and is mother and had patched up their differences and he had moved back home to live. As Alice put it John and Joyce had been `walking out` for a couple of weeks now. So that was the end of that I was a bit disappointed but tried not to show it. I liked the girl and we got on well together but as Alice said I had another three and half years to do in the army. She reckoned Joyce was looking for a husband and didn't want to wait that long. I wandered over to Jeff Slater's and spent an hour yapping to him. I did alright his wife Mini made me a big sausage sandwich and a mug of tea. It was as much as I could eat but I managed it. I called in The Fullbrook Pub on my way back home just to say hello to Uncle George and Aunty Maude. I didn't want a drink after Minis blow-out I was too full. They insisted so I had a half of mild and I got it down and made a quick farewell to them. Bill was home tucking into a pile of chips he had brought, he was surprised to see me. I asked him about Fanny and he said he said he thinks she's now living with Blondie in Rushall. Bill reckoned she hadn't slept here since last January. He shows me the famous buff envelope with O.H.M.S. along the top they were is call-up papers. He had already been for his medical and he had got to report to a training camp down near Bournemouth next week. That begged the question what to do with the house if no one was living here I said I would see Jeff. Knowing Jeff would be off working feeding Haynes pigs in the morning I nipped over at lunch time. Jeff was not too happy to see me his lunch was nearly ready perhaps he thought I was hoping to get invited. As soon as I mentioned about Bill being called-up Jeff said he had it all in hand. A Council housing official was coming to see him and Austin next Wednesday. When it was all finalised he would write to me with the details.

It was a bit early to go and visit Granny Mac so I went and bought Uncle George a pint in the Fullbrook.

I made my way along the Broadway up to Birmingham Road to visit Granny. There were quite a few others visiting with it being Sunday afternoon so Granny put her coat on and we had a little walk. She reckoned coming into this home was one of the best moves she had ever made. She asked me if I had any contact with Mary I had to tell her no. Granny then told me she had tried to get in touch with Mary at an address in Chase Town as she had a bible to mark Mary's confirmation for her. Granny had received a letter telling her Mary didn't want the bible and not try contacting her again. I could see that had upset Granny. I spent over an hour with her and promised to take her down Patterson's tea rooms on my next leave.

With it being Sunday and everywhere closed I had to survive on a diet of toast until Monday morning. With not taking Joyce out I was able to have the full breakfast in the café. That would last me until tonight when I was planning to get a feed of chips in Liverpool before I caught the night ferry. I wasn't due back at Ballykinler Camp until Tuesday evening but I didn't know if there was a morning ferry. Anyway my return ticket was marked evening ferry. I went Back home after my feed and got my kit, called in Alice's and said goodbye and off. Caught the train from Walsall to Wolverhampton. I thought it would save me walking from the bus station to the Wolverhampton high level station. There was a train going north at one thirty but I had to change at Crewe for the Liverpool train. There was a café on Crewe station so I had myself a mug of tea while I was waiting for the Liverpool train. It was gone seven o'clock when I got to Lime Street station and wandered out into Lime Street. A search of the side streets and I found a chip shop with a tables in. They had a special on the notice board cod and chips with a round of bread and butter and a mug of tea one and a tanner. This was just the place I was looking for so I dived in. It was a popular place as there were a lot of men eating in there. Mainly seamen from what I could hear of their conversations. It was warm in there so I made the meal last and had another mug of tea. Went and spent an hour in the station waiting room before walking up to the ferry dock It wasn't due out until ten o'clock but passengers were boarding so I got on. Found my way down to the deck with the café and shops an got a seat in the corner. I had learnt for Friday nights crossing it got crowded and you need to grab a seat early. The crossing was about eight hours and I had done it once stuck on deck, never again. Slept most of the way and awoke about six thirty as the boat was docking in Belfast. It was midmorning before I got back to camp and I hadn't enjoyed my leave it was fifty bob wasted I think.

Preparations were now afoot for the M.M.G. platoon competition this was going to take place on Salisbury plain. The carriers and a fifteen hundred weight truck with my motor bike in the back went off on Friday morning. The rest of us collected our haversack rations after lunch then loaded into Lorries and taken to the port of Larne. It was only a two hour crossing to Stranraer in Scotland from here. As soon as we got out of the transport Sgt Chapel was after us, don't put your rifles down anywhere make sure you have always have them on your shoulder. Corporal Vale was the first to get Chapel wrath when he lent his rife against the Ferry rail while he lit a fag and Vale was the R.E.M.E (Royal Electrical Mechanical Engineers) carrier fitter. Apparently the I.R.A. was known to lurk in ships railings. However we had a good crossing and past the time flipping our fag ends in the air for the seagulls to catch. The train was waiting at Stranraer and we were instructed to go in the first coach as the train split at Carlisle. The train set off and we were all a bit disappointed none of us had been to Scotland before. We expected mountains, rivers, stags like you see on all the picture of Scotland. The county side was dead flat you could have been anywhere in the British Isles. The army had forgotten to book us into the dinning car so we stuffed our haversack rations down us. When the train reached Carlisle it changes the coaches at the back before setting of for London. It was getting dark by now and over the next hour the talking gradually stopped and we nodded of. By breakfast time we were in London with Chapel shouting disembark down the carriage. There was a check just to see we all had our rifles and kit bags before being marched out of the station. There were lorries on the road outside the station waiting to pick us up and take us for a breakfast. The transport didn't take us far we were still in central London and dropped us off in what looked like an ordinary street. An Officer waiting took us into a doorway and down a long spiral staircase. When we got to the bottom what a surprise there was a whole army camp in the passages down there. It turned out to be well worth clomping up and down the stairs as we were given a grand breakfast down there. While we were stuffing ourselves Lieutent Ball rolled up an announced we would be going from here to Kings Cross station. From there we would catch the train to Salisbury or as he put it, entrain for Salisbury where we would be picked up and taken to a place called Netheravon. When we arrived at the camp it was only a smallish place but it had a N.A.A.F.I. so we were all happy. The whole platoon was billeted in one Romney Hut it was the first time the platoon had all been together in one room. We had arrived here about twelve thirty just in time for lunch so once we had handed our rifles in to the store we soon found the cookhouse. When we got there a Corporal on the door demanded to know what regiment we were from and on the ration strength before ticking us off and letting us in the dinning room. I would have thought a look at our cap badges would have shown him our regiment. The place its self was sparkling clean and painted in pastel colours with some tables at the top end of it with white table cloths on. These were not for the likes of us, there were civilians and girls from the W.R.A.C. (Women's Royal Army Corps) worked at the camp. The food itself was better than average and well cooked much better that the usual swill. First parade two o'clock and Sgt Chapel said the platoon would clean and oil the guns before handing them into the stores. After this had been done the rest of the afternoon would be left for us to settle in our new quarters, well it was Saturday. As soon as we had got our kit sorted out it was time to have a mooch around the camp. There were all sorts of funny things around this camp as it was a place where new weapons were tested before going into service with the army. On a little field below or hut was what looked like a tank, and behind it an aeroplane. Closer inspection revealed them to be only blown up rubber models. Giler reckoned they were a cunning War Office plan. When the enemy fired at them shot just bounced off them. However we found the N.A.A.F.I. some where to spend Saturday night so everyone was happy. On Sunday afternoon some of us had a wander down into Netheravon for a look. It was a typical English country village the sort you see on post cards. A few thatched cottages couple of pubs and a church. Reading the church notice board we saw they held a Saturday night dance in the village hall. We made a note of that.

Monday morning parade after the inspection to make sure we had all stood close enough to the razor while shaving. Lieutenant Ball got us back into the hut to give us a talk. At the end wall of the Romney hut we were staying in was a black board with a little stage in front of it. Lieutenant Ball and the Sergeants got on the stage. Balls and the three stooges some one at the back said. Chapel heard it. Who said that he barked but no one owned up. Lieutenant Ball then explained that for most of the exercises we did this week we would have observers watching us. We had spent months training for this and he expected a good show from us all. Sergeant Chapel then announced or first exercise would be gun training for us all. Although half the platoon did different things like wireless operators, carrier drivers and range finders. We all had to do the gun drills like mounting the weapon aiming it and zeroing up the dial sights, so we would be interchangeable. By the time it had all been accomplished to Chapels satisfaction it was lunch time. I went up the transport section with the carrier drivers after lunch and my motorbike was still in the back of the fifteen hundredweight truck. With the help of Bill Brough and the truck diver we got it out and I gave it a run round the yard just to check it still worked. The truck driver had to have ago on the motor bike didn't he. The driver was a lot older than the rest of us and had been in the army since the nineteen thirties. He was not a regular member of the M.M.G. platoon but from the M.T. platoon and had been sent with us just to cart the ammunition around.

Things started in earnest on Tuesday as we spent the day out on Salisbury Plain. Setting up positions and racing about while two officers with binoculars and clip boards followed us in jeeps. On the Wednesday morning the platoon was going to do some live firing, two officers gave Lieutenant Ball some map references of targets. The platoon set of on to the plain after a while we stopped in some trees and Ball and the Sergeants held a conference. After some pouring over the map each Sergeant called his gun number ones in and had discussions with them. Each section now set of for a different area and I had to take note of the map references as I would have to carry messages between them. I had just taken a message to three section when they started firing. Their target was a patch of Broom bushes and as soon as they fired at it hundreds of rabbits came flying out of it. The whole exercise seemed to go of to everyone's satisfaction although the binocular and clip board pair never said any thing. By lunch time it was all over and the afternoon was spent cleaning the guns. The following day the guns were on the firing range in the morning and the carriers along with me taken out on the plain accompanied by one of the clip board brigade. We were taken to a place with a few small trees were growing. The art of camouflage was what we were going to do. The carriers were driven in amongst the trees and the camouflage nets put over them and tied to the trees a bit of bracken thrown on top. We were all marched about three hundred yards to a little hillock to view or handy work. I must say it looked just what it was Brengun carriers under nets. The army's camouflage nets didn't help they were dark green and brown, the trees light green. However the men with clip boards seemed happy so we all went home. Friday afternoon was to be the big event firing at a target blind using the dial sights. The clip boards had been out on the morning and laid panels on the ground in a valley somewhere. Map references of them and where the guns are to fire from given to Lieutenant Ball before we left camp. Each gun would fire five hundred rounds and a time was given to complete the whole exercise. Off we dash for about a mile or so set up fire and with draw without any mishaps. Lieutenant Ball and the Sergeants were taken to see the panels and they had one or two holes in them, not many but it counted as a success. Lieutenant Ball got us together and said he was pleased with how we had performed and would let us know the results of the completion later. It was all go now to clean and boil out the guns before our evening meal.

Saturday morning parade was a bit easy going well it was all over now. Lieutenant Ball rolled up and told us we were runners up in the competition we had been beaten by The Royal Scotch Regiment serving in Germany. He thanked us for our efforts and said he wouldn't be going back to Ireland with us he was taking up a new posting as an acting Captain. We discovered later the truck driver would be staying here also with the M.T. The move back to Ireland would be on Monday so we had the weekend to pack our kit. The Saturday dance down Netheravon was our goal now. That turned out a bit of a giggle. We called in the pub and had a couple of pints before going over the church hall. The old buffer on the door smelt everyone's breathe before he would let them in. If he could smell beer on you he wouldn't let you in so we danced our way back to camp.

Monday morning we drew haversack rations and started our journey back. It was uneventful until we reached Stranraer station about eight o'clock in the evening. The station was only a booking office toilet and a wall with a bench along it and a canopy over it. As we all stood around waiting for the ferry someone noticed a rifle propped up against the wall. A quick check revealed it was Sergeant Chapel's, he had gone to the toilet. Corporal Vale saw his chance and grabbed it and put it under the bench. He got some of us to sit on the bench and hide it with our legs. Chapel came back and didn't say any thing just walked up and down looking. He then held a conference with the other two Sergeants and they had a wander round before going into a huddle at the end of the platform. While they were discussing what to do Fred Baker one of Vales boozing partners shouted out I've found a rifle. Sergeant Chapel red faced grabbed it off him but didn't say a word. There was mutterings in the crowd like you've got to watch these I.R.A. But Sergeant Chapel just ignored the comments. It was after midnight before we got back to Ballykinler and we could have eaten a horse between two bread carts but we were getting nothing until breakfast.

Chapter Eighteen

At first parade on Tuesday morning Sergeant Chapel introduced us to our new platoon commander, Captain Gregg. He was a sporty looking individual with and handlebar moustache and as soon as he opened his mouth you could tell he was an easy going, relaxed sort of a bloke. Most of the platoon was more interested in the car he had come in; it was an old nineteen thirties Alvis sports car.

Now that our cappers at Netheravon were over we were back to normal and that meant Saturday morning on R.S.M's parade and with it being early summer it was warmer than the last time we were on the square.

The M.M.G. platoon was not the battalion conquering heroes but was the football team who had won the Northern Ireland cup. The main reason being that during the battalions build up to full strength a few lads drafted were professional football apprentices; one lad had actually played for the Wolves first team a few times. We were back to normal training now and did a couple of schemes with the whole regiment moving across country to take up positions. One day we even got as far as surrounding Belfast Airport, although most of us squaddies couldn't understand what was going on half the time as every bit of information was on a need to know basis and our job was to follow the pointing finger and me to do the errands on my bike.

All the talk now was of our move to West Germany as a couple of the carrier drivers along with Sergent Burrows had already gone on the advance party. The week before we were due to go Support Company was the week's duty company. I had done one guard duty on Tuesday but on the Friday night's Company orders I was down to report along with nine others to the guard room at fourteen hundred hours (tomorrow) Saturday. Dress should be best uniform and we were to have our rifles. We were all intrigued and asked Cpl Wallbanks if he knew where we were going but he didn't. Dave found out from the company clerk who he had met in the N.A.A.F.I that The Northern Ireland Show was on at a showground at Belfast and we were going to be the Saturday night guard. After our lunch we all reported to the guardroom togged in our Sunday best boots bulled brass dazzling. The provost Sgt lined us up and gave us the once over just to make sure. We were loaded onto a truck and drove off to Belfast which was only thirty five miles away. We were dropped off at and army camp by the showground and shown in to an empty barrack room with a few beds in. The afternoon was spent in there smoking and talking until Corporal Wallbanks marched us over to the showground about five o'clock. The guard post was in the main grand stand and run by the Royal Ulster Constabulary. I could see there was some confusion as soon as we had marched in, you could sense there was a 'what's that lot doing here?' attitude. A Lieutenant Colonel showed up and we were told to go and sit down in a room next door while discussions went on. When we got in the room there was a table at the end loaded with sandwiches and other goodies. After about half an hour the Lieutenant Colonel along with the chief of the police came into the room and we all sprung to attention. Now we were told that the guard detail would be taken back to the army camp where we would spend the night before returning to Ballykinler. It seems the Royal Ulster Constabulary had decided they were quite capable of guarding the showground without the army's interference. The police chief now thanked us for coming and said 'you lads help your selves to some food before you go', the tea in the urn might be a bit cool by now but I bet you lads would sooner have a bottle of beer!'. You could see that got up the Lieutenant Colonel's nose a bit but we had made a start on the sandwiches when a copper came with a bottle of beer for each of us. The sandwiches were very dainty with the crusts cut off, so we ate them with our little fingers cocked up. Corporal Wallbanks marched us back to the barracks after we had done justice to the goodies. The whole group of us decided to go and have a look round Belfast while we were there. There didn't seem a lot of night life going on and most of us ended up at the funfair by the show ground. Dave, Giler and I had a go on the bumping cars and got in with three girls. We spent a very pleasant evening with them going round the fair, although they had to leave for home at nine thirty as they lived in Portadown and the last bus was nine forty five. Anyway we had a good night and with the sandwiches, we found out how the other half live.

The beds in the barrack room allotted to us had no blankets on them; however they all had a paliases or friendly donkeys as we always called them so with it being summer we just slept in our shirts. A hearty breakfast was eaten before our trip back to camp on Sunday morning.

Our move to Germany was now on and everything was being packed up ready, even the rifles although we would have enough to carry with out them as well. It was late afternoon before we set off and didn't draw haversack rations so we knew we were being fed along the way. The Larne - Stranraer was the route again and I think that the ferry was just for us to cross on. The train was just for the regiment so wouldn't be direct like the one we went to Netheravon on. Food was dished up in our mess tins on Stranraer station before we entrained as they put it. It was nearly dark when the train started off and it wasn't long before most of us were asleep. The only trouble was that the army had neglected to book us a sleeping car. Breakfast was served at Manchester along with haversack rations for our lunch. I don't know if the army had a haversack ration menu because wherever you were it was the same; two rounds of prairie chicken (corned beef) and two rounds of bungy (cheese). As the train chugged on through Crewe, Stoke then Wolverhampton I realised we would be passing the old farm. By mid morning the train was passing the fields and the pool where we had so much fun as kids. To my surprise although most of the farm had been knocked down, the old barn by the field was still standing, so I gave it a wave just for old time's sake. This would be my highlight of the journey. The train puffed its way across the country sometimes slow and sometimes fast.

It was evening when we got to the port of Harwich and we were all starving but there was a meal slopped up in our mess tins. The cooks serving it thought they were very clever as they managed to catch one or two out. A few of us were yapping to our mates and not concentrating when we walked along the food line. The servers grabbed the chance to act the giddy goat and some got the rice pudding dumped in with their meat and veg. Very funny.

The battalion boarded the night ferry for the Hook of Holland and my first move was to find a corner to curl up in for the night. I needn't have bothered as down below deck there were rows of bunks for us. There was no bedding on them but they were alright to kip on.

Once I was stretched out on the bunk I wasn't going to move again so I never even went back up on deck for a look. Morning saw us docked at the Hook of Holland where were we were told to disembark and line up on the dock. There was a count of each company just to make sure no one had jumped overboard in the night. The whole battalion was then taken in a large hut and given some breakfast. Haversack rations issued to us on the way out with our Colour Sergeant standing there shouting 'who wants ham and pickle and who wants the smoked salmon'. It was the usual prairie chicken and bungy.

The train was on the other side of the dock and each company was allotted two carriages and being S company we were at the back of the train. Once we were loaded the train pulled forward off the dock and stopped in a station. The hawkers were waiting for us selling sweets mainly. They were still on ration in England but there didn't seem and shortage of them here. They would take English money for them but they were expensive, several hawkers had boxes of Mars bars selling at a tanner a time - they made us giggle as they couldn't pronounce it and they were calling them Muzz Buzzes.

We gathered from some of the old soldiers who had been here before that Minden was just over two hundred miles in land for the Hook. The journey was uneventful until we passed Osnabruck where all along the side of the line were factories totally wrecked by bomb damage. The war had been over seven years and it was still all rubble.

It was just about two o'clock in the afternoon when we got to Minden, a town on the river Wesser. Our kit bags were loaded onto trucks and we were left to march up to the camp about a mile away. Off we marched, columns of three of course and over the river up to camp.

The camp was a modern one with the HQ on the left as you went into the main gate and over the door was an eagle holding a shield with what had been a swastika on it. Some one had tried to chisel it off but you could still see what it had been. There was a large square, oh joy, with three two story barrack blocks each side of it. At bottom of the square was a large gym and behind that the M.T garages. S company got put in the far barracks on the right-hand side; very handy as the next building along was the N.A.A.F.I. The rooms only held eight beds and were centrally heated and across the passage from the rooms were the ablutions with showers and baths. All the widows had two sets of window frames an outer and an inner to keep out the cold. You can say what you like about poor old Hitler but he knew how to look after his troops.

It was bright and sunny for our first morning parade at Minden and the Colour Sergeant announced we would all call at the stores and draw a tin of dubbing each after we fell out. In future our normal working boots would be cleaned with dubbing, not polished or best boots kept bulled for parades. This would cause us some problems as you had to wear your best boots while your others were repaired. It was a right job trying to get a shine back on them once they had been dubbed.

After we had dubbed our boots to Sergeant Chapel's satisfaction I was rounded up by Corporal Wallbanks along with the carrier driver and marched to the M.T offices. We were going to be introduced to our vehicles, in my case an old side valve B.S.A motorbike. The carriers were the same two universals for each section making six for the platoon and one Tee Sixteen for the platoon commander. Captain Gregg had now shown up and reminded us that we would now have to get used to driving on the left-hand side of the road, or as he put it 'the wrong side of the road'. Gregg then got all the drivers to start their carrier to make sure it worked. Corporal Vale the platoons R.E.M.E fitter gave the nod and we all signed for our vehicles. By now it was Thursday pay day and we would be paid with B.A.F (British Armed Forces) money. It was all paper money even the pennies were paper notes. The pay clerk announced that if any one wanted German marks they would need to order them on the Monday before the next pay parade. These would be at the rate of twelve marks to the pound. A voucher would also be issued to us with our pay and this would allow us to purchase one hundred and forty cigarettes from the N.A.A.F.I.

Within a few days things got back to normal and by Saturday it was C.O's barrack room inspection and then R.S.M's parade. It was a very hot day and there was a swimming pool on a patch of ground at the side of the gym, so after lunch half the battalion decided that they were going to have a dip; trouble was it had never been maintained and was only full of rain water and there must have been six inches of mud on the bottom. It wasn't long before everyone was trying to swim in what looked like brown soup. Someone must have complained as the Provost Sergeant came and turfed us all out. The pool was abandoned after that and on Monday night Battalion orders declared it out of bounds to us.

With the large gym we now had a regular session in there two periods a week. There was plenty of P.T.I's as all the football team had been made Psychical Training Instructors. Some times to end the session the instructors would have us boxing one minute rounds. They would split the platoon in two halves and when he blew his whistle one from each side would jump into the ring and fight each other. When they had done their minute he would blow his whistle the pair fighting would throw their gloves to the next couple. This went on until we had all had a go. If our gym session didn't end this way it would be the old knights on horses. You got some one to piggy back you and then tried to knock each other off until the last pair standing were the winners.

This game was for us short arses as the lower your centre of gravity the more stable you were therefore harder to knock over.

A lot of our time was now being spent out of camp at the training area a wooded district on the edge of Minden. The town itself was a nice little place with a nice old town hall and lot of Army camps in the area. The place was famous for a battle that took place during the seven year war. Down where the river Wesser ran through a gap in the hills was a large statue of the prince who won the battle.

At the end of August a group of us were sent to the training area with a couple of Bren gun carriers. With the help of Corporal Wallbanks and a couple of drivers we were going to learn to drive them. Our first job was to set up a camp with a couple of tarpaulin's borrowed from the M.T. The carriers were the type known as universals and had a steering wheel that only moved half a turn. Being tracked vehicles you steered them by applying the brakes to one track. Most of us had some idea of how to drive them as we had all played about in them when no one was looking. Corporal Wallbanks split us into two groups, one would go with Fred Harris and the gang, I was with Bill Brough. The carriers were easy to drive but changing gear was the tricky bit as you had to double clutch. You couldn't just put the clutch in and pull it out of first gear and slip into second gear. It was clutch in, out of gear, clutch out then clutch in again and into second gear. With the carriers being tracked they didn't freewheel very well so you had to be quick. We all soon got the hang of it and had a right old time practising in the woods and on the county roads. Most days our last call would be up an old lane to what looked like had once been a farm but was now a cigar factory. The young girls who worked there would hear us coming and hang out of the windows waving and shouting to us. The man in charge would get them back in but as soon as he did some more of them would be waving out of another window and yapping to us.

As we got better at driving Corporal Wallbanks took us down by Minden one morning to give us some experience on the cobbled roads. Most of the roads around the town were coddled and you had to be careful with a tracked vehicle. If you tried to turn going too fast, the carrier would spin round like a top on the cobbles. However there were no accidents and we all passed according to Corporal Wallbanks.

By Saturday we were ready to return to our camp but we had an invite from the girls at the cigar factory to the Apple Feistier on Saturday night. A conference was held and we decided to stay and go back first thing Sunday morning in time for breakfast. With it being the weekend no one would miss us anyway.

The feistier was held in a field by the cigar factory and we must have looked a pretty sight at the Feistier wearing the denims we had been in all week. All the locals were there, especially the girl's mothers to see that no hanky panky was going on - obviously they had the wrong idea about us young squaddies. They were all very friendly and with a chap playing the accordion it was a nice atmosphere. There was cider with apple pips in it, which was a bit rough, but the apple juice was nice. Cheese and that dark brown bread the Germans seemed to like was also laid on. It was a great evening and we danced with the girls and some brave souls even did a turn with their mothers. By nine thirty it was starting to get dark and the show was winding down. Some of the squaddies had exchanged addresses with some of the girls. I don't know what they would do with them as most of the girls spoke very little English and the squaddies no German. However it had been a very pleasant evening and we all had a good time.

Chapter Nineteen

Most of the jobs around the barracks were done by the locals, the girls in the N.A.F.F.I were all Germans, so when it was our turn to do Duty Company there was only the camp guard to do. However we did a lot more playing soldiers and spent a lot of time doing manoeuvres of one sort or another. Some of these would last a week or more and we would do miles over the German countryside with units from other N.T.O. countries involved. We did most of our moving about under the cover of darkness and I recall one cold wet night when we were going over some heath land. Major Dillon company commander who was travelling with us in one of the carriers called a stop. He got us all out to look at what in the dark looked like a large grave stone. This was the spot where Field Marshall Montgomery had taken the surrender of the German army in nineteen forty five. We couldn't have cared less, all we wanted to do was to get where ever we were going and get our heads down. It was probably two o'clock in the morning when we stopped by what looked like a timber yard and Sergeant Chapel was running around shouting 'make sure your vehicles are all well camouflaged!' One of the main things when we were on these schemes was finding somewhere to sleep and most times it would be under your poncho. Keeping out of the way of the tanks was another must. You think of them as slow moving things but the Centurion tank can move a bit when it needs to and the drivers could only see what was right in front of them. It was on one of these schemes that we had our first casualty, one of the carrier drivers, a lad in the mortar platoon. He had tried to drive his carrier up a near vertical bank and it had tipped over. He must have tried to jump out at the last minute but the vehicle had fallen across his chest killing him. Popeye who I was at school with came with the Medical Officer and his jeep ambulance to fetch the body. They loaded him on the stretcher feet first and Popeye, still the clown said 'can you turn him round his feet smell!' The M.O then gave Popeye a right dressing down for being disrespectful, it and reduced Popeye to tears. When we got back to camp after the scheme had finished it was suggested that the M.M.G. platoon all donate five bob each towards a wreath for him. However his parents decided to pay to have his body brought back home to England for burial so our donations were not used. Captain. Gregg said the money had been offered to the lad's parents but they had said they would sooner the platoon do something with it. Sergeant Burrows suggested we have a coach trip; apparently we could get an army coach for a recreational trip out. One of the old soldiers who had been in this part of Germany before suggested a place on a lake about fifty miles away as a nice place to visit. As no one had any other ideas this was agreed by all but one of us, Ruthven the platoon's religious maniac was not happy about it. He did some chuntering, we would all end up in hell and as the trip would be on a Sunday that made it worse. Sgt Burrows said he would see our company office and organise it.

If we were not out on a divisional scheme we would be performing up on one of the training areas. This usually meant I would be sent back up there on my motorbike the following day to look for things we had left behind; usually Captain. Gregg's map case or his binoculars he had left hanging on a tree. I didn't mind as I made the job last me all morning.

Most of us were now used to being in Germany, the barracks were good and there was a recreation room on our floor. News papers were put in most days, they were delivered by a little aeroplane that would drop them on the square early in the morning there was also table tennis but no balls to play with. There were football pitches at the back of our barrack block and Dave was a keen player, he was always playing Saturday afternoon matches. I preferred to go down the town.

The N.A.A.F.I. had a great place on the edge of Minden, I think it had been a old mansion as the rooms were large and they all had chandeliers in them. All the charities like the Church Army and the W.V.S. had places for squaddies to go and you seemed to be in the centre of things there as the H.Q. B.A.O.R. (British Army on the Rine) was only at Bielafeld a few miles away. Randolph Turpin the once world champion boxer had paid us a visit. He had given boxing demonstrations in Minden football stadium against some of the army lads. I didn't get to see any of it as it was in late September while I was learning to drive carriers up the training area.

There were all sorts of activities you could spend your spare time doing and I got into small bore shooting. There was a notice on the battalion orders one night that a small bore shooting contest was to be held. They would award prizes for first, second and third best scores although it didn't say what they would be. The contest would be on the twenty five yard indoor range situated on the floor above the battalion armoury and anyone wishing to try their luck should leave their name at the company office. I put my name down and was detailed to report to the indoor range the following Thursday afternoon. When I got up there the regiment's adjutant, a Captain Waters seemed to be in charge of proceedings, with the battalion armourer a R.E.M.E Sgt overseeing the shooting. He explained to us that we would each be firing twenty rounds, ten to practice and then ten to score. The targets would be unfamiliar to most of us as they would not be the single bull targets we were used to but we would be firing at five bull competition ones. There were a few up there and only two small bore rifles between us. When my turn came I fired my ten practise shots and the Sgt inspected my target. When I got down to fire my ten to count the Sergeant came and moved my shooting position and showed me the best way to use the sling. I fired my shots, cleared the rifle and handed it back to the Sergeant. No more was said, you could sense it was you've had your go now clear off. So, no one was more surprised than me when a few weeks later I was on battalion orders to report to the indoor range at eleven o'clock on Sunday morning. When I rolled up the Adjutant the Sergeant Major of A company, a well known crack shot, the R.E.M.E Sergeant, and a Corporal were there. He looked like he had been in the army since the First World War. I was told that this was just a practise shoot and another two rifles had been issued although the R.E.M.E Sergeant had his own target rifle. I fired my twenty rounds, the target was inspected and I got a well done. I gathered from the conversation that we were going to be the battalion small bore shooting team, I wasn't going to be asked to join, just detailed to do shooting. I made a few discreet enquiries as to who had won the shooting competition but it fell on deaf ears, so I shot when company orders said I was to report to the range and never found out how the team was doing; the usual army need to know bullshit, like who won the shooting competition mystery. However it got me off a few duties so it was a good skive really. The target shooting was about the limits of my sporting prowess.

The battalion football team were the heroes beating all the other regiments by four, five and six nil's. However, like all unbeatables they would come unstuck later.

There were some changes during October the first being the retirement of our beloved Regimental Sergeant Major, according to battalion orders he had been in the army for thirty years. It was a sad announcement and most of us squddies cried our eyes out. He was to be replaced by an R.S.M Marshall from Lichfield, another one of

Dave's Dad's mates. He wasn't the only one retiring, our company commander Major Dillon was off as well; our new one was a Major La Rue and he was different altogether. Where Dillon had been an old father figure, La Rue was a 'hello chappies' sort of a bloke like Captain Gregg.

Our first parade with the New R.S.M was on a Wednesday morning since we didn't have the regular Saturday parades now. Saturday mornings was cross country run morning, well around the outskirts of Minden run. A visit from the fifth armoured division commander was due. The South Stafford's were part of the infantry brigade attached to that division and of course we had to show him how good the South Stafford's were so Marshall had us on the square practicing for a week. Instead of the usual march past we were going to do it in columns and do open order on the march. This turned out to be a bit tricky with the front column marching on, the middle column marking time two paces and the rear column four paces just before we reached the saluting Dias. After us all being driven half mad for a week, it was eventually decided that when the big day arrived we would do a normal march past. On the day it all went off like a well oiled clock with the general and our brigade commander taking the salute. Our brigade commander was a Scotchman with a military moustache one half brown and the other white. This took everyone's attention but being on parade you couldn't have a giggle. This was on bonfire day November the fifth because on the evening the regiment had a bonfire on the sports field. This was only for the married quarters and their kids and didn't have proper fire works; the entertainment was put on by the Sergeants mess shooting very-lights and Para illuminators into the air.

The coach trip was set for the second Sunday in November which was a bit late for any decent weather. When the platoon was all together do a bit of gun training Sergeant Burrows gave us the details; we would have the coach from one in the morning until six in the evening and there was enough money left to buy us a bottle of beer each to take on the trip. I couldn't figure out how he had managed this as there were thirty four of us in the M.M.G platoon. Assuming every one had paid up at five bob each, it only came to eight pounds ten shillings but I bet one or two had dodged paying it.

Sunday morning was wet, cold and misty. Ruthven said it was judgment on us but I noticed he joined us for the trip and off we set. The driver went out of his way a bit just to give a ride on the auto-bahn as none of us have ever been on a road like it - two carriage ways dead straight and no halt signs or traffic lights, every motor going flat out. The weather hadn't improved by the time we got to the lake; it was a typical north European November day although on a better day it would have been a nice place. There were a couple of stalls selling raw fish which seemed to be a local delicacy, a café and a restaurant but as no one had any marks to spend we couldn't go in the café. And being it was a trip organised by ourselves we didn't get haversack rations to take with us so by two o'clock we were all cold, wet and hungry. Most of us got back on the coach and by two thirty we were on our way back to camp via another little ride on the auto-ban. That had been the most enjoyable part of the trip. Ruthven was the only one happy, his predictions had come to pass; we had got off lightly for our wickedness.

The first one to in our platoon to get any leave was Badger. He was to marry a girl who he had got into trouble. Badger was rather proud of it as he explained; there were two sisters and he had been seeing to both of their needs with the promise he would marry the first one he put up the stick. The one who he had been sent for to marry was the one he liked best. The thing that seemed to please him most was the fact he was getting a weeks leave, the marriage bit was inevitable anyway sooner or later. We all drove him up the wall suggesting names for the kid and a lot of them he certainly couldn't have put on a birth certificate. By Sunday he got some relief from all the ribbing he was getting as it became Dave's turn. We were doing our usual Sunday afternoon exercise like laying on our beds reading and listening to the wireless when we noticed Dave togging himself up in his best battle dress uniform 'I've got an important appointment' was all we could get out of him. So we all ganged up on him and refused to let him out of the barrack room until we found out what he was up to. He had only been invited to Sunday tea at the Regimental Sergeant Major's house hadn't he? Dave pleaded Marshall was a friend of the family and he couldn't refuse the invitation. What made the situation worse was that the Marshall had two teenage daughters, so we reckoned it was probably operation catch Dave old Marshall had in mind. However we let him out in good time saying he was to see Badger if he need any tips on getting wed. It was all taken in good part and we all got our legs pulled from time to time.

The platoon had now got into a routine with gun training drill and our separate jobs. If we weren't out on a scheme I would be down the

M.T cleaning my bike. I was busy doing this one morning when Sergeant Chapel arrived. 'Come with me, Power you can drive a carrier' he said and took me to a row of garages by some stables. There in the corner was a universal carrier with a flame thrower on it. 'It's been put onto the M.M.G. platoon strength' he explained and 'we don't have a spare driver. Its got to have a driver so you've got the job but don't worry you will probably never be asked to take on the road, the bloody things are obsolete'. He was right; I only drove it round the garage block once just to check it worked. My total mileage must have been all of two hundred yards.

As the weather got colder it was decided that for battalion parades on the square overcoats would be worn or as the army call them great coats. We still had to turn out for our morning company parade and roll call in our denims and stand there while we turned blue. The first do with our great coats on turned out to be a bit of a giggle. Some of the lads who had been in Hong Kong had been issued with new great coats before we left there. These had just been handed out as an overcoat to make up their kit, size didn't mater as long as you got a coat. A lot of them were large sizes and the old Indian contractor had cut them down to fit. The result was that on some of the shorter lads the little belt on the coat came across their behinds and in a couple of cases below it. The flaps on the pockets were a few inches above the bottom of the coat and the shoulders overhanging the arms. After a quick inspection by Lieutenant Colonel Degg along with the Regimental Sergeant Major the parade was fallen out and we were marched back to our company's area where our Sergeant Major along with the Colour Sergeant sorted out who needed coats changing or altering to fit them. In a couple of cases there was a bit of an argument with the Colour Sergeant claiming they had never been issued with the coat they were wearing. "You didn't get that in this mans army son!' the Colour Sergeant claimed but our company commander Major La Rue said "just get them changed Sergeant." One or two of us had great coats with plastic buttons which had to be handed in to have brass buttons sewn on. We were lucky I suppose with all the coats going as a job lot, I was surprised they didn't just give us the brass buttons to sew on ourselves.

Chapter Twenty

I hadn't had a letter off anyone for a while so I wrote to Alice asking about my brother Bill. I got a letter back informing me Bill was serving in the Pioneer Corps and was stationed at a camp on the South Coast. If I ever needed somewhere to stay when I went on leave I could stay with her. The letter went on to tell me that Alice's son and Joyce were now engaged and would be married next year. I'm glad I had written to her as Jeff hadn't bothered to let me know about the house we had lived in; there were new tenants living in our old house now, a young couple with a baby. I sent a letter to him asking for information and got a reply. The house had been handed back to Walsall Council on the understanding that they would find us another house when we needed one. That turned out to be like most council promises, not worth the paper it was written on. Jeff was sorry he hadn't written before but would have told me on my next leave.

In late November both the M.M.G platoon and the Mortar platoon were taken up to the Baltic coast to do live firing. Before we went all the carrier drivers and I got a change of uniform. We handed over our denims in exchange for a tank suit, a denim one and a thick waterproof over one. With the weather getting much colder now this was gratefully accepted by me. On the Friday afternoon we took my motorbike and the carriers to Minden station and loaded them on to railway wagons. After our evening meal we were all taken to the station for an overnight trip north and given the usual five man ration packs for tomorrow's food.

The train made a slow journey through the night and while we were having breakfast we came to a stop. There then some shunting back and forward for a while then silence. We had been shunted into a siding at Lubeck. Nothing happened for over an hour and Captain Gregg along with Lieutenant Blake of the Mortar platoon decided to go and find out what was going on. With it being Saturday we had been put in the sidings until Monday. This lead to some heated arguments and arm waving on the station platform when a Major from the Service Corps showed up. Captain Gregg and his party came back to inform us we would be moving again by two o'clock. As there was now three hours to wait it was suggested we stretch our legs around Lubeck.

Captain Gregg got us all together before we went and told us we must keep to the main road in the centre of Lubeck. If it had been left to him he would rather us not go. He explained that Lubeck had been used as one of the terror bombing targets to draw the Luftwaffe away from our airfields during the battle of Britain. Most of the local people were alright but a lot of the older ones were not well disposed towards the British. He had to admit that Lubeck was well worth seeing as it still had a lot of medieval buildings left standing. Most of us went for a look and no one encountered any trouble, it must have been a lovely town before Churchill's hooligans bombed it.

The train started off again and we made our destination before dark. It was not a proper railway station it was what they call a 'halt' just a platform with a lean-to shed. The carriers and my bike were unloaded and we drove to the camp about two miles distant. The camp accommodations were good and there were garages to put the carriers in. From looking at the height of the exhaust marks on the walls it seems it had been a tank training area for the German army.

The good part was that we had got there in time for an evening meal. It was the usual army high table stuff but well cooked, mind by now we could have eaten a scabby eyed monkey. The only unusual thing was the camp had no N.A.A.F.I.

We had all Sunday to settle in before our attack on the Baltic Sea or so I thought I had. Breakfast had finished and we were all lying on our chariots listening to the forces wireless and talking when Sergeant Burrows stuck his head round the door and shouted 'Power, Captain Gregg wants to see you over the officer's mess'. I got togged up and wandered over there, 'Power we have a little job for you' said Gregg. Lieutenant Blake and I would like you to fetch us some Sunday papers. There's a N.A.A.F.I. shop at a Royal Artillery camp about fifteen miles west of here'. He gets the map out and shows me the route. It was mainly a straight run except for having to go through two little towns. 'We would like a Sunday Times a Sunday Mail and a News of The World if you can get them, if not bring what they have. And Power with us being at the end of the world up here they may not have very early deliveries so have your lunch before you go.' I set off at one thirty and I was glad of the outer tank suit the army issued before we came and the long johns and woolly vests we got in Ireland. It was dry but the wind off the Baltic was bitter.

I found the Artillery camp alright, it was an easy if cold run. I got the papers then had a mug of tea in the N.A.A.F.I and sat in there until I got warm again. The run back was even colder so I stopped on the way back to stamp my feet to get some feeling back in them. All I got when I got back with the papers was 'well done Power,' I could have done with a double brandy.

There were other country's armies using the ranges along with us. The Americans had an anti aircraft battalion shooting at aerial targets. These targets were towed over the Baltic Sea by a Mitchell bomber. The Danish troops seemed at bit old fashioned to us. They had motorbikes and side cars with a Browning machine gun mounted on the side car. We spent the week training but only got to do live firing twice. Our first do was a night firing exercise. This was all done off a map and aimed using two line makers, once one gun was set up all the rest zeroed up to it. It was the first time we had ever done night firing and Gregg was pleased by the performance, but to me, if you couldn't see what you were firing at how do you know when you have hit it? The next bit of fun was firing off the carrier. There was a mounting on the back of the drivers and passengers compartment where we normally carried the gun. This mount could be swivelled round to enable you to fire the gun from the carrier. The targets for this little caper were some old rusting tank hauls down near the beach. This little manoeuvre had not been done before not even by some of the old soldiers in the platoon. All the gun number ones had a shoot at the tank hauls with the carriers standing. Partridge, our range finder and now a full Cpl was checking the fall of shot through his range finder. It was now decided to try the same thing with the carriers moving and this started off very well while the carrier was passing the target at right angles. Once you had passed the target and still firing the rear of the gun was over the driver, so every time the gunner gave a bust of fire the driver got a shower of red hot bullet cases down the back of his neck. However after poor old Bockey got the first shower down his neck Gregg put a marker at which point they were to stop firing.

We had an interesting week and there was a N.A.A.F.I van came round the ranges most mornings and we usually got a break and a mug of tea. The exercise had all but finished by Friday but we were not going back to Minden until Monday. That meant I was on the Sunday paper run again.

The week before Christmas a dance had been arranged in the gym for Saturday night. I was not really interested but Dave kidded me into going with him. Some of the wives from the married quarters had decked the place out with bunting and it was a big improvement from the smelly place we knew. On the night a couple of coach loads of girls from the W.R.A.C were bussed in for dancing partners. Dave did a bit of dancing and I spent my time trying to chat them up. Most of them had heard it all before, they were old boiling pieces and they must have left the young ones at home. The proceedings were brought to a close at ten thirty but it had been a pleasant evening.

The weather was colder now and it was hard going on the parade ground even with our greatcoats on. The worry was that you would drop your rifle with your hands being so cold. The army issue gloves didn't help much. Our first parade in greatcoats coincided with us having new bayonets as well. These had been issued during the week and they were like little hunting knives without the handle and not Sharpe enough to cut anything with. They were about the same length as the old ones that we handed in and the boss to fix them to your rifle was the same. The next thing was a parade and inspection by the Commanding Officer to check our great coats were now up to standard. Once this had been done we had an hour's drilling just to make sure we could do it in our coats.

Another week of night manoeuvres in the woods up the training area was done on the up to before Christmas. Our return to Minden was on the Monday and on the Battalion order Tuesday night. Wednesday (which was Christmas Eve) would be holiday until the following Monday the twenty eighth of December. Company orders were still posted and I saw I was down to report to the indoor range on Christmas morning. Perhaps they were going to give me a present but no, they wanted me to shoot a match card. I did ask why I was needed to shoot Christmas morning and was told one of them was going on leave tomorrow and the cards had to be shot and sent in by the end of the month.

The lunch was a bit of a giggle as by tradition it is served by the officers so all the Company commanders were slapping the food on our plates with Degg the Battalion Commander overseeing proceedings. It was a good feed with turkey and a slice of beef, probably horse and a bottle of Herforder beer each, courtesy of the P.R.I. When we had all been served, Degg stood on a chair and wished us all a happy Christmas. That started the chant we used to hear at the impromptu concerts on the troopship when they wanted someone to sing. We called on our CO to sing us a song, 'sing, sing or show us your ring!'. He obliged with a little ditty he didn't learn off his mother about wishing he was in Wigan sweeping Mrs Jones's flue. He was going well until someone threw an orange at him, it missed but it brought the song to an abrupt end. The officers were all watching Degg so no one saw anything.

The N.A.A.F.I had been closed for the day but would be opened for our tea at five o'clock. When we got down there it was all covered up with sheets of paper and we had to wait for the cook Sergeant to unveil it. Half the crowd were pissed up on the local brews like Schnapps and Steinhager and when the Sgt took the cover off it just went wild. It had been a lovely spread with iced Christmas cake and mince pies, sandwiches and trifles. It had obviously been done by the civilian staff in the cook house. The drunken gang just charged it knocking tables over and fighting one another to get at it. Most of it ended up on the floor and we just salvaged what we could. I enjoyed it anyway, it was the best Christmas food wise I'd had for three years.

There was a few ended up in the clink during the holiday due to the booze. The Medical Officer had to be called and battalion orders were posted, any one caught with the local steinhager would be charged. It seems that although Steinhager was a German gin the cheap local stuff was just wood alcohol. Off course it didn't stop the boozers guzzling it out of camp.

With Christmas nineteen fifty two over several of us regulars were called to our company office. The Sergeant Major explained to us that we were all now three star privates and if we wanted to get higher grading, up to five stars, we would need our third class army education certificate.

Each star we got meant we got higher pay. He was putting us all down for an education course running in the New Year and anyone not wishing to do it should fallout now. A couple did as they were old soldiers who had tried and failed a couple of times before.

On Friday's company orders, the second week in January, we were all to report to H.Q block on Monday morning. After first parade we went over and joined squaddies for other companies also doing the course. There were forty of us and two Sergeants' from the Education Corps so they split us into two classes. The Sergeants took us up to two rooms on the first floor and issued us with an exercise book and a pencil each. They then explained that we would be here every morning after our first parade for the next two weeks. Our main emphasis would be on English and basic maths with a bit of geography and history as well. After our fortnight was up we would take an exam at a camp at Bielefelt, the Army on the Rine H.Q. Our morning education session was great, well it was warm in the class for a start. The Sgts teaching us didn't expect too much off us but by the end of our course I think we had all learnt a bit. We did our first exam on our final Friday afternoon; taken one at a time into another room and asked to read a passage from a book. This was a reading and comprehension test and we were asked questions as to the meaning of what we had just read. The one I got was about a man talking about being in a prison but he wasn't in jail. His prison was the fact that he was blind, it was a tricky one but I passed. We were all going down Bielefelt in the morning to do the rest of the exam. That meant we were going to miss the cross country run, I could have cried over that.

We were taken down to Bielefelt on Saturday morning in two Lorries. There were squaddies for other regiment there to take the exams as well as us. The maths was taken first and we had an hour to do it and they were easy enough for me. The English was next and I found that a bit hard going but I think I did alright. The last hour was geography, mainly questions like capital cities of Europe and which river flowed through them. It had just gone twelve o'clock when we finished and we just made it back to Minden before lunch was taken off in the cookhouse. After our morning exertions we were laid out on our beds after lunch listening to the wireless. About three o'clock Broughie got a visitor an old soldier like himself. They greeted each other like long lost brothers and sat on the bed talking for half an hour. After the visitor had gone Broughie said they had been mates when a battalion of the Stafford's had been stationed in Berlin in nineteen forty six. When Broughie told us who he was a chap named Baker and he had just been released from the army jail after serving five years for desertion, I and a couple more of us remembered reading about him in the News of the World about his capture by the Russian secret police. He was kept in solitary confinement, beaten and hung up by his thumbs. He had a hell of a time but eventually managed to escape back to the west. Broughie now gave us the true facts about what happened. Baker had met a German girl and she lived in the Russian zone of Berlin and he had gone over there with her. She had a flat and he had lived with her for six months. Eventually they fell out and she chucked him out of the flat so Baker had come back. The News of the World had made up the secret police story and paid Baker five hundred quid to use his name on it. It made me think and I question a lot of the things I read in the papers even now.

The results of our exams came thorough a fortnight later and all the Support Company squaddies who had taken the exam had got a pass.

Chapter Twenty One

January was cold and wet although we didn't get much snow. At the end of the month we were off on manoeuvres again and this time we were out for nearly a fortnight. As usual we did most of our moving about at night. We squaddies never knew much of what was going on, we just followed the pointing finger and kept out of the way of the tanks. We did have one three day break when we bivouacked under our ponchos in some woods along with a Dutch infantry regiment and a squadron of the Royal Horse Artillery. They were the poor relations of the armoured division as they still had the old Cromwell tanks. I got knocked of my motorbike while we were camped here. I was sent down to battalion H.Q one afternoon to fetch the mail. H.Q was in some woods about a mile from us and the dirt track to it had a stream across it. The Sappers had built a pontoon bridge over the stream to allow vehicles to cross. When I got to it there was a stationary convoy of Canadian half tracks with one stopped on the bridge. There were a couple of feet between the half track and the edge of the pontoon so I tried to sneak along it. I had almost got over the pontoon when the vehicle started to move forward and the rear end of it slewed towards me. The back end of the half track hit me knocking me and the bike off the pontoon. Both I and the motorbike ended up in the reeds at the side of the stream, luckily the bike fell at the side of me, it could have dropped on top of me but I wasn't hurt, just shuck up. None of the half tracks stopped to help, they just whizzed off down the track. A couple of the Sappers got my bike back up on the track which fortunately was alright as we both had a soft landing in the reed bed. When I got back I found I had lost the mail so I had to go back and I found it in the reeds.

That evening we moved out of the woods near to a town called Celle and then down past Bergen. Just outside this town had been the infamous concentration camp Belsen. All that was left of it now was the row of long mounds, the mass graves. It was a sad place even in the half light of dawn.

We had been moving around on this scheme for nearly a fortnight now and most of us had had enough, it had been cold and wet. 'These are the conditions you would experience if you were fighting a war' we were constantly told. However we soon got over it once we were back in camp and we never saw the east European gentleman with the hairy jotter who had been chasing us since our training days, although now we were in Germany we must be very close to him.

By now most of us could speak a few German words, like please (bitte) thank you, (danke schon), I don't understand (ich versten nicht). Of course when we were trying to chat the girls up down by the river Minden we were not very good. Spraziergang fraulein was the only line I remember. However we managed alright especially on a Sunday when the weather was nice and a lot of the girls dressed up in traditional German dress and walked down by the river. Some of the lads had German girl friends. Our platoon interpreter when we were out training was Joe Minton who had learnt the language at school. He was Captain Gregg's batman and could speak good German.

After my Christmas day target shooting appointment I was never called to shoot again so I think the small bore shooting team was just abandoned. Whether we ever won anything or how we did I never found out, so now our hopes of glory rested with the football team. These were to be dashed in the spring. They had beaten all the teams they played in the B.A.O.R Cup, some with double figure scores and it was just a formality they would win the cup. In the semi final they drew the H.L.I Highland Light Infantry in a home match to be played at Minden. Their recruiting area was Glasgow and where we had lads form our local teams like Wolves and West Bromwich. They had them from the likes of Celtic and Glasgow Rangers. The Goal keeper was the star as the word going round was he had played a couple of times for Scotland. The Stafford's team put up a good fight but lost two one in the end. The whole camp was in mourning for a week.

I got a letter off Alice in which she mentioned her son and Joyce were getting married on the twenty ninth of March. They would like to invite me to come if I could get leave and I was welcome to stay with her, so I put in for a fourteen day leave pass to start from the middle of March, and got it.

A week later a battalion parade was called and when we were all lined up on the square the battalion Adjutant explained the North Staffordshire Regiment now serving in Trieste would be going to Korea in the autumn and troops for the South Stafford's would be used to reinforce them; 'any one on parade who still had eighteen months or more to serve take one pace forward now'. He then asked if any one had reason not to go. A couple of chaps who had been there with the Middlesex Regiment when we were in Hong Kong put their hands up, and he told them to fall out. Each company Sergeant Major, along with the company clerk now took the name of all who stepped forward. It seemed a funny way of sorting us out, I'd have thought they could have done it by looking at our records.

A few days before my leave was due we went to Sennelager ranges to do some live firing.

It was near Detmold and was one of the Rhine army's main training areas. I was only there two days before I was due to go on leave. The only thing I remember was going to the cinema in the evening to see Mogli and the Wolves. The next morning I was on a lorry and back to Elizabeth barracks in Minden.

I had drawn some German marks with my pay to buy a present to take home for the wedding. After lunch I walked down into Minden town and splashed out fifteen marks on a cuckoo clock, a whole twenty five bob blown on a wedding present. The following morning I handed my kit into the company stores where there was only the Colour Sergeant and the store man as all the rest of the company were at Sennelager. I got over to the guard room and joined the rest of the squaddies going on leave. A three ton lorry took us all down to Minden station. There were lots of squaddies already on the train from stations further up the line and we were all destined for the Hook of Holland. The night ferry was well loaded, not only with troops from B.A.O.R but squaddies from Austria and Trieste and all stations south. We were joined by an old soldier from the Service Corps, probably because he thought we were young and daft enough to listen to his tales of how he won the last war. There were a lot of chaps like him in the British army. We had them in our regiment and they were usually store men or they worked in the officer's mess and did jobs like that. They had been in the army most of their lives and never made any rank. The army was the only life they knew and they didn't seem to have anywhere else to go. However we lost him in the customs shed when we disembarked at Harwich next morning.

After getting though customs (I don't know what they thought we would be trying to smuggle into the country on army pay) I caught the train for London. It only went to Liverpool Street station, so you couldn't miss it. I went on the underground to Euston station and then got a train on to Birmingham New Street. I usually went to Wolverhampton but there were another two chaps from Walsall and we were travelling together and they thought it would be a good idea to get off at Brum. We got a Midland Red bus from New Street Station into Walsall where we each went our separate ways.

It was late afternoon when I got to Alice's and the first thing I noticed was the carpet. It was the one mother had bought for the posh room at the farm, we had it down in the house we had given up and Jeff had given it to Alice when he cleared the place out. He had also given her a single bed with a mattress. The council had carted all the other sticks of furniture off to the tip.

It wasn't long before I found out why Alice needed another single bed. She had got herself a lodger, a chap named Fred and he had a six year old son with him call Johnny. Alice explained that I would have to share a bedroom with them, Fred and Johnny in one single bed and me in the other. Fred was a cripple, he had been wounded in his right leg during the last war. Of course Fred had been a commando hadn't he, and over the next couple of weeks he got on my wick a bit with his tales of daring do. He could tell a good story could Fred. Luckily he had a job polishing at a works on the Pleck Road so I only had to suffer his tales in the evening.

It was now I realised I had made a mistake in booking my leave as I was due to return to Germany on the Thursday before John and Joyce's wedding on the Saturday. I didn't say anything to anyone about it as I thought I would sort it out when I was due to go back.

The next fortnight soon went by, with me visiting all my relations and I even had a day at Dudley Zoo. I got Granny Mac out and down to Patterson's café on the Bridge; she loved visiting that place for tea and a fancy cake. I think it was the only café left in Walsall where the waitresses still wore black dresses with white aprons and hats.

As the day of my return to camp approached I mentioned to Alice that I would not be attending the wedding. She was not at all happy and got a bit nasty, saying she had found me accommodation and now I was letting her down. I couldn't see how I was letting her down as she was not the one getting married. If I stayed another couple of days would it matter? After I thought about it, if I upset Alice I would have nowhere to go when I had my next leave, so I agreed to stay until Sunday. The wedding took place at Bath Street Chapel. Joyce lived in the next street. The reception or bun struggle was held in an upstairs room at the Newport Arms on the Pleck Road. Alice paid for a barrel of beer to be put in the room for the guests to help themselves. It was just as well because I only had a ten bob note left out of my leave pay. However, I along with Bill Clements the brother of Alice's eldest daughter's husband made full use of it although there was still some beer left when they threw us out at ten thirty. Bill only lived with his parents up the road so he went and fetched a bucket. We poured what was left of the beer in and took it back to Alice's making a night of it.

Sunday morning I said my goodbyes and set off back to Germany. Being Sunday there was only a limited bus and train service operating. I got the bus to Birmingham and had to wait for two and half hours for a train to London. I reached Paddington Station and then went on the underground tube to Liverpool Street Station. When I showed my ticket there I was called inside the office. The ticket clerk got on the phone and a few minutes later a Sergeant and a couple of squaddies from the military police showed up. The Sergeant explained that I was being arrested for being A.W.O.L, absent without leave. I would now be taken down to Harwich under escort and handed over to the authorities there and they put me in a little cell at the back of the office to await the next train for Harwich. When the train came I was marched across the station between the two Military Police squaddies and sat in a compartment to ourselves. At Harwich I was handed over at the office on the dock to a Sergeant who seemed to be in charge of proceedings. When I had been signed for and the paperwork done the M.Ps went to catch the train back to London. Once they had gone the Sergeant gave me a mug of tea and after some paper shuffling said 'I can't get you on the ferry tonight son, you'll be on tomorrow nights sailing, so in the mean time I've got to lock you up. Before I do I've got to take your neck tie and shoe laces off you. The rules say you are entitled to have three fags a day while you are in custody and I suppose you get three for today'. He gets a packet of Players out of the desk and gives me my three fags before taking me out of the back of the building and locking me in a cell. There were a row of cells out there and some more criminals locked up, but I couldn't see them. The cell only had a bed with a mattress and an old army biscuit tin to wee in, however I slept alright and was awoken next morning by the Sergeant shouting. We were escorted from our cell one at a time to have a wash and shave and then breakfast was delivered to our cells. It wasn't a bad meal by army standards and I enjoyed it. I was a long day locked in the cell with nothing to do but just lie on the bunk.

At around six in the evening we were waiting for our evening meal to be delivered when we were fetched out of our cells and taken back to the office. Our tie and shoe laces were returned to us and we were told we would be going on the night's ferry; escorts were being arranged and would escort us back to Germany. I had two chaps from the Royal Tank Corps to escort me, it seems they just found squaddies returning to the same area as the prisoner and detailed them as escorts. They were doing their National Service and I promised I would not try to escape by jumping in the North Sea. I had to suffer their nonsense, they both had heard of squaddies who had been shot for being a day A.W.O.L. When we reached the Hook of Holland next morning I had to go and find them to escort me off the boat.

The train chugged its way across Holland and into Germany and my escorts got off at the first stop in Germany, leaving me to escort myself to Minden.

I got there by early afternoon and walked up to the barracks. I reported to the guard room and was promptly arrested and locked up again. The cell was very small and the heating pipes for the guard room ran through it. I spent the hottest night of my life in there, it was air less and the little window at the back was screwed shut. Even stripped down to my underwear I was still sweating like a pig so it was a relief when the Provost Corporal opened the door at seven thirty next morning. The prisoners in there had fetched the breakfast and gave me a mug of tea and some porridge. After my bit of breakfast I was marched over to Support company stores to collect my kit and then marched back to the clink. The Provost Sergeant came and told me I would be on C.O's orders at three this afternoon and I should smarten myself up for the event. When the time came I was marched round to the C.O's office by the Sergeant and the Corporal which was in the same block as the guard room and handed over to the R.S.M. He marched me into Colonel. Deggs office and the clerk read out the charge. Degg ask if I had any thing to say for myself and I said no, I just took the extra three days knowing the consequences. Colonel Degg just grunted and said 'twenty eight days detention'. I was marched back to the nick and told to lay all my kit out on the bed for inspection. After I had done that I was given a bucket and a scrubbing brush and told to scrub all the Blanco off my belt and gaiters. Discipline was strict and we got a kit inspection every morning except Sundays. We were taken everywhere at the double and if there were any dirty jobs to be done around the camp we did them at the double, of course. There were two other chaps in the nick both for A.O.W.L and one was awaiting a Courts Marshall. He was an old soldier and was a regular absconder; he was one of the gang who only seemed to be in the army because he had nowhere else to go. He reckoned he would get a D.D (dishonourable discharge) this time. After a few days in there I got used to the routine and found it a bit boring.

While I was in there I learnt that a lot of the chaps had already gone to join the North Staffs in Trieste.

Chapter Twenty Two

I still had another three days to do of my twenty eight day sentence when the Provost Corporal came and told me to pack my kit bag. There was another draft leaving to join the North Staffs in the morning and I would be with them. At nine o'clock the next morning I was marched out with my kit bag to join forty eight other Squaddies waiting out side the H.Q office. After a roll call we were loaded onto two lorries and taken to Minden station. There, as the army put it we were entrained for Cologne. From there we would get the army train which ran from Austria to the Hook of Holland. I think it was called the Medlok C route. It was lunch time when we were transferred to the train going south and it was great by the usual army standards as it had a dinning car. All of us were given a meal card for the last sitting so we got some lunch and you could buy yourself a bottle of beer to have with it. It's a pity the food wasn't up to dinning car standards. The train ride south was one of the best journeys I've ever been on. It went all down the Rhine valley past all the castles and vineyards so I spent most of the day glued to the train windows. The train trundled on through the night and by morning we were in Austria. The country was flat now but as we got further on we started to get into the mountains. Our destination was a place called Villach; the Medlok C train ran between here and the Hook of Holland. At Villach we were lined up on the platform for a roll call just to make sure none of us had jumped into the river Rhine. The Captain who seemed to be in charge told us we would proceed to Trieste about one hundred and twenty miles distant in a motor coach. From a distance there looked like there were two little coaches waiting for us but when we got close we could see the rear coach was a trailer attached to the front coach by a tow bar. Our names were called and we were told which coach to get onto; I was in the trailer. It stopped the punch-up that would have happened if we had been left to our own devices since everyone wanted to ride in the trailer. The driver was an old Italian man and after only half an hour we made a stop at a pretty little village in the mountains. The driver had been here before hadn't he, and they were waiting for us. Chocolate, sweets, bottles of pop all at rip-off prices, mind you they would take any money B.A.F, Lire, Marks, anything spendable. Some of the chaps splashed out and most filled their water bottles from the village pump. After the driver and locals figured they had taken us for all they were going to get we went on our way. We now were in for the ride of our lives round some of the narrow roads and the driver was not wasting any time. With the coach pulling the trailer it made hard work of it going uphill but it made up for that when going downhill. A few of the more nervous lads crouched at the back of the trailer as white as sheets. I think we all got a bit frightened on some of the bends and it was a relief when we got back on the main road. Our next problem was that we had guzzled lots of water before we left the village stop. Now we were all crossing our legs and there was no way of communicating with the driver. There were only little vents at the top of the coach windows and we couldn't reach even standing on the seats. Desperate times call for desperate measures so we did it in our mess tins and chucked it through the vents.

It was late afternoon when we reached Trieste and unloaded at a large building. We were taken inside, names checked off and told if any one had B.A.F they could change it to Italian Lire here. Two Lorries from the North Staffs were on the car park and we were loaded into them for the journey to camp. We left the town of Trieste through a short tunnel and as we emerged from it there was a large oil refinery by the shore of the Adriatic Sea. The beach next to it made us stare. It was almost covered by large ship's anchors; they couldn't have been washed up there. The road followed the shore line and we passed through Muggia a little fishing town and on up to Gibraltar Barracks at a place called Lazaretto. We entered the camp through an arched gateway and unloaded in front of a large white plastered building which looked like it may have been a hospital at some time in the past but was now battalion H.Q. We were all lined up and the adjutant, a Captain came out with his clip board. He walked up to me and asked what I had been in detention for and I told him A.W.O.L. He just grunted and walked off. It seems it had already been decided which companies we would be in and the squaddies from the rifle companies would join us here. The support company squaddies would join the same platoons as they did in the South Staffs and do the same jobs. That meant only two of us for support company, John Rudd. for the assault pioneer platoon and me for the M.M.G. A Corporal Martin had been sent down to collect us and take us back to the company office. As soon as we got there we were met by Sergeant Major Hillman and got the 'what you been in clink for' again. The Colour Sergeant issued us with our bedding and the Corporal showed us to our huts. There were a few lads from the old platoon there, Dave, Joe Brooke, Tuddy

Phillips, Sailor Bowden and Don Perry. Perry had only joined our platoon while we were in Germany. His farther was a Sergeant Major at Lichfield barracks and Perry along with his brother would spend their whole working life in the army.

I joined Dave and Joe for the evening meal and was warned the cooking was a bit rough here. The cook house and dinning room was attached to the large plastered building. It was just like our training days at Lichfield; a dangerous looking flat footed Cook Sergeant stalked the dining area during meal times. You were given the usual two choice army menus; take it or leave it. My first job after the meal was to get some Blanco to cover up my belt and gaiters, so I spent my first lira buying a block from the N.A.A.F.I. The camp had a high wall surrounding it with only one way in. The large building contained the H.Q Company as well as the M.O, N.A.A.F.I, The Officers Mess and a shop run by some Italians. All the rest of the camp was billeted in Nissen huts. At the bottom end of the camp behind the gym was a little dock and the Adriatic Sea. Support Company was billeted at the opposite end of the camp furthest away from the gate. At the end of our row of huts there was an old cemetery behind a high wall.

It was now late spring and I had got here at the right time as the swimming in the sea had started and we spent a lot of our spare time swimming in the Adriatic Sea. The sea came round the side of the camp to a little beach by the road. Where the land jutted out on the far side of the little bay was Yugoslavia. It was only about one hundred yards away so we all had to swim over and touch the beach so we could say we had been to Yugoslavia.

On Friday night's Company orders all the Squaddies who had come from Germany earlier in the week were to report to battalion H.Q at eight thirty in the morning. We were met by a Sergeant from our Intelligence Platoon. This platoon only consisted of a few chaps mainly N.C.O's and a Captain who could speak the local lingo. He took is into a hut were the Captain was waiting with a map spread on the black board. The Captain explained we were in Trieste along with the Americans and we were called B.E.T.FOR. (British Element Trieste Force) since the area at the top east corner of Italy was an area of disputed land. Negotiations were going on between Italy, Austria and Yugoslavia the countries that border Trieste as to who would take over the area. The Captain said that we had probably noticed the border check point just down the road. The border was not very well defined in our area and the Sergeant and a Corporal would take us and show us exactly where it was. In the past squaddies had strayed over it and the Yugoslav's had sent them back, apparently they once shot one in the leg. Crossing the border caused a diplomatic incident with the 'Jugs' as the Captain put it and we must avoid that at all costs. The Sergeant and Corporal walked us down to the border post and the 'Jug' border post was about fifty yards further on. Both the guards had met half way between their posts and were leaning on their rifles yapping to one another. As we walked along there was a barbed wire fence in some places and in others just a line of pickets painted yellow.

By about eleven we had reached a little village in the hills. As we approached the Sergeant and Corporal were greeted like long lost brothers. A grey haired old buffer opened the barn doors to reveal a little bar and anyone with Lire could buy a bottle of beer. The Sergeant and Corporal had been here before and so got a free drink. Most of us bought a drink and those who couldn't run to the cost of beer were given some orange cordial. The village was as far as we would be going so it was all back to camp in time for lunch. The camp wasn't a bad place and of course if you liked swimming it was ideally placed on the Adriatic. Another good thing was it was a lot warmer down there.

Monday morning's parade and we new comers were introduced to the section Sergeants. We had already met one Sergeant Hardcastle or Jim as every one called him. He was a bit of a comic book character and was about as bright as an N.A.A.F.I candle. He had been in the army since the year dot and one of the nowhere else to go gang who had made it to Sergeant. His first party piece was on our pay parade. He had appointed himself in charge and as he prowled the queue he saw Tubby Philips standing in front of me. He grabbed Tubby by the collar, pulled him out and stuffed him in front of Kenny Foster.

Sergeant Jones in charge of two section wasn't much better. The senior Sergeant was a man named Bridge and he seemed to hold the whole platoon together. Our platoon commander was a Captain Bow and easy going sort of a man more interested in cricket than the army. He was another called up at the start of the last war that made it to officer rank and was now waiting for his pension to mature.

Those of us from Germany would do the same jobs here as we had done there, so I became a motorcycle orderly but with out a bike. Things would be sorted out when we started the training for Korea but in the mean time I had to just muck-in with the gun drill.

The training area was in the lime stone hills above Trieste. The place was riddled with under ground caves and we were forbidden to go into them. It was the usual story; people had gone in them and had never been seen again. This of course meant that when no one was looking, in we went.

Being a spare man I had to drive a carrier up there one morning and explained that I had only ever driven one solo round a garage block. 'You've got a W.D permit to drive one Power, so get driving.' Luckily I didn't kill anybody.

At the weekend on Saturday afternoons the Battalion ran recreation Lorries down to Trieste city so I thought I would go and have a look and was surprised; it was quite a nicely laid out place with lovely squares, very Italian in fact and it was Italy who took the place over eventually.

It was a bit of a drunken scrum on the lorry back to camp as a lot had been at the vino. I had my share one Saturday night a few weeks later. Although the main gate was the only way out of the camp you could escape at the end of the cemetery wall. There was a row of rocks there that jutted out into the sea. When the tide was low you could climb over them on to the beach. A group of us climbed over and went to a little café come bar on the beach about half way between the camp and the border. We ordered a jug of vino as this was the best way to get a drink when money was short because you could get a litre of the local plonk for less than the cost of a bottle of beer. We had a good night and by ten thirty we'd had enough and decided to get back over the rocks. As we were making our way towards them the Provost Sergeant came whizzing down the road in a jeep with some of the camp guard and rounded us up. All of us were marched back to camp and locked in a large bare room opposite the guard room along with the night's drunks from Trieste. Next morning the drunks were sent back to their companies but we were kept in custody. None of us knew why, all that we were told is that we would be interviewed by the Field Security Branch.

When the army detectives arrived we were taken to see them one at a time. All they seemed interested in was why had we been in the old cemetery and what we had been doing in there though none of us had ever been in the cemetery, we had only sneaked out over the rocks to get to the beach bar.

After the question session we were sent back to support company none the wiser of why we had been arrested in the first place. We reported back to our company office and Sergeant Major Hillman told us to go and get cleaned up. It was some time later when we found out what our arrest was all about. Someone had been thieving things from around the camp and stashing it in the cemetery. The provost platoon had to come up with some suspects and we fitted the bill. I don't think the crime was ever solved.

The Queen's coronation was declared a day's holiday so I got stuck with guard duties didn't I. The Sergeant Major said it was an honour to be a Guard on coronation day. I was quite prepared to let some one else have the honour but that didn't wash, I had to do it.

The date for the battalion to leave Trieste was now announced and we would go to Trawsfynydd for battle training prior to embarking for Korea.

When I'd had my last leave Alice had asked me to look out for a table cloth; Alice's eldest daughter was married to a chap who had done his national service in Trieste and he had bought Alice some table runners when he got demobbed. Now she wanted to see if I could get a table cloth to match. I knew I could because I had seen them in the camp shop two thousand five hundred lire. So I bought one as a sweetener for my next leave to get my foot in!

We didn't have to go back up to Villach to get the train as it came down to Trieste. A band from the American army came to play us off; it was a change from the usual army bands as they played popular tunes. Also the staff from the camp shop came handing out flowers so it was quite a send off.

It was a two day journey back up along the Rine valley and across Holland then onto the night ferry to Harwich. We had a shock going through customs since the officer on the door was asking 'are you going to Korea son?' When we said yes he just waved us straight through.

The train was a special and we didn't change at London but went right to Trent Valley station.

Our kit was loaded on to Lorries and that started an argument. Spud Murphy who was a keen cyclist had nursed a racing bike frame all the way home from Trieste. Sergeant Hardcastle said he couldn't have it on the coach back to camp; it must go on the lorry and chucked it on one of them. Of course when we got back to Whittington barracks it had gone missing.

We were now billeted in the old blocks along the square where we had been to do our basic training. There had been some changes; new toilets had been built between the old barrack blocks. These had showers, a bath, toilets and a row of wash basins.

A company parade was called and the Sergeant Major said we would now have seven days disembarkation leave so any one needing travel warrants were to apply to the company office. Those who lived locally could go home but must be back for first parade at eight o'clock in the morning.

A lot of the lads went home before the evening meal and all were back next morning. It wasn't worth unpacking our kit bags and after pay parade and sorting out bedding we were just hanging about and after lunch word came from company office that we all may as well go on leave. It was not officially due to start until tomorrow but there was nothing for us to do there.

When I flashed the table cloth, I was in at Alice's.

Chapter Twenty Three

It was a bit crowded at Alice's although her husband Jim didn't live there anymore. I never heard the full story but there had been a punch-up between him and Fred the lodger. Jim now had a new woman, a fellow bus conductress and was living with her. I suggested that I go and find somewhere else to spend my leave but Alice wouldn't hear of it and I was offered the settee to sleep on. It was better than nothing and I had nowhere else to go.

Every one was surprised to see me as it had only been fourteen weeks since my last leave.

I did my usual round of visiting and had a shock when I got to Uncle Bustys as my aunt Sarah, Bustys wife had died while I was in Trieste. It was sudden and she had been rushed into hospital with stomach pains but had died while being admitted; a twisted gut was the reason. I could see Busty was still cut up about it although he was still running the butchers shop. His youngest son Gordon was helping him on Saturday but he was working full time in engineering during the week. It was a sad visit for me as Aunty Sarah or Sally as everyone called her had always been good to us when we were kids. During the school holidays she would have our Mary to stay with her for a while.

Granny Mac had been to Bournemouth the week before I came on leave with the old folk's holiday scheme. She showed me a photo of her sitting on a bench cozening up to some old buffer. She assured me she was not courting, just good friends. Anyway, she seemed happy enough and was even happier when I took her down to Patterson's Café.

One of the high-lights was a trip to the Caldmore Tory Club. John, Alice's son was a member there although he didn't have two pennies to rub together most of the week. He had expectations as he spent half his waking life doing complicated perms on the Littlewoods football pools coupon. He never won anything that I knew about. On Sunday morning he would tog himself up in what he called his black and whites, obviously the Tory uniform. He looked smart but it was a pity he wore a Scotch plaid shirt with it. I was taken to the club and signed to be his snooker partner. I must say the beer and the locals were O.K. and I enjoyed the couple of hours we had there.

With it now being summer you could sit outside on the wall at the Fullbrook pub and drink your beer. I got chatting to a girl named Silvia who worked at Orgiles laundry; she was a nice enough girl but not very bright. I took her to the pictures one night as she was someone to talk to and have a drink with.

All too soon the leave was over and I paid Granny a visit on my way back to camp. I got the usual 'don't marry any Korean girls' and if I saw any silk cloth while I was out there I should send her some to make a blouse with.

There were now a few days before we were due to go to Trawsfynydd in Wales for a month's battle training. We had an easy time with a bit of drill just to keep us in order and our afternoons were spent on the firing range. As I didn't have a motorbike to ride I was roped in as a number two on a machine gun. On the following morning after our trip to the firing range the platoon had a training session on a new anti tank weapon. This was the three point five rocket launcher known as a `Bazooka` to the Yanks. This was just a length of tube with sights on and a trumpet shaped front end. The whole thing was about four feet long and it broke down into two halves for easy carrying. The trigger mechanism gave an electric charge when you pulled and this was how it fired the rocket. The rocket which was about two feet long was the heaviest part. It had two wires sticking out of the back that you attached to contacts on the side of the tube. When you pulled the trigger, the charge generated fired the rocket. A couple of hours were spent practising the drill for using the weapon but it would be another two years before any of us actually fired the thing.

We spent a couple of evenings down Lichfield in the Malt Shovel pub. Upstairs they had a room for us common squaddies and the local girls. It had a Juke Box with all the latest songs on it. We would have a few pints when we had the money and a bag of chips before getting the bus back to camp. Boy this was really living!

The day before we were due to go to Wales the Colour Sergeant got us all in an empty barrack room. He explained that we would require different equipment for Korea and this afternoon he would measure us up for it. Some of the kit that was white like our towels, housewives and any other kit would be changed for green coloured. The uniforms would be bagged up and waiting for us when we got to Korea. First thing to sort out would be our cold wet weather boots (C.W.W). These had a double thickness of leather and a thick cleated rubber sole, christened `boots gravity` by us squaddies. These would need to be a size bigger than our normal boots to allow two pairs of socks and a plastic mesh insert. The next items were two sets of combat jackets and trousers - these would be our normal sizes; a parker lined with imitation lamb's wool and a wired hood to go over it all to keep out the cold. There was also a pair of short long johns with imitation lamb wool linings. Our webbing would be changed to the new equipment now being introduced into the army. This didn't require blancoing and had sheradised buckles and only one large back pack. The aluminium water bottle had a mug on it other wise it was much the same as the old kit. This would also be issued on our arrival in Korea.

The store man had samples of the uniforms and we were allowed to inspect them. The combat jackets were dark green or olive drab as the army liked to call it and made of a shower proof material. They had a zip up the front and two large side pockets. The store man had a short woolly scarf thing called a cap comforter which you could fold in and use as a hat plus a pair of canvas and leather gloves which would also be issued. The best part of the whole thing as far as us squaddies were concerned was the new webbing. No blancoing and no brass buttons to polish although we would still keep our old belts and gaiters for poncing about in on parade.

On the morning of our move to Trawsfynydd we paraded on the square with our kit bags packed. These we loaded on to lorries, one lorry for each company. We squaddies would be travelling to Wolverhampton low level station on coaches. It was a pleasant ride to Wolverhampton with house wives choice playing on the coach radio. There we would as the army always put it, entrain for Porthmadog in Wales. It was only a two hour journey to Porthmadog and we still had our haversack rations to eat. So we got them down us knowing it would probably be about two o'clock before we got another chance. There was no luxury travel at this end of the journey; it was back on the old army Q.L lorries for the trip to camp.

There were no surprises when we got there it was still the bog hole I left over two years ago.

Support Company had got the luck of the draw for accommodation as we were in the Nissen huts on the hill, the same huts we had used during our basic training. The rifle companies were down in the valley between the main camp and us in hundred and eighty pounded tents. It was a nice day as we arrived and with it now being late June we were hoping it would stay that way. But of course it didn't last, did it.

Our first day of the battle training was given over to sorting out what was what. The first thing was the drivers had no Bren carriers and would use jeeps with a trailer for their gun crews. The only platoon to have carriers would be the Anti tank platoon and they would still use their large Oxford carriers. Their only difference would be that they now had the new Battalion Anti Tank gun in place of the old seventeen pounder. This B.A.T gun was the weapon we saw them testing when we were at Netheravon last year. The job everyone would be doing had been posted on the company orders notice board but I wasn't down for anything. I didn't have a motorbike, it seems the motorcycle orderly job had been done away with so I fully expected to be transferred back to a rifle company until Capt. Bow came and said 'I'm keeping you in the platoon Power as a spare man, we can use your experience'. I don't know what experience that would be, but I was chuffed anyway. The first few days were spent doing gun drills and the whole platoon did this, drivers, wireless operators, everyone. Aiming at targets using a map was gone into at some detail and angles of elevation worked out on a crude army slide rule. It turned into a bit of a snigger when Sergeant. Jim started performing. How he ever made sergeant was a mystery to most of us but he always seemed to get away with it. He was married with three kids and I think his wife had most of his money because by Tuesday most weeks he would be cadging fags off us squaddies.

On the Friday of our first week I was on company orders to report to the cook house on Monday morning. At the time I just thought it was the usual fatigues party job for the day.

On the Saturday afternoon a gang of us caught the recreation lorry down to Blaenau Ffestiniog and went to the pictures to see Gary Cooper in High Noon. I don't know whether it was the shock of the film or what but Sid Fletcher came back with the tooth ache. With the next day being Sunday there was no sick parade so Dave, Joe and Kenny took him round to the hut the platoon was using as a store, got some pliers out of the gun kit tool box and while Joe held his head Dave and Ken tried to get Sid's tooth out. They ended up making things a lot worse as they broke the tooth off so he still had to wait for Monday morning sick parade.

I reported to the cook house on Monday and was told I would be working in there while we were training. There had been two cooks in there, a corporal who was in charge and a squaddie. The squaddie was a National service chap and was due for demob and I would take his place.

I couldn't see anyway of getting out of it so I just had to get on with it. The A.C.C corporal named Ward was an old soldier and a grumpy old sort of a cuss and whatever I did I was doing it wrong in his book.

The cooking range was coal fired and worked better some days than others depending on which way the wind was blowing. The corporal had a bunk in a little room at the back of the cook house and banked the fire up before he went to bed. This meant the oven could be used to cook the breakfasts. We managed to rub along for the next week the only trouble being it was six o'clock in the morning until eight o'clock at night seven days a week.

On the Monday of the next week Corporal Ward told me he would be moving to the main cook house and I would be left on my own with some one from the daily fatigue party to help me. The Sergeant Major came and said that I would have the fatigue party to help peel vegetables and clean up. He was detailing the spare man from the mortar platoon to permanently work with me. His name was Harry Saunders and he came from Wetly Rocks in north Staffordshire.

By lunch time Corporal Ward had packed his kit and moved out and I was left to it. After the lunch break I went to the company office as I was concerned about keeping the cook house fire going all night. The Sergeant Major said he would see that the guard were detailed to keep it stoked during the night. He also suggested that both I and Harry move into the room vacated by the corporal. I was not very happy with that as the place was damp and had no light in and it rained in on one corner. Sergeant Major Hillman made it plain it was an order, not a suggestion so we had to do it. I don't know what Corporal Ward had been sleeping on but there was no bed in the place. We couldn't just put our paliase on the bare floor as it was too damp so the Colour Sergeant found us some empty ammo boxes to make our beds on.

It's a good job it was summer and light at four o'clock in the morning or we'd have had a struggle. Being down in the cook house away from the huts meant we didn't get all the latest news just snippets from the fatigue party and the talk in the dinning room. However we learnt that Sergeant Jim had done his party piece. The M.M.G along with the mortar platoon had been giving live covering fire to a company attack on a hill. The range had been two thousand five hundred yards and using tracer for safety. The trouble was that tracer ammunition burns out after about fifteen hundred yards which was near the top of the trajectory at that range. Jim sees this and orders his section to drop their range by one thousand yards. The gun number ones knew this would put the shot in among the advancing squaddies and refused to fire their guns. Jim then started his usual bluster having them shot at dawn courts martial. It seems things were on the verge of a punch-up when Captain Bow arrived to see why they were not firing. It was all hushed up of course and Jim got away with it.

The next bit of fun happened on the twenty seventh of July when armistice was signed in Korea. This made the lads question why they needed to train for Korea if the war was over. I think what made it worse was we had a week of very wet weather and everyone was cheesed off. Battalion orders were put up that anyone found shirking would be severely dealt with. The fighting had stopped for now but it could start up again at any time.

We were on our last week of training now and the weather had picked up. On the Saturday morning most of the company returned to Lichfield. Leaving half a dozen of us as cleaning up party, we would return on Monday. The cook house would be closed and we would go to the main cook house for our food. On the Saturday afternoon I had my first outing for a month and along with Harry and Joe we caught the recreation lorry to Porthmadog. We did the pictures on the afternoon, had a bite to eat in a café and then into the pub. Well, I was flush wasn't I? as I'd been drawing my pay and couldn't get out to spend it. Harry kept telling us the lorry back to camp was going but Joe and I cocked a deaf-un and we missed it. We were both quite merry when the pub closed and had the mad idea of walking back to camp. After walking for half an hour we had enough and took refuge in a workmen's hut by the side of the road. It wasn't long before we were asleep and it was day light when we both awoke feeling perished. We must have been walking in the wrong direction last night because the signs pointed to Criccieth. I don't how far we had come but the cafes had started to open when we got there this was a surprise to us, being Wales and a Sunday most things closed down. However Criccieth was a little seaside town and a lot of people from the Midlands came here on Sundays for a day out. Our first priority was a hot cup of tea to warm us up a bit and some toast, toast being the cheapest thing on the menu. We did consider trying to get a bus back to camp but the weather looked well so we decided to stay a while; may as well make a day of it and catch the recreation truck back tonight.

After a stroll along the beach and a lie in the sun it got a bit boring as there were no pubs open so we decided to go to the bus station and try to get a bus back but there was a recreation truck there. The driver, one of the R.A.O.C squaddies said he would be leaving at five o'clock and if there was room once his own chaps had got on the lorry he would take us. That was nice of him so we gave him a couple of fags just to butter him up a bit. He was as good as his word and we were back in time for our evening meal.

Harry had moved back into the huts so I joined him for the night and we packed our kit ready for tomorrows move back to Lichfield.

What a surprise on Monday morning, our return had been postponed and we had been detailed to take the tents down and roll them up. Sergeant Hartley from the mortar platoon would be in charge of the tent party. A lot of the tents had been struck when we got down there and Sergeant Hartley said we should take it steady and make the job last. But by lunch time there were only about a dozen tents left to strike. It was a hot sunny day so after lunch the Sergeant suggested we have five in the tents before taking them down. Harry and I settled down in the first tent and the next thing I was aware of was some one kicking me in the ribs. As I awoke I could see Harry standing to attention and I still had a mallet in my hand. There stood a Captain of the R.A.O.C looking down at me and I sprang to attention. The commotion had got the sergeant up and he came running round. The Captain now took the Sergeant to task on what we were supposed to be doing. He seemed more concerned that I had gone to sleep with a mallet in my hand than the fact I had been asleep. The officer said he would report the matter and marched off. We finished taking the tents down and went and had a nap on our bunks until food time.

Tuesday morning we went back to Lichfield in a lorry and never heard anymore about the tent sleeping incident.

Chapter Twenty Four

Now we were back at Whittington barracks we had a week left before getting fourteen days embarkation leave. It was hardly worth unpacking our kit bags, however there was a good laugh waiting for us. On the battalion's return on Saturday the cells in the guard room were full so cells in the old block had to be used. A squaddie named Dawson who was a regular guard room customer had been put in one of these cells. I think he would have had a dishonourable discharge by now but for the battle of the wills; the C.O was determined he would do his national service and Dawson was determined he wouldn't. With the old block being used as a store for years the locks on the doors had been changed, so instead of them being on the out side of the door they were on the inside. The Regimental Sergeant Major had left his boots, belt and gaiters in the guard room for the prisoners to bull up ready for Monday morning. Dawson managed to escape and got down to Lichfield where he flogged the R.S.M's boots and had a couple of pints with the proceeds. It gave the whole battalion a good giggle, all except the R.S.M of course.

On the Wednesday evening the band and corps of drums beat the retreat on the barracks square. Some of the local bigwigs came for the event along with most of the married quarter's people. It was a lovely balmy summer evening and the band and drums put on a good show; marching up and down the square twirling their drum sticks with the drum major throwing his baton in the air and he never dropped it once.

The kit change was done with us who had white towels and house wives handing them in for green ones. A holdall for our washing kit was also issued which contained a chromium plated mirror, the thing named holdall ablutions G.S. However we had never had one before so we couldn't grumble.

The days were spent training and on the square but it was all half hearted just waiting for our embarkation leave. We were paid off on Thursday afternoon and we still had a few ration coupons to collect as sugar and meat were still rationed. These would be given out with the travel warrants tomorrow afternoon and as soon as we had them we could go. After first parade on Friday morning the rest of the morning was spent packing our kit up and handing it into the stores. They made us wait until after three o'clock before we got our passes but once we had them we were soon off.

Accommodation arrangements were as usual when I got to Alice's, I would be kipping on the settee but I didn't mind as I slept like a log after a pint or two in the Fullbrook Pub. The weather was still great and I certainly got around a bit. I took Sylvie to the pictures two or three times, well we went together really as she always insisted on buying her own ticket.

I had a trip to Stratford one day; John, Alice's son had bought an old Austin car. He couldn't afford to run it but after screwing five bob out of me and some money off his mother he decided to take us to Stratford on Avon. Joyce, Alice, Pat and me all piled into the car and off we went. The old car went alright and when we reached Stratford they decided to visit Shakespeare's house. I had been there with the school, so after arranging to meet them later I went off down by the river Avon. It was very pleasant down there and I spent an hour talking to an old soldier who had been in both world wars. I bought myself an ice-cream the first one I'd had since Hong Kong two years ago. Later, I met Alice and her gang in the tea rooms as arranged and had a cup of tea before setting off. All in all, not a bad day out for five bob.

I met Ray Thurstance in Walsall one afternoon. He was in my class at school and left the same time as I did. He had been the Hostler's assistant at Scribbans bakery since leaving school, but was now doing his National Service. Ray was still looking after horses at the Royal Army Vetinery Corps depot. The pubs were not yet open so we had a yap over a mug of tea in the Bridge Café.

I had a drink in the Fullbrook with Sylvia and promised to write to her, knowing I probably never would.

I got Granny Mac down to Patterson's for tea and a cake before my leave ended and got warned not to marry a foreign girl again as we parted.

I had enjoyed my leave, it was the best one I'd had probably due to it being summer. All the other leave I had taken had been in the winter or spring.

It was about nine o'clock when I got back to the barracks and there were a few back from their leave. The night turned out to be a long hard one with squaddies clomping in all through the night. At the roll call next morning everyone was there or as Sgt Bridge said to Capt Bow, 'all present and correct sir'.

We had no rifles so the Sgts marched us up and down doing various drill movements just to get us back into the swing of things. After an hour on the square we got a lecture on avoiding tropical diseases, V.D being the main one of course. The battalion was due to move out tomorrow morning and I think they were stuck with just finding something to keep us out of mischief. Everything had an air of waiting for something to happen.

By eleven o'clock we were back out side lined up. It was a lovely warm sunny day and we were given the order for short sleeve dress and back out on parade in ten minutes. This meant taking your jacket off and rolling your shirt sleeves up just above the elbows. Once back out each support company platoon would do its own thing. Captain Bow decided we would have a cross country march, with hour out and an hour back this would get us back in time for lunch at one o'clock. Now at this point Captain Bow and Sergeants Bridge and Jones found they had other appointments. This left Sergeant Hardcastle to take us on the march and the trouble with Jim on his own was you never knew what he would do. He marched us out of the barracks down through Whittington Village and after about three quarters of an hour we came out by Trent Valley railway station. By now it was twelve o'clock and the station hotel pub was just opening. Some one, I can't remember who, offered to buy Jim a pint so we all ended up in the pub. Once Jim got started on the beer one wasn't enough for him and half an hour later and after he had got a couple of pints down him he decided it was time we started back to camp. Jim started hooting 'get out side on parade' but no one took any notice of him, like Jim they were having a couple of pints and some were buying more beer. With the weather being so nice all the pub doors were propped open so Jim tried shoving some of us out the front door. We didn't resist him and just walked round the pub and came back in through the back door. The pub landlord didn't seem to mind, he was enjoying it all and selling more beer. Jim was going barmy and by now a lot of us were quite merry. By about quarter to one we had enough and lined up out side the pub ready for the march back. Lunch had been finished a good while by the time we got back to Whittington barracks.

At 2pm sharp Sgt Bridge came in the barrack room shouting those three little words, 'Get fell in'. The platoon paraded outside smelling like fly traps and some a bit wobbly. Captain Bow rolled up and could see the state of some of us. He questioned Sgt Hardcastle as to what we had been up to. Jim cracked on he didn't know anything 'it looks like they have all been in the N.A.A.F.I Sir', was Jim's reply. 'Well' said Captain Bow 'you had better march them down the back of the Spiders and hide them for the afternoon before the C.O sees them'. So the platoon spent its last afternoon at Whittington barrack sun bathing in the long grass down the Spiders.

When we got back for our evening meal there was an elderly chap waiting in our barrack room. He was looking for Sergeant Jones and Dave said he had seen this chap before; he was from a Christian Mission. Dave told us that while we were training in Wales Sergeant Jones had had taken a religious turn and got mixed up with them and they had got the him to order enough little prayer books for the whole battalion. Of course when Jones tried to distribute the books everyone just laughed at him. Dave reckoned to his knowledge they were left in two sand bags in the stores at Trawsfynydd. Whether Sergeant Jones thought they were free we never found out but this little chap wanted some money so they couldn't have been. We all thought it a great giggle and was only too happy to point him in the direction of the Sergeant's mess. Whether the chap got his money we would never know, but Dave said he didn't think it was much only about seven or eight quid at most.

Haversack rations were drawn after our breakfast ready for our move and we were lined up on the road with our kit by nine o'clock. This was a bit early for the transport but it was to give time to check for any barrack room damage before we moved off. Fag burns on the windowsill's was one of the main things they charged us for, one and a tanner each I seem to remember. However we got an all clear.

We would depart from the Lichfield City station this time not from the usual Trent Valley Station, this was probably because the Regiment had a train to ourselves.

Each company loaded their kit bags on to a lorry but we would be marched down to the station, it wasn't far only about three miles. The carriages were the old type with no corridors and we were loaded eight to each carriage. There were lots of the families of local lads there to see us off plus the married quarter people.

The train made good time for a military train as they usually took the roundabout way. However we were lined up on the Liverpool docks by mid afternoon ready to embark on the Empire Austurias. Reunited with our kit bags, we embarked a company at a time. Once on board it was a surprise as it was all cabins of four or six bunks per cabin with a wash basin in. This was a great improvement from the old standees.

The word was that the ship had been converted to carry immigrants to Australia. Support Company being the last company to embark got the cabins near the deck, so we had a port hole to look through. The dining area was small and there were three sittings for meals and we were issued with coloured disks; red, white, and blue which we had to show before being let into the dining room. We got white the middle sitting and when the Colour Sergeant issued them he gave us a warning 'if we lost it we would not be getting another one, so look after it'. Korea was five weeks away so it would be a long time without food if we lost it.

By the time we had boarded and sorted our bunks out it was meal time. There may have been a big improvement in troop ship accommodation, the food hadn't got any better but after only having the haversack rations all day we got it down us. Our main concern now was when the duty free shop was going to open but by bed time the ship was still in the dock. When we woke the next morning the ship was out in the Irish Sea steaming south. It seemed like hours between our breakfast and the duty free shop opening at ten o'clock. Every one wanted fags and they were still half a crown for fifty. The chocolate and sweets were still pretty dear and they had been off ration since last spring. The beer was sold at a different counter where they sold vouchers which you handed in for beer. Two pints a day was our ration and the bar only opened between seven and nine thirty each evenig. The ship had the usual recreation room with a piano in it and it wasn't long before the first crown and anchor board appeared.

If we thought it was going to be a leisurely cruise out to Korea we soon got a rude awakening. A training program was posted on the notice board and it would all start tomorrow with our first parade at eight o'clock on deck wearing plimsolls. A lot of the program would be lectures as there was not enough room on the deck for us all to prance about. Areas of the deck had to be booked well in advance. Overall it wasn't too bad as everything went on in the mornings leaving the afternoons for us to skive.

On our first afternoon at sea our company commander Major Lowens came round the company cabins just to have a nose, I think. The only other time we would ever see him would be with the Sergeant Major on the Saturday inspection.

Once we had got our cheap fags the rest of the day was spent settling in. Some of us swapped cabins as mates wanted to be with their mates and Corporal's wanted their own cabin, too grand to mix with us squaddies.

Jim was with them now. I think a combination the firing incident while we were training in Wales and the Trent Valley march had lost him a stripe. However he was still in charge of three section and remained his usual objectionable self.

This was the first time I had been sailing out in the summer. My last trip was late winter going out and mid winter on my return. By the time we had reached the Bay of Biscay it was quite warm and calm.

The recreation room was a good one but with the battalion on the boat it was kept in order. It was being run as though we were in barracks with the orderly Sergeant on the prowl. Crown and anchor board operators always had a look-out so they came and went as he did. Even on our first night out, the place was going full swing; there seemed to be no shortage of piano players and singers. There were squaddies from other regiments going to postings in Egypt and out east, a few W.R.A.C's and a couple of the Queen Alexander nurses were on board. With our afternoons off and the weekends we settled in to enjoy the five week cruise.

Our training program got underway usually in the area outside our cabins, although we always had our first morning parade on the main deck. Training sessions on the main deck had to be booked in advance as there were troops from other regiments going to postings so the North Stafford's couldn't have all the deck to themselves.

We thought that with the magic Jim now being a Corporal we would be having another Sergeant in the platoon. On our third day out during a map reading session Captain Bow told us Corporal Hardcastle would still be three section leader.

Two P.T. sessions a week were on our schedule and we had a new Physical Training instructor a Sergeant Powell. With all the training and moving about we hadn't done any P.T. since leaving Trieste. Sergeant Powell was a lot different from the old P.T. Sergeant, he was only a small man with muscles like knots in cotton. How he passed the medical for the army is a mystery as he wore glasses with lenses like the bottoms of milk bottles. He soon became known by all and sundry as Billy Muscles. All the P.T. classes were held on the forecastle of the ship or as we all called it, the raised bit at the pointed end. Push-ups, stars and running on the spot were about all we could do on there. At the end of our first session knights on horses was tried but sooner or later some one was going to end up over the side so it was abandoned.

Chapter Twenty Five

The day before we were due at Port Said, our last training period for the morning was a talk by Lieutenant Godwin of the Anti Tank platoon on the history of Port Said and how it was founded in eighteen fifty nine as a working camp by Said Pasha to house men working on the canal. A lot of the city was built on Lake Manzala which had been reclaimed by landfill. Now it was now one of the world's major ports with all the leading maritime powers having consulates there. Lieutenant Godwin went on to point out some of the notable buildings in the city and that's when most of us lost interest; telling a load of eighteen to twenty year old squaddies about architectural gems was a complete waste of time. We got a bit more interested when he explained that the Statue of Liberty was originally designed to go on the start of the canal at Port Said. The statue was inspired by the huge statues at Abu Simbel. Auguste Bartholdi, the sculptor designed the statue as `Egypt carrying the light of Asia`. After the statue had been made the Khedive Ismail decided the whole project was too expensive and abandoned it. `The Light of Asia` was sent to America to become the Statue of Liberty.

As soon as the ship had docked in the port it was surrounded by the usual `bun boats` selling tatty leather goods. The game was to get them to throw their string up on the pretence you wanted to buy something and then tie it to the rail, but most of them were wise to this little trick and wanted the money first. The best entertainment was throwing the pennies in and watching the kids dive for them. You could throw the coins as far away from the boats as you could manage, they would still get them. Shore leave was posted for the following afternoon so on the fist parade the following morning we got the usual warnings, 'You represent the regiment when on shore and all will show the decorum expected from an English man abroad'. We would be inspected before we left the ship, no suede or canvas shoes allowed and we had four hours, from two until six o'clock. As soon as we hit the quay we were surrounded by the hawkers selling wallets with camels embossed on them, Tins of `Spanish Fly` it looked like axel grease to me, and cardboard fezzes plus offers to come and see his sister. There were one or two fruit sellers but we had been told not to buy. The old soldier's tale was that they soaked it in the Sweetwater Canal to plump it up, The Sweetwater Canal being the city's sewer outlet into the sea.

Dave and I strolled down into the town once we had run the gauntlet of hawkers. We didn't look for any of Lieutenant Godwin's architectural gems and just had a stroll round and had a drink in an army club, The Church Army I think. I had been here before and Dave had lived in the army married quarters when his Dad had been stationed here. However it made a break from being on the ship and passed an afternoon. When we all got back one or two had the wallet with the camel on, but it looked like the cardboard fez had been the best seller. There were tales of daring do being told all evening, mind you it's the first time most of the squaddies had trod on foreign soil. Every one was back on the ship in time for their evening meal.

The boat started its passage up the canal in the early hours of the morning. We had a P.T. session after our first morning parade followed by a bit of gun drill. Our final session was another talk on the Suez Canal by Lieutenant Godwin. This was given to all of Support Company sitting cross legged on the deck. Lieutenant Godwin explained that attempts to build a canal were made by the ancient Egyptians. The first modern efforts came from Napoleon Bonaparte's Egypt expedition. He thought a canal would be a trade problem for the British. The first attempt to build it was started in seventeen ninety nine but was abandoned when the experts reckoned the Red Sea was ten meters higher than the Mediterranean. In eighteen thirty three a Fence group known as the Saint Simoniens arrived in Cairo and became interested in building the canal but by then Mohammed Ali had lost interest in the project. The Saint Simonies returned to Paris leaving a Ferdinand de Lesseps the Fence vice-council in Alexandria behind. In eighteen forty six the Saint Simoniens created another association to study the possibility of building the Suez Canal once again. Linant de Bourdaloue drew up a technical report in eighteen forty seven and confirmed there was no difference in the sea levels of the Mediterranean and Red Seas. At this time there was considerable British opposition to the project. However, Said Pasha who had been a childhood friend to Ferdinand de Lesseps founded The Universal Company of the Maritime Suez Canal to build the canal in eighteen fifty eight. This was a private company, which would build the canal under the agreement that it would operate it for ninety nine years after which it would revert to Egyptian government ownership. The company ran into financial trouble and Said Pasha purchased forty four percent of the company to keep it going. However the British and the Turks managed to get the work on it suspended but after the intervention of Napoleon the third work started on the twenty fifth of April eighteen fifty nine. Work on the canal was suspended again when Ismail succeeded Said Pasha in eighteen sixty three. Napoleon again intervened and an international commission was set up in eighteen sixty four. The commission resolved the problems and the canal was completed on the seventeenth of November eighteen sixty nine. Like all great schemes it cost twice as much as the original estimates. The opening of the canal was cause for great celebrations attended by many heads of state, the Prince of Wales was the British representative. The canal had a dramatic effect on world trade from the time it opened, and even on world politics. It was now much easier for European nations to penetrate and colonise Africa. In eighteen seventy five the British government purchased all the shares belonging to the Egyptian interests for four hundred thousand pounds but France still held the majority interest. Under a treaty signed in eighteen eighty eight (The Convention of Constantinople), the canal would be open to vessels of all nations without discrimination. Britain considered the canal vital to its maritime power and colonial interests. This seems to be the point were Britain got involved, well you can't trust the French can you? Lieutenant Godwin finished off with the things most of us learnt at school like the length of the canal and the fact it had a railway running alongside it. By the time he had finished giving the talk we were sailing through the Bitter Lakes past the north bound convoy that were anchored there.

By late afternoon we went through Port Suez and out into the Red Sea. It was hot now and most of us lay on our bunks in the afternoons until it cooled a bit in the early evening. Some played cards but most of the cigarettes used as our gambling stake were now only paper tubes due to the heat drying the tobacco in them.

A concert had been organised for Saturday night to be held on the stern of the ship. The recreation room was not big enough to accommodate all the spectators. Although with the North Stafford's going to Korea we had no married quarter's people with us, there were quite a few going to other postings. Company orders pointed out that any one attending the Concert must be properly dressed in trousers, shirt and beret, not our normal wear of P.T shorts and bush hats. As usual the whole proceedings were dominated by singers with three of the W.R.A.C. girls doing an Andrew sisters act. There was one comedian on the bill, he got booed off. The band came up with a string quartet but I think that was for the officers' mess benefit, it was wasted on us squaddies. All in all it was a very pleasant evening with the ship floating down the Red Sea on a balmy star light night.

It took about five days to get down to Aden and on the morning before we arrived we got the now familiar talk. This time it was by Captain Pyke of the Mortar platoon who had apparently been stationed at Aden some time. The first British involvement was when the British East India Company landed Royal Marines there in eighteen thirty nine. This was to occupy the territory and stop attacks by pirates on British shipping. Once on shore with their foot in the door the British managed to expand both east and west to establish the Aden protectorate, this included the island of Socotra. After the Suez Canal opened Aden became an important coaling station for British shipping. In nineteen thirty six Aden became separated for the British India Empire and became a Crown colony in its own right but still retained the rupee as its currency. Although Aden was a Muslim area Sharia law was never used. All matters were dealt with in the secular courts of the colony. The present population for those of us who were interested, most of us wasn't, was one hundred and thirty eight thousand four hundred and forty one.

It was afternoon when we docked and we were told shore leave for those who wanted to go would be after our evening meal. There was the standard inspection just to check you were fit to represent the regiment while on shore. I didn't feel like going as I had been there before and it wasn't much of a place. All the others in our cabin decided to go just for the walk round while I spent the evening leaning on the ships rail watching events on the dock side. Ten o'clock was the time for every one to be back on board but it was a last minute rush for some. A couple of the Royal Artillery lads were bought back to the boat by the Military Police, we never found out what they had been up to. When Joe got back to the cabin we chucked him out again, he stunk blind. His trousers were plastered with goat muck. He had been up to his usual getting his end away. Brownie said he had seen Joe chatting up what looked like his Granny. It must have been while performing with her that he got the goat shit on him. Joe had to take his trousers off up on deck, luckily there was a separate wash-house at the end of the passage so he could rinse them out. The handkerchiefs portraying the fifty ways of doing it were still good sellers. It seems everyone had bought one to send home to 'our kid'.

When we woke next morning the ship was back at sea in the Indian Ocean and the flying fish were jumping out of the water as the ship passed. Things got back into the normal routine for the next few days until we reached the port of Colombo in Ceylon. We didn't get a talk on Colombo so I took it none of the Officers had ever been there before. Shore leave was posted on Company orders the night before docking. It would be from two until six tomorrow afternoon or as they would have it, fourteen hundred until eighteen hundred hours. I decided, along with Dave and Brownie, to go if it was only just for a change. After the normal inspection to make sure we were smart enough to visit a former colony, off we went. The hawkers main stock seemed to be little carved Elephants and coconut shell fiddles. Of course me being more on the exotic side, bought myself a bunch of bananas. Once you had got through the docks the city was about the most civilized place we had stopped at so far. But I knew that as I been here before. Perhaps I should have given the talk on the place but all I knew was that tea comes from Ceylon. We had an uneventful wander around the more salubrious town centre and were back to the ship for eighteen hundred hours. The bananas were good but they were smaller and sweeter than ones we at home from the West Indies at home.

The following morning we were on our way again. After our first parade it was decided that the rest of the morning would be used for dial sight practice and what happened became a bit of a giggle. The forecastle (or the raised bit at the pointed end to us) had been booked for the morning. The practise was mainly for the gun number ones and twos the rest of us were to watch and learn. It was decided that only two guns with their sights and tripods would be needed and each Sergeant would take his own section. Sergeant Bridge detailed four men and off they went down into the bowels of the ship to draw the stuff from the stores. They made it back lathered in sweat as they had to carry the guns up five flights of steps and it's a bit warm in the Indian Ocean in August. The training started with one section performing and when they had done, number two took over. Three section was the last to go and once they had zeroed their sights the fun began; Corporal Martin, Corporal Hardcastle's main number one knowing how bright Jim was said his sights were no good, the level was moving. Jim takes a look at it and growls out of the side of his mouth the bloody things U.S. and sends Brownie to get another one. Brownie tried to explain it was the ship moving that caused the level to move back and forth. 'Don't you back chat me young man, you'll do as you're told or you will find yourself on a charge a bit quick. Now get going at the double'. Brownie gets the dial sight and sets off while

Sergeants Bridge and Jones lean on the ships rail grinning. Brownie comes back half a stone lighter and Corporal Martin puts the sight on his gun and announces it's just the same. Corporal Hardcastle was about to send poor old Brownie off again when Sergeant Bridge stepped in. The sea looked dead calm and Jim took some convincing that the boat rocked a bit even on a calm sea. We all had a bit of a laugh except poor old Brownie however he was excused taking the stuff back to the stores.

Singapore was our next stop and we didn't get a talk on there either. I thought we may have got one off our company commander Major Lowends as he had been a prisoner of war here. I could see there had been a lot of building done since I was last here; a lot of the war damage had now been repaired. The N.A.A.F.I had built a new club with a swimming pool in Singapore. That's where most of us who went on our shore leave went for the afternoon. It was quite a large place with a big pool and plenty of people in it. The bar had closed before we got there so we spent the afternoon binging on tea and orange juice while watching the girls of the W.R.A.C. swimming in the pool waggling their arses at the squaddies. Then all back to the boat for our evening meal.

On our way up to Hong Kong we had the first bit of rough weather and high winds. It seems we had sailed into the tail end of a summer typhoon. One or two of us got seasick but there was nothing anyone could do about it. However after a couple of days we had steamed out of it.

The day before we hit Hong Kong it was back to the talk on the colony, this time by Lieutenant Butcher of the Assault Pioneer platoon. There were three of us, Joe, Sailor and me who had been there with the South Stafford's so we got told again what we already knew. It was still the same place we had left nearly three years ago. Joe and I were first in the queue when shore leave came up and we took Dave with us to show him around; all the high spots down the Nathan Road and back. You could see a few changes had been made and the security car park in front of the Peninsular Hotel had gone. The Star ferry was still ten cents so we took Dave over to Hong Kong Island and had a drink in the Services Club over there. It had been a whirlwind tour but we all enjoyed it.

We left Hong Kong in the night and it would be another six days to Pusan in Korea. Most days we would see patrolling American warships and aircraft. We were told the aircraft were Neptune recognisance planes keeping an eye on China. I bet there would be some howling and gnashing of teeth if the Chinese had planes keeping an eye on America. On the late afternoon of the sixth day we were escorted into Pusan by a navy frigate. Then we had to wait while they lowered the anti submarine net before we could get into the dock.

Chapter Twenty Six

Our first impression of Korea from the ship was not good. If Pusan was a guide we had come to the end of the world. There was an announcement over the tannoy that we must all collect our personal weapons and carry them off the ship. As we disembarked on to the quayside there were several army Officers from neutral countries ticking off what weapons we were carrying. This was part off the agreement to stop the fighting and ensure no side bought in more arms. It made me wonder who was checking the Chinese. Standing on the quay you could see the American army was in charge by their stuff piled up on it.

We were all lined up by company and awaited the unloading of our kit bags. Once we had them we were loaded into Lorries of the New Zealand army Service Corps all driven by young Maori squaddies. The camp was only a couple of miles up the road and by the look of the tents had been an American army camp. They were canvas tents on a wooden frame and quite comfortable, it was a nice camp. With it being Thursday it was pay day and once we had settled in our tents the next thing was pay parade. We got paid in B.A.F the money we had used while stationed in Germany. This was being used as the currency of the British Commonwealth Division in Korea. Getting paid meant we could get some fags; the only problem was the N.A.A.F.I only had the Marcovitch Black and White fags in the twenty five tins. The fags were not very nice but at least you got a little flat tin to keep your money in. One or two of us started to get the diarrhoe`e after our evening meal and we ended up trotting over to the latrines all night. It seems we weren't the only ones as there was a queue at the M.O's tent next morning. The Corporal in charge of the medical tent lined all of us up with 'the shits' as he put it. The M.O came out and went along the line just checking we all had the same symptoms. Once he was satisfied the medical room orderly started filling half pint bottles of thick white liquid from a large gallon bottle. He then doled them out, we got one each, with the instructions to take 10ml of it every four hours. 'What's 10ml?' was the cry, 'two of your standard army issue spoons' was the reply. In practice a good swig every four hours turned out to be our normal dosage. This complaint must be a regular thing by the way the M.O had dealt with it, and I must say after a couple of doses it cured the problem. Some of us never went to the latrines again for a week.

During the afternoon we were busy handing in our normal kit and collecting our combat uniforms. They were already in kit bags as we had all been measured up for them at Lichfield. The Colour Sergeant told us to go back to our tents and check we had it all; two combat suits, one parker, a pair of imitation lamb's wool long johns and two string vests (these were like medieval chain mail and designed to let air circulate around your body in cold weather); two pairs of space boots complete with mess insoles, a cap comforter and a tin of face cream. Not the sort you could send home to your girlfriend, just plain lanolin to rub on your face when it got really cold. The only surprise was everyone had the right stuff, so it must have been packed by civilians.

Battalion orders posted that evening said we would be moving from camp on Sunday afternoon and there would be a cross country run in the morning. No one could figure out where we were supposed to do the running as there was a large American air base over the road and on our side a big hill. Come Saturday morning we soon found out, it would be up the bloody hill. To make sure none of us would find a short-cut or hide half way Billy Mussels the P.T.I Sergeant, together with several other NCOs had been sent off earlier. These would be posted at the top of the hill with an ink pad and stamp. As we reached them they would stamp the back of our hand and we would show it on our return as proof we had been to the top of the hill. The run was hard going after five weeks on the ship but we all made it back alive. Any way we had until tomorrow afternoon to recover.

After our Sunday lunch which was a bit earlier than usual the battalion paraded on the edge of the camp. Our kit bags had been loaded onto the lorries but we would march down to the station about half a mile down the road. The station was as tumble down as the rest of the place with the local hawkers selling Coca-Cola, cigarette lighters and dirty photos. One of them had no legs and was getting round by putting his knuckles on the ground and swinging through his arms. Of course this prompted one or to of the kinder members of the Battalion to ask him what he was 'arsing' about at. The Support company commander Major Lowends came and told us we would be going to an area on the Imjin River just north of Seoul. This was the place that the battle of the Imjin had taken place in April of fifty one. The battalion entrained as they say and off we went through countryside that was very hilly, much like Hong Kong had been. By six o'clock we were all starving but it was half seven before we got anything. What a pantomime it turned out to be. The store man and Colour Sergeant came with the boxes of five man rations. They took all the breakfast rations out of them first. Six squaddies were detailed to go with the Colour Sergeant and came back with dixie's of hot water. The tins of food were then put in the hot water to warm up. It was a waste of time as the water wasn't very hot in the first place and putting the tins in only made it colder. Instructions were given that when hot enough, which they were never going to get, we would collect one tin each. Those who got a tin of stewed steak would share it with some one who had a tin of vegetables. Those with the tins of vegetables could swap a bit for other vegetables. However we managed to get fed and the best part of the meal was the packet of hard tack biscuits.

The train seemed to be stop starting all the while and by about ten o'clock in the evening we came to a halt in a little town. The hawkers soon came round with what seemed to be the main goods for sale in Korea, Coca cola and dirty post cards. No one was interested except Paigie and he was in negotiations with one of the hawkers. As the train got underway again Paigie showed us the fruits of his dealing. He was the proud owner of an old American army forty five calibre automatic pistol, dated nineteen fourteen. The cost of which had been nine pence in B.A.F. and a tin of bacon! He must have pinched the bacon when the Colour Sergeant and his store man were sorting the rations out.

The train puffed north stopping and starting all through the night. Breakfast was to be another gourmet meal but at least we did get a mug of tea this time. The tins of bacon were left to warn in a dixie of hot water The Colour Ssergeant and his store man gave out little individual boxes of corn flakes, these had perforated flaps so you could eat them out of the box. We even got some milk to put on them as the store man had tipped some tins of the carnation milk in a dixie and thinned it down with water. They were spoiling us now. The bacon was rationed out, one tin to four men and it was not very warm but it still went down well with the hardtack biscuits. The water in the dixes was still warm so we filled one of our mess tins to shave in.

It was just before lunch when we reached the rail head at Kaesong. It was a small town of what appeared to be mainly wattle and daub houses and a collection of Romney huts around the rail head. This place had been the supply depot for The British Commonwealth

Division during the war. The battalion detrained and lined up by company and a roll-call taken. The camp was about fifteen miles north of here, so we were loaded on to lorries and taken through the hills to a tented camp that had been set up in a valley. The camp itself was divided in two by a road and a stream that ran down to the Imjin River. All the rifle company's were on the north side just below the last positions occupied when the war had ended. H.Q and Support Company were on the south side of the road and stream. All the tents were the American heavy marquees which had eighteen beds, so were a bit crowded. A steep bank with a flight of steps up it split the support company lines.

On top of the bank was the cook house, the dinning tent, the senior N.C.O's lines and two marquees to be occupied by the Mortar platoon. The company paraded and the Sergeant Major along with the Colour Sergeant sorted out who would be in which tent. The M.M.G platoon got the two tents next to the company office tent. Having sorted that out the Sergeant Major announced that a meal had been prepared for us. The cook house had been cobbled together with a bit of corrugated sheeting and was manned by two cooks of the A.C.C. An old stiff legged Corporal who looked like he had been in the army since the days of Napoleon was in charge, assisted by Wilf, a national service private. The Corporal must have had a name by was always known by all and sundry as Old Dead Legs. The meal was alright the vegetables being the freeze dried chips with Pom for the spuds but we got a right chunk of beef steak with it. It seems the Americans were supplying the meat and we would be getting boxes of all sorts including boxes of chickens and legs of ham. All the boxes it came in had where it had come from stamped all over them like 'from the big corn country of Idaho' and various other parts of the states. On the tables in the dinning tent were tins of butter and cheese, a present from the New Zealand Government. They didn't last long we soon got stuck into them with butter on your Pom and anything else we could put it on. However it was a good meal finished off with a knob of cheese.

At our first afternoon parade we noticed that there were several squaddies from The Duke of Wellingtons Regiment, together with a couple of Korean squaddies present. Lieutenant. Godwin who had come up on the advance party a couple of days before, explained to us that the Yorkshire lads had only just come out and would stay with the North Stafford's to finish their time. The two Korean lads would be attached to the Assault platoon but rifle companies would each have a platoon of the Korean army attached to them.

The next thing was the issue of sleeping bags and this turned into a bit of a giggle. When the Korean lads came to sign for theirs the Colour Sergeant started shouting 'Sergeant Major they are drawing little patterns', 'that's what they do said the Sergeant Major' He wasn't the brightest one around, our Colour Sergeant.

The tents were a bit crowed so we didn't have much room, only about two feet between the cots and with them being thick canvas it was a bit dark. We stacked our kit in what space we had before handing our rifles into the armoury for security. That was a laugh as it was only a tent and our rifle secured with a bit of chain through the trigger guard. There were one or two interesting rifles already in there, mainly American and Russian captured from the Chinese army. The rest of the afternoon was given over to settling in.

The evening meal was another good one, with old hand Dead Legs in charge he had done it all before and seeing they only had two hydra burners to cook on did a marvellous job. What bit was left of the butter and cheese got polished off and we didn't see any more until Christmas.

There was no N.A.A.F.I but the last regiment here had knocked up a bit of a hut out of corrugated sheets to use as a canteen. They had made a counter, some seats and little tables out of the empty beer crates and all lit, like everywhere else, by candles. The main sale of course was beer; Guinness and Ind Coope but the best seller was Asahi, a Japanese beer. Fags and other odds and ends we had to get from the P.R.I shop on the other side of the camp.

On first parade Tuesday morning Sergeant Major Hillman told us he would be organising some fatigue parties to get the company lines into good order. The first thing would be the latrines as the present one was only a slit trench with a pole to ledge your arse on screened with elephant grass woven in telephone wire. 'There's not much in the way of comforts in this mans army, surely we are entitled to a comfortable crap' he said. Beer crates would be used to make the toilet seats or thunder boxes as the Sergeant Major called then. As well as the toilet we needed some urinals one at each level of the camp and one by the canteen. Once these were in place, relieving yourself through the tent flap in the middle of the night would be a chargeable offence. I was on the detail for the building of the urinals and our first job was to scour the area for something suitable to make them with. Along the side of the upper part of our company lines was what had been a terrace of paddy fields. At the top of the terrace by an abandoned house there had been an artillery position with the old packing for the shells still there. Among the rubbish were some metal tubes about eight inches in diameter and two and a half feet long. Looking at the writing on them they had contained one hundred and seventy-five millimetre shells. 'Just what we are looking for,' said the Sergeant Major 'bring four back to camp'. Our next task was digging little holes three feet deep which we half filled with stones to make soak ways. The tubes were then placed on top at an angle and the earth filled in to keep them upright. Screens were made from field telephone wire which was lying about everywhere. Some fine mess wire was found from somewhere and bound on top of the tubes, with telephone wire of course, to keep the flies out. There were two on the upper level and two at the lower which we christened 'pissaphones'.

By the end of the week the platoon was sent up to their defensive positions in the hills. I was with one section and the bunker was on a hill covering the plain running down to the Imjin river. These had been the positions occupied for the last two years of the war so the gun bunkers had already been done. Our job was to finish digging a covered connecting trench between them. Number two section were higher up the ridge on top of the hill, marked castle hill on our maps. This was because the remains of a small castle were on it, built by Kubla Khan no less, according to Captain Bow. Their connecting trench was nearly done except for a great lump of rock in the middle of it. Jim's section number three was on the other side of the valley and were almost completed. There were still a lot of the debris of war scattered about and Captain Bow pointed out that this was the place where the Gloucestershire Regiment made their last stand. It was the battle of the Imjin in April nineteen fifty one when the British twenty ninth brigade tried to stop the Chinese army crossing the Imjin River. It made me think, if both John Rudd and I had been a few months older we would have been here. We had a lucky escape! We worked up there all day and lunch was brought up to us in a jeep. A halt was called to the digging at four o'clock and we marched back to camp in time for pay parade.

Another surprise awaited us as we drew our pay; we got a fifty tin of fags with it, free.

What happened next when we got back in our tents Jim would fall for on several occasions over the next few weeks; the mail would be delivered to the company office and it was the job of one of the Corporal's in the tent to go and collect it. Corporal Martin would say to Corporal Hardcastle 'go see if there's any mail Jim'. Jim would say 'am I the only `c—t` around here?' Corporal Martin would stand up and look slowly round the tent and say 'yes Jim, I think you are'.

Chapter Twenty Seven

It didn't take us long to settle in our tents, although there wasn't much room so you could just about get an empty beer box between each bed. The boxes the Asahi beer came in made great bed side lockers and there was a waiting list to get one. The food was good except for the freeze dried vegetables but the meat was great thanks mainly to the Americans. Sergeant Major Hillman had got one of his fatigue parties to knock up a bit of a wash house but it only had cold water. This was delivered to us in a little tanker lorry and stored in old fifty gallon drums. If you wanted a shower this was on the stream back along the valley at the foot of Mount Kamak San by the R.T.R. `Royal Tank Regiment` camp. It was here you also got your clean clothes. You walked in the first tent and undressed, then through into the showers which were warm and running all the while. Once you had dried yourself you handed your dirty clothes in and were given clean ones in exchange. The only trouble was they inspected your socks and if they found a hole in. they wouldn't exchange them. After a few weeks floors for the tents were delivered all the way from Malaya. These came in packs of floor panels and two doors, one for each end of the tent. The assault platoon got the job of installing them but the tents were already on level ground so they only needed laying. The doors were hinged to the frames and they didn't take a lot of fitting either. The tents seemed warmer with the wooden floors down and it was somewhere else for the rats to hide. A few lads had been bitten by rats while asleep, always on the lobe of their ear. At about the same time as the floor fitting was going on a small Romney hut was erected on the high ground. Everyone thought this would be the new company office but to our surprise it was to be a canteen. The Sergeant Major took charge of fitting it out with the old beer crate chairs and tables. He got a lad from the mortar platoon who had been an apprentice sign writer in Civiy Street to make a sign. It had a letter S lying on its side asleep and the `lazy S` saloon above it. I think he fancied himself as Wyatt Earp our Sergeant Major.

A lot of our time was spent on schemes like practicing a stand too at night and other military manoeuvres in conjunction with the Commonwealth Division. I got landed with any job Captain. Bow wanted a man for. If the platoon was together I would be the cook but a lot of times each section would be in different areas and then I would probably be a gun crew member. We liked it like that because we would then get the American one man ration bags. These were great and contained all sorts of goodies. A little packet of breakfast cereal, tin of bacon or sausage, tin of stew or something like that for lunch and a tin for the evening meal plus a tin of fruit, some packets of coffee, powdered milk and packets of sugar. Along with this was toilet paper a book of matches, water purifying tablets, a little hexamine stove and some tablets to burn on it. The goodies were a block of chocolate, a pack of jammy biscuits or cookies as they called them. Some of the food in the tins was different to what we were used to like ground beef and spaghetti but I enjoyed it. The prize bit was they always had a packet of twenty fags usually Lucky Strike, Chesterfield or Camel.

Being out and about doing the manoeuvres took us all round the area which was still littered with the debris of war. We came across some little field guns one day left by the Chinese army. They were with skeletons of mules or horses obviously hit by an air strike. The guns were in three separate parts, breach, barrel which clipped on to the breach like a bren gun and iron tired wooden wheels. On close inspection stamped on the breaches was `Armstrong England 1904` so they had been around a while. Occasionally some one would find the odd skeleton of what was left of a Chinese solider hidden in the elephant grass. When this happened the officer in change made a map reference and reported the find to H.Q. who would send people to collect it.

The pioneer platoon got into some trouble over not doing this when they found one. It was their job to maintain the mine fields down towards the river crossings and while doing this one day they found a skeleton of a Chinese solider tangled up in the barbed wire. O'Brian one of the old soldiers in the platoon brought the skull back to camp and hung it in the platoon tent and put a candle in it. Every one thought it a great novelty until there were claims that the tent was now haunted. When the Sergeant Major found out there was hell to pay and the Padre was sent for. He blessed the tent and took the skull away. I don't ever remember any one getting charged over it, just dire warnings of the consequences if it ever happened again.

If we weren't out playing soldiers a lot of the M.M.G platoons time was spent working on the gun positions, each section working on their own bunkers. Me being a spare man usually got sent up to help two section on castle hill. This overlooked a little village called Choksong on the road that ran down to the river. It was on this road just out of the village the N.A.A.F.I were building a canteen with a little hall on the side. The one thing that always stands out in my memory is how clear the air was on these autumn mornings. You could see the Chinese army positions clearly and Captain. Bow reckoned they were over thirty miles away. It seemed like you could see forever. Another thing that surprised me was the amount of wild Chinese Pheasants there were flying around.

Our next comfort for the troop's project was a little open air cinema. This was built on a sloping bank that ran up towards the officer's mess. The screen was a bit of old white washed tent and the seating empty ammo boxes. The P.R.I, thinking they were going to make a few bob got an usherette with a tray selling chocolate bars. He was a lad named Walters who worked in the P.R.I shop and looked more like a girl than a lad. He only lasted about ten minutes as everyone was feeling his arse and as he tried to stop them they pinched his chocolate bars. The films were a bit ancient but they were always well attended. Colbert, one of the lads from Yorkshire was in his element with them. He was a proper film buff, you only had to mention the name of a film and he would tell you who starred in it and the supporting cast.

The only patch of level ground you could play football on was by the P.R.I on the other side of camp at the end of the aircraft landing strip. A lot of the keener lads used to go over there playing but the ground was littered with bits of broken rock. This resulted in a queue at the Medical hut with cuts to the knees so the M.O had it stopped. A few days later there was a note on battalion orders that if people wanted to go and pick the bits of rock off the patch in their spare time, football would be allowed again. There was no shortage of volunteers and it was all done with the guidance of the Regimental Sergeant Major. This is where they should have smelt a rat if he was involved, because he had no interest in playing football. As soon as it was all cleared to his satisfaction football was allowed again and we now had a parade ground as well. It wasn't long before we were testing it out with a Saturday morning parade, bulled boots and all.

The weather was getting a lot colder now and there were frosts in the mornings. The washing water had ice on it but the cook house took pity on us and warmed a dixie of water so we could go and fill a mess tin to shave in. By the middle of December the inside of the tent would be white with hoar frost first thing and we had to keep our boot insoles in our sleeping bags. The sleeping bags were old and not very good for this sort of weather. Another bag was issued and we were told to stuff one bag inside the other. A week later Sergeant Bridge told Sailor Bowden and me to report to the Colour Sergeant with our sleeping bags. The Colour Sergeant had some new green sleeping bags much lighter than the old ones and they were on test for the winter. There would be two to each platoon; Sailor and me for the M.M.G platoon and we would note any problems we had with them and be asked to make out a report in the spring. We found a lot of difference the first night, as they were a lot warmer yet didn't seem as thick as the old bags.

Our next improvement was electric lights powered by a little single stroke engine generator. They were made in Japan and several of them were to be installed around the camp. Support companies generator was put against the bank outside our company office. The signals platoon did the wiring up, putting two forty watt bulbs in each tent. They were not very bright but a lot better than the candles and hurricane lamps. Extra bulbs were installed in the canteen and it was quite good, if you wanted to write a letter that was the place to do it.

Just before Christmas a concert was arranged in the canteen, H.Q Company had held one in their canteen last week. The concert party was some local boys and girls mainly singing and dancing to the local squeaky music. The final highlight of the show was one of the girls pretending to be nailed to a cross with the iron dogs we used to hammer in the frames of the gun bunkers to hold them together. The whole show only lasted about an hour and the place was packed until the Provost Sergeant along with the Corporal in charge of the night guard arrived and called a halt. They rounded the concert party up and took them away.

They were not the only ones who had come to entertain as they had brought with them more than the singers and dancers. While the concert party was keeping us busy on our side of the camp their mates were over the other side in the rifle company lines offering services not normally available on a cold night in Korea. That was the end of the entertainment program for the whole year - even the out door cinema had lost its appeal, too cold.

Christmas day arrived and we got the Padre coming round wishing everyone a Merry Christmas and giving out fags, I think he was looking for customers. The Duke of Wellingtons had built him a little church before they had left with a spire and a shell case to ring for a bell. He did get a few more than the usual Sunday morning brigade. The company officers came and served us lunch as is the army tradition with the company commander Major Lowens wandering around merry Christmasing. The meal was alright as we got two lots of meat, chicken and some pork plus a small bottle of beer each. Some roast potatoes would have been nice but we had to make do with the Pom. However we did get some Christmas pudding and custard and to top it all off there was another issue of the New Zealand cheese and butter on the tables. Before the officers all cleared off back to their mess Major. Lowens announced there would be some rum punch in the canteen tonight.

The afternoon was spent keeping warm until our evening meal. Dead legs and Wilf had put on a bit of a buffet with some hot soup, cold meat and tinned salmon. A chunk of Australian tinned Christmas cake was given to all and with a mug of tea it all went down well. All we had to do now was wait for the company commanders punch bowl. It was seven o'clock when he rolled up at the canteen with a two gallon dixie half full of hot water from the cook house. With great ceremony he tipped half a bottle of red wine in it. The word on this was he had it with his dinner in the mess, it was rubbish and this was his way of getting rid of it. Next to go in the pot was a bottle of cordial followed by the crowning glory, a half bottle of rum. 'Right lads get your mugs' was the shout before the surprise; it wasn't free the bugger charged us three pence a time for it and you only got a small ladle full. There we were, daring each other not to buy any but none of us had the nerve to refuse did we? There was plenty of beer at one and three pence a bottle and some one came up with a bottle of Lucky Seven Korean whiskey so we had a good night anyway.

It was back to the grindstone on Boxing Day and Jim became a Sergeant again in the New Year Honours. It was a pleasure to see the back of the fag scrounging old fool out of our tent. As January came in the weather seemed to be getting colder and some nights the temperature was down below twenty degrees. If the weather was bright and sunny it would be freezing all day. If it was misty and over cast it would just struggle to get above freezing. The wind was the main chill factor and you needed to apply the army face cream (lanolin) around your lips and nose. You had to be careful of what you touched especially at night and early morning. Touching metal with the bare skin it would stick to you and when you pulled it of it took the skin off. These were called cold metal burns and took some time to heal in these conditions. The M.T had to put on a nightshift to run the lorry's and jeeps for half and hour in the night to stop them freezing up although they all had anti freeze in them.

In spite of the conditions things carried on just the same, digging the trenches although the ground was now frozen solid for a foot depth. The only extras we got for the cold was if you were on guard or out playing soldiers at night you got a tin of soup. This had a tube though the middle of the tin and when you pulled the tab off it fizzed and heated the soup. It got red hot and you spent more time warming yourself up on it than eating it. Help arrived in the middle of January in the form of things called space heaters. These were installed two to a tent and we had to cut a square out of the tent roof to put a meal plate in to take the chimney. The heaters ran on petrol and we were given strict instructions of how to operate them any deviation would result in the heaters being confiscated. A five gallon jerry can of petrol per day would be issued for each heater and this would give five hours running time. They were great and warmed the tent although we were still frost covered in the mornings. Most of us had them on for about four hours in the evening and finished what was left of the fuel in the morning. They were a god send as you could heat a drink up on them and in the mornings warm up empty dried vegetable tins of water to wash in. With all of us in the tent washing and shaving in them they got a bit soupy by the time the last man had shaven.

Support Company was Duty Company at the end of the month and I got a guard duty. There were two places we had to guard the camp and a check point down the valley in a narrow pass by Kamak Sam. I got the camp guard which was stationed in the guard room, a tent by the main gate. The jail part was separated from guard post by some barbed wire but there was nothing to stop the inmates escaping out of the back of the tent. It was the barbed wire between the jail and guard post that had been the source of some amusement in the battalion a few weeks ago. It was the practice of the duty bugler to hang is bugle on it. He had blown first post at seven o'clock alright but when he came to blow last post at ten o'clock he couldn't. The Provost Sergeants favourite jail bird, Mr Dawson had been in residence and had the usual Pom with his evening meal. Dawson had rolled some up in a ball and stuffed it down the bugle while no one was looking. Everyone thought it hilarious except the poor old bugler.

Chapter Twenty Eight

At the end of January we were out in the field playing soldiers with the rest of the twenty nine brigade. The whole scheme was for five days and would end with us doing some live firing at night. The platoon would be together for most of this exercise so I would be the cook. Captain Bow had scrounged a hydra burner from some where for me to cook on but I had a cooker of my own. This was an old ammo tin with some holes knocked in it and a piece of expanded metal on top. The fuel was the old thick grease soaked cardboard tuxes that shells and mortar bombs had been packed in. These burnt long and well and a bit too fierce to fry on but for boiling things were great. Plus you got a warm off it.

We spent the days moving around the district along with the rest of the brigade; The Argyle and Southerland Islanders, an Australian infantry regiment, supported by tanks and a battery of Royal Artillery twenty five pounders. With me being the cook for the platoon I usually got to move around in the back of the platoon commander's jeep along with Somers his wireless operator and Mock his driver. Mocks proper name was Cooks but his had earned the name Mock as when we had a soup issue he always wanted the Mock Turtle.

It was very cold and we didn't get a lot of sleep. Captain. Bow and Mock tried to sleep in the jeep. Somers and I clipped our ponchos together and made a little bivouac to kip in. There was a self heating soup issue most nights and we got a rum ration. The soup we saved until bed time to warm our feet on before we drank it. It was while on this scheme that I nearly got my first metal burn early one morning. I brushed my hand on one of my mess tins and it stuck to my hand. I didn't try to pull it off since if you did it would take the skin off so I let it warm up a bit until it dropped off with out doing any damage.

The whole scheme came to an end with a night firing exercise covering a river crossing. One section set up their guns and the rest of the platoon zeroed off them. I got roped in as a number three on a gun as Baxter; Corporal. Campbell's usual number three had gone sick. The Mortars were doing their firing at the same time and probably at the same target.

It was all over by one in the morning and we bivouacked down for the night. As the grey light of dawn came I was the cook again and did the breakfast. We couldn't just pack up and go back to camp but had to withdraw as per the military hand book. As our jeep went back up the road it started to misfire and it wasn't long before it stopped altogether. Mock got out and looked under the bonnet and tried to start the jeep. It wouldn't go and at this point Captain. Bow asked Mock what was wrong with it. Mock said 'the f--king f--kers f--king f—ked Sir', Captain Bow looked at Mock in amazement. 'That's the best bit of English I've heard in a long time, can you repeat it so I can write it down'.

The M.T towed us back to camp with a fifteen hundred weight truck and we spent what was left of the day cleaning the guns and our equipment.

As the weather got warmer it got wetter and we got freezing rain. It had been dry over most of the winter although we had snow on a couple of occasions but only just enough to just whiten the ground. By March the rains were quite heavy and I got caught proper. I was twenty one on the ninth of March. Most them in our tent reckoned it was traditional to be given the day off so after breakfast I went to the company office and saw the Sergeant. Major. He asked what our platoon was doing that day- working on the gun positions in the hills. 'Good' said the Sergeant Major 'you are excused that now go to the stores and draw a pick and a spade then report back here'.

When I got back to the office I was given the job of digging a monsoon trench around the outside of it. To add insult to injury no one had sent me a birthday card, not even Granny Mac.

One day at the start of April it had pored down all day and as we returned from the digging we found ourselves cut off. The stream that ran through the camp had swollen to a river fifty yards wide. It had been well up when we crossed it this morning but nothing like the torrent it was now it had started to flood the rifle companies lines and the airstrip. I think the brass was more concerned about the airstrip than the rifle companies as all the mail, papers and correspondence came and went by plane. Sergeant Bridge decided we should wade across and it was chest deep and pushed us side ways as we crossed. As we reached the other side the assault pioneer platoon arrived to blow up the fancy bridge they had built between the camps last autumn. As Sergeant Bridge lined us up to march us back to our lines a squaddie caught my arm it was Dickey Henley a lad I was at school with, he had just come out from Lichfield. How he recognised me under a soggy bush hat and poncho I don't know.

Captain. Bow suggested we should go to the showers where we could change our wet clothes for dry ones but as that was on the same stream that had probably been overwhelmed as well. Once the assault platoon had blown the bridge it relieved it a bit and we never had it that bad again. After it had subsided the remains of a couple of squaddies had been washed out, Australians according to the Dracula squad who came to collect then. Although the rains went on into May things carried on as normal only with your poncho on.

Since before Christmas some squaddies had been going on leave to Japan and at the end of May it was my turn. It was for five days at a camp in Tokyo. Now this leave had been a bit of a hit and miss arrangement as you might not go on the day you were supposed to. You travelled there on an American transport plane and if they had the room you went if they didn't you had to wait. There were three of us from Support Company, Spud Murphy, Norman Brightwell and myself down to go on the five day leave. On the morning of the great day we boarded the lorry along with squaddies from the rifle companies and set of for Seoul. At the American airbase we were taken to the Commonwealth Forces office photo graft and given an identity card in Japanese with our picture stapled to it. The plane we were to travel on was the main American army transport plane at the time, a Globe Master which we boarded by walking up a ramp at the front of the plane. The cabin had two decks and the seating was just canvas slings in a row along the side of the plane and two rows back to back down the middle on both upper and lower decks. I along with the other squaddies from the Stafford's was on the top deck and it was the first time in a plane for all of us. Were we nervous, but we were certainly not going to show it were we? A sick bag was given to each of us and the plane took off and we were on our way. The flight was uneventful and you couldn't see a lot out of the portholes. Things changed as we got towards the coast of Japan as we flew into a thunder storm and the plane started shuddering and going up and down. I was fascinated by the overhead crane rails that ran along the roof of the plane as they were twisting and bending as the plane went up and down. You could feel the relief of everybody when the plane landed at Tokyo.

All British army squaddies together with a Maori squaddie, several Australians and a lad from the Indian army were picked up by a lorry and taken to the British Common Wealth Camp in Tokyo. It was still pouring with rain when we got there. A Sgt showed us to a barrack room and said he had arranged with the cook house to put us some food on. None of us had eaten since our breakfast this morning, probably a good thing given our flight over Japan. The food was pretty good and tasted better for being on a plate and not out of a mess tin. After we had stuffed ourselves we went to the recreation room bar for a drink. While we were drinking our beer a lady of the W.V.S. came and told us about the trips out they ran. These were to places of interest around Tokyo but we needed to book these trips early as they only had one motor coach. She also pointed out places of interest were we could go ourselves, like Ginza Market. Although we were in a large barrack room with squaddies from several countries it was comfortable and had clean sheets on the beds and we had a good night.

Next morning we were overloaded with information on the high spots around Tokyo. We had heard all about it by the squaddies back at camp who had been before us. However we had already decided our first trip would be to Ginza Market on the Tokyo underground. Before we could set off we needed to change our B.A.F. in Japanese yen. There was a post office and shop by the recreation room and we changed it there, I think we got two thousand and four hundred yen to the pound. There was a station just out side the camp and armed with all the advice from our barrack room clientele, off we went.

Ginza Market was much larger than we had expected and had stalls selling every thing. The cameras, wireless and electrical goods were all much more modern and better quality than we could get back home. I splashed out on a box of fishing tackle; rod, reel, lines, hooks and a load of flies all for five thousand yen. After spending a couple of hours around the market we wandered down the shops in Shibuya and came across one selling cloth. I remembered Granny Mac saying if I ever got to Japan send her some silk. I went in and looked for silk and found something that looked like it. It might have been nylon for all I know. There was I pointing at it saying silk and the shop assistants grinning and nodding their heads. I indicated that I wanted to buy some and they got a stick out which looked about a yard to me so I bought three brightly coloured pieces. These I posted off to Granny Mac as soon as we got back to camp.

Before I did anything else I went and put my name down for tomorrow's trip to a place called Kamakura. After our evening meal we decided to go out for the night. There were some bars in the street outside the camp but the word in our barrack room was that all the high spots are down Shibuya. So, on the underground again but the journey

184

we made seemed more over ground than underground. At the first bar we came to we were dragged in by the girls waiting outside we knew this was the normal thing, hostesses they called them. When you bought a drink you had to buy them one as well. For this you could sit with your hand on her thigh anything else was an optional extra of course. Most of the other clientele in the bar seemed to be American squaddies. There was a bit of a band and a topless dancer with tassels on her tits with most of her dancing just swinging the tassels in different directions. The girls fetched us a beer each and something coloured in a glass for themselves. When we saw the bill for the drinks we nearly passed out. To get our money's worth of entertainment we made the beer last us over an hour with the girls trying to get us to drink up. It was a struggle to make good our escape with the hostesses trying to drag us back and although they couldn't speak a lot of English they seemed to know Anglo Saxon pretty well by what they were calling us. It was back to the bars by the camp gate where they still had the hostesses but it was much cheaper. We would come out here for a drink at night for the rest of our stay in Tokyo. The drill was to have a few drinks in the camp canteen bar until it closed at ten o'clock then we would have an hour down an outside bar.

I was first on the coach for our trip to a place called Kamakura with a Korean lady who was married to a Sgt in the Australian army, she was our guide for the day. As we drove through the outskirts of Tokyo and into Yokohama it was all heavy industry. Japan was a far cry from Korea. This was a modern country geared up to produce modern things. This was pretty evident by the electrical goods on sale in the markets. Our first stop in Kamakura was at the Hasedera shrine. This housed an eleven headed statue carved in the year seven eleven A.D. There had been two carved out of a large camphor tree some where else in Japan. One had been set adrift in the sea with prayers for it to bring good luck to where ever it got washed up. This one had landed at Kamakura in seven thirty-six A.D. and had been set up in a shrine by a local noble man. There were hundreds of little statues of kids outside. The lady told us were Jizo statues dedicated to the souls of unborn children.

The next stop was at a Buddhist Shrine with a statue of Budda about fifty feet tall. This had been cast in the eleventh century and was hollow inside and you could walk up the steps into the head, which we all did of course. After the Buddhist shrine visit we were left to wander round until four o'clock. There were several other shrines to see but the two we had visited were the high spots. We soon got tired of wandering round in the rain and all ended up in a bar. To most of us it had been a very interesting day and there were other trips to come.

The next day we decided to have a day in the camp. As well as a good recreation room with a large record collection the camp had a large lake. You could swim in it or have a boat out or borrow draw rods and fish in it all for free. At the end nearest the barracks there were some concrete towers in the deep water. These had been used to train the Japanese sub-mariners during the last world war according to what we were told. Well we just had to have a swim just for a better look didn't we.

Thursday was an interesting day as we did the high spots of Tokyo. Our first call was their houses of parliament the Diet as the guide called it. My main memories of it were a pool outside with the biggest gold fish I'd ever seen in it and the box where the Emperor sat. It was positioned so the Emperor could see the parliament and they couldn't see him. Apparently he had been treated as some sort of deity up until the last world war. The Christian Cathedral was our next port of call and after that one or two shrines but it had been another great day. The trip on our final day was only a half day one to the Judo school. Once there we were taken up to a balcony above a large hall where they were teaching the students various holds and throws. Later we were taken down into the hall and given a demonstration on Jujitsu and shown some holds and throws. Most of the squaddies thought this the best trip we had done, I liked the one to Kamakura myself.

The leave was over all too soon and early next morning we were lined up waiting for the lorry to take us to the American air base. When we got to the air base which was some way out of Tokyo the plane was waiting, so we were marched onto a Globe Master straight away. With in a couple of minutes we were on the run-way. The plane revved up and sped off down the run-way but came to a shuddering stop at the end. The plane taxied round to the airport building and we were all told to file off. The lot of us were lined up and told the plane had a fault in one of its engines and we would have to wait while it was repaired. The next thing was that after it had been repaired it would have to wait for another take off slot. The officer pointed out that the airport was very busy as they were flying military equipment to Indo China. From this we all gathered that this was were the next war was going to be.

After we had sat around for a few hours the officer came and said we would be given some lunch. All the Commonwealth squaddies had to sign a docket before we got severed. This was so the Americans could recover the cost of the lunch from the Commonwealth Division. It was a great lunch served on a tray divided into compartments and if this was the usual American menu, we were in the wrong army. The only complaint was there was no mug of tea; coffee, iced chocolate or orange juice was the only choice.

It was late afternoon when we got back on the plane and we took off alright this time. The flight was uneventful this time; well we were old hands at flying now. It was late in the evening when we landed at Seoul and as we filed through the airport building were given tins of food. These were tins out of the American one man packs and we got a tin of dinner and one of fruit each. Mine was a tin of spaghetti and ground beef and a tin of pears. I'd had the beef and spaghetti before and I liked it mind you anything would have tasted good. There was a lorry from the Stafford's waiting for us and he had been there since early afternoon.

It was well after midnight when we got back to camp but it had been a great experience.

Chapter Twenty Nine

As the wet season gradually petered out it became very warm. The R.S.M's parades were back on with a new 'get us fit after the winter' scheme i.e. cross county runs. These were a bit embarrassing for us British army super squaddies as the Korean squaddies left us all standing. They went over the hills like mountain goats. Another thing that got us annoyed was Henry (the Korean P.T.I) Billy Muscles had with him. He had introduced us to Korean wrestling which was like arm wrestling standing up and the object was to throw your opponent off his feet. Henry was like all the Korean squaddies, about six stone soaking wet. We all had a go at him and even chaps twice his weight couldn't throw him, apparently he had been the China games champion before the war. Dai Evens took it a bit hard and made plans of how he could beat Henry by lifting him as well as pushing side ways. Dai was a big lad, well built and about six feet tall. No one knew why we called him Dai as he wasn't Welsh, he came from Tamworth. At the end of our next P.T session which usually ended with the wrestling we gave Dai first go at Henry. It lasted about two seconds with Dai ending up on the floor with a dislocated knee. That finished the Korean wrestling, it was banned after that.

At our next P.T session Billy Muscles started by lining us up and looking closely at our eyebrows. This was his way of sorting out who had done some boxing. He had decided it was time the battalion had a boxing team. The only volunteer he got from Support Company was a chap named Froggot in the assault platoon. However Billy did get his boxing team and he even got them excused duties for his training. Though the summer they were quite a success in the fights in the boxing competitions against other regiments.

If Billy had a boxing team, Captain Bow had to have a cricket team didn't he? He came up with a bat and wickets from somewhere and advertised on battalion orders, a trial for would be players on the football pitch. There were quite a few turned up for Bows' trial and he sorted out a first eleven. They were not quite as successful as the boxers as they only played one match and that was a disaster. A team from the Canadian army, all big lads, came to play them one Sunday morning. The Canadians batted first and instead of bending down and batting normal they stood up like baseball players do. They knocked the ball everywhere scoring sixes with nearly every ball; Bow was tearing his hair out. The Canadians won by a large margin and the cricket team never played again.

Boxing and hockey were the main sports now the football season was over. It made life a little quieter now there wasn't the arguing between the Baggies, Wolves and Manchester supporters clubs. Tommy Dankes had to find something else to make a book on. He had been taking a few bets on the outcome of matches over the winter. Toms Dad was a local bookmaker in Wednesbury and Tom was just carrying on the family tradition and as he said there was some easy money to be had. There were always wild claims as to how many goals the team they supported were going to win by. So if they wanted to back their fancy Tom would take their money.

My only sporting achievement was to play in goal for the support company hockey team on a couple of occasions and we lost both times. It was while playing hockey that I got a smack in the teeth with a stick. One tooth got broken and the other knocked lose. I reported sick the following morning and was sent to the little field hospital about half a mile down the valley from our camp. I walked down there, which was a bit disappointing as most of the patients arrived on a stretcher strapped to a helicopter. The dentist got me in the chair as soon as I arrived and got to work. His assistant held my head while he pulled both the teeth out and it was all over in a couple of minutes. It was a bit sharp while he was doing it and a little anaesthetic would have been nice but he did give me some aspirins. Before I left the hospital a Cpl told me to wash my mouth out twice a day with salt water and to report back there in twelve weeks time.

The weather was mainly dry and sunny now and we were back in tropical dress. To cool down on hot days after parades we would have a dip in a little pool by the M.T. This was formed by the stream that flowed down the valley to the river Imjin. After a while the sick parade queue got a lot longer with squaddies with ear problems. The M.O reckoned it was probably swimming in the M.T pool that was the cause so that got banned. It was on the same stream that the shower unit was on and we didn't get ear problems from that.

But as the weather got hotter, so did we and Sid was the first to fall victim. After he had been to see the M.O and came back with the cure we couldn't keep our faces straight. They had given him a seven pound tin of D.D.T powder. Sid had got the 'Sandy MacNabs' crabs and he had to powder himself and his underwear with the D.D.T. Quite a few

189

in the battalion went sick with them and the source of the infection was traced back to the clothes exchange at the showers. We could still use the showers but changing our underwear was forbidden. Arrangements were made for us to boil all our underwear and hence forth we would be responsible for washing them. At first the boiling was done by using an empty biscuit tin but eventually the Sergeant Major set up a half fifty gallon drum with a hydro burner to warm the water for our washing.

The Sergeant Major was also instrumental in making the company a shower. He got an empty tin that the chipped vegetables came in and knocked a row of holes in it about a third of the way down the side of the tin. He then knocked a hole just above them each side of the tin and put a bar through for it to swing on. He then scrounged two tent poles from somewhere, knocked them in the ground and mounted the biscuit tin on top with a bit of cord dangling down so you could tip the tin forward. You filled the tin up to the shower holes then pulled the cord forward until the water reached the shower holes. You wet and soaped your self up and washed it off with the rest of the water; mind you if you pulled the cord too hard you got it all in one go.

Most Sunday afternoons if I wasn't on duty I would go fishing down the Imjin. I would scrounge a couple of bread crusts off Wilf the cook on the understanding I didn't bring any fish back to camp for him to cook. The fishing was good and we always caught a few Mirror Carp; most of them quite large, about eighteen inches was probably the best we ever caught. Another little treat while we were down the river and out of site of the camp was to have a shoot with the pistol Pagie had acquired on our way here. It had passed through a few hands in the time we had been here, usually when the current owner was short of money but anyway I was the present owner. The surprising thing was that the powers that be hadn't found out we had it because they would have taken it off us. There were always sounds of shooting going on so our few shots at things floating down the river never got noticed. I soon got tired of it and scrounging around for ammo and sold it to Harold Mayes for a couple of quid when I was short of beer money. He would come to grief with it later.

The war had been over for twelve months now and the locals seemed to be getting back to normal. It was funny to see them walking out at the weekend; the husband wearing a white robe and a stove pipe hat, his wife walking behind him with the kids following in order of precedence. All in a line down the road bowing to every one they met. I could see that happening back home.

We were doing more battalion parades and having tent inspections now and we even got a C.O's inspection one Saturday morning. This turned into a bit of a giggle due to Pagie who had always been a bit of a 'nutter'. Pagie had found a bit of tube from somewhere and tied it to the front rail of his bed. He would sit on his on the bed and pretend it was a motor bike making all the noises. On the morning of the C.O's inspection Corporal. Woodall had told Pagie to get rid of it. But when the C.O arrived accompanied by the M.O our company commander and Sergeant Major it was still tied to his bed. It was our company commander Major. Lowends who asked Pagie what it was doing tied to his bed rail. 'It's my little motor bike Sir' and proceeded to show the C.O how it worked even kick starting it. The C.O and our company commander didn't know whether to laugh or cry but we could see the Sergeant Major turning purple. He was about to get Pagie marched off to the guard room when to M.O stepped in and detailed Corporal. Woodall to bring Pagie to the Medical Room when the inspection ended. The outcome was that Pagie got excused duties for a week with strict instructions that he be kept out of the sun. After his week inside he was never to leave the tent without wearing his bush hat.

It was unusual to see the M.O accompanying the C.O on an inspection and when battalion orders were posted on Monday we found out why. Several squddies in the division had been taken ill with something called Haemorrhagic fever, known as Songo. This was carried by the rats who had been brought south with the Chinese army supplies during the conflict. This disease turned your white blood cells green or something like that. If anyone had headaches or felt dizzy they were to report sick immediately. From now on our beds would be sprayed on a weekly basis and arrangements to do it were put in place. Ken Foster got the job in our platoon and with it being a very important job got made up to Lance Corporal; He was issued with a Flit gun and charged with making sure all the beds were sprayed each Sunday morning. Ken now became known as Songo ever after.

The regiment decided it was going to show off a bit, but of course we squaddies were only invited to do the dirty work. It was announced that the band and corps of drums would beat the retreat. On the day a couple of marquees were set up, one each end of the football pitch come parade ground. On the evening all the knobs from the

Commonwealth Div plus the American army were there. Our officers were strutting about with the arrogance of empire builders wearing their white monkey jackets with their medals dangling. The flunkies from the officers and Sergeant's Messes were all in white jackets waiting on them. The band wearing full ceremonial rig beat the retreat and it ended with searchlight lighting up a cross on the hill where the Gloucestershire regiment made their last stand during the battle of the Imjin while a lone bugler blew the last post.

As we got into July an E.N.S.A concert party put on a show in the N.A.A.F.I road house they had built below Castle Hill. They were out from the U.K to entertain the troops. The N.A.A.F.I hall wasn't very large so we were carted down to see them two companies at a time. It was a good show but I can't remember who was on the program so they couldn't have been very famous. Other than the concert party our main entertainment was the pictures or following the boxing team. One of the highlights I remember was the news reporter from the Reynolds news giving a talk. He was a regular visitor when we went out on manoeuvres or were digging in the hills; he would come and talk to the squaddies and take some photos of what we were doing. His talk was very interesting as he explained how Korea had been ruled by Japan from nineteen ten until after the Second World War. Following the surrender of Japan in nineteen forty five, American administrators divided the country along the thirty eight parallel, with American troops occupying the south and Soviet troops the north. A new house of parliament was built in Seoul and reunification talks held but a failure to hold elections in nineteen forty eight deepened divisions between the both sides. The North established a Communist government and the thirty eight parallel became a political border between the two Koreas. Reunification talks continued but there were skirmishes along the border until the twenty fifth of June nineteen fifty when North Korea invaded the south. America came to their aid but the armies of the north pushed them back to a small area around Pusan in the south of the country. A lot of other countries now came to the aid of the Americans and an amphibious landing was made at Inchon to cut off the retreating North Korean army. The North Korea army were pushed back over the thirty eight parallel and up to the Yalu River, the border with China. It was now the Chinese who became involved and pushed the united Nations force back over the over the thirty eight parallel in April nineteen fifty one. From then on it became a stable trench war until the armistice was signed on the twenty seventh of July nineteen fifty three. He gave us the details of why General Macarthur was removed as supreme commander and replaced by a General Ridgeway. He reckoned Macarthur had dreams of invading China and had a lot of support in America to try and do it. He rambled on for an hour about Korean history and politics but it was all very interesting.

Our main pastime was still digging new positions in the hills and as Dave and I was extending a trench we dug into a grave. By the look of the bones it was a few hundred years old. Sergeant Jones who was in charge of us at the time said just chuck the bones down the bank. When you find the skull bury it before some idiot takes it back to camp. The funny bit was we never did find a skull. Whoever it was got buried without a head.

It was while up in the hills digging one day that we got introduced to a new lunch time beverage. Our lunch would be brought up in a jeep and trailer and always come with a dixie of tea. This day we didn't get any tea, instead we got a dixie of green liquid which the driver called citrus juice. The stuff was horrible; it put your teeth on edge and made you screw your arse up. It soon got a different name that rhymes with citrus juice. This was to be the only lunch time drink available from now on and we must drink it to stop us catching scurvy, so they told us.

Some of the company squaddies were now due to get demobbed; Joe Brookes and two of the lads who the East Yorkshire regiment left behind from our platoon. Sailor Bowden was another and I don't think he was to keen to go home. He was in the canteen moaning about his girlfriend wanting to get married when he got home. Sailor reckoned she was rushing things as they had only been engaged for fourteen years. However he didn't sign on again so home he went to the slaughter.

With squaddies now getting demobbed new trainees would be brought into the platoon and to make room for them some of us would be transferred back to rifle companies. Names of the chaps to be transferred were posted on company orders; five or six squaddies for each platoon in Support Company would go. I would be one from the M.M.G platoon together with Cpl. Bird, Tom Dankes, Billy Green and Lambert. John Rudd, now a Cpl who had joined the army the same day as me was one to go from the assault pioneer platoon.

After our normal morning parade on the day of our move we were told to pack our kit and report to the company office. As I arrived at the office with my kit packed and ready to learn which company I would be going to, Captain. Dow arrived on the scene. 'Where you off to Power?' he asked me, "I'm being transferred, Sir" I replied. "Are you" he said, 'we will see about that!' and dived into the company office. After a few minutes he came out and said 'go and put your kit back Power you're going nowhere! You're my spare man and can do most of the jobs in the platoon, so you're staying put.'

I was still in the M.M.G. platoon when I got demobbed fifteen months later.

Chapter Thirty

Now that I was back in the platoon I got detailed for guard duty. This time it would be on the route eleven check point up the valley. The road was very narrow at this point and Sgt. Bridge reckoned it was where the Chinese army had a lot of their soldiers run over by the tanks of The Kings Royal Irish Hussars. Apparently the some of the Chinese squaddies had just stud on the road and tried to stop the tanks with their small arms. The tanks had ran over them as they rushed down the valley to support the Northumberland Fusiliers, Ulster Rifles and a Belgian infantry battalion during the battle of the Imjin in nineteen fifty one. This of course gave rise to tales of Chinese squaddies patrolling the road at midnight but I wasn't on stag at midnight to find out and the chap who was didn't see them either. The check point must have been set up during the war to check vehicles going up to the front and there didn't seem any point in it being there any more. We just stopped vehicles and asked where they were going and that was all there was to it. We did the normal guard roster of two hours on and four hours off. There was a bit of traffic during the day but after about eight o'clock in the evening very little. It was while on duty here that I was amused by watching the locals fishing. I'd often wondered why they collected our old wireless batteries; they used them to catch fish. The stream was fairly deep along past the guard post and gin clear as it hadn't reached the shower tents yet. The locals would get an empty biscuit tin and cut the bottom out of it, fix a length of the old telephone wire to opposite sides of the tin and plug one into the negative terminal of the battery. They placed the tin in the water and threw some bait into it. When the fish swam in to investigate they would plug the other wire into the positive battery terminal. The fish would flip over on its side and float to the surface. They had to be quick scooping the fish up as they usually recovered and swam off after a few seconds. They were only little fish about four or five inches long but they cooked them with their rice. Why they didn't go down the Imjin and catch some bigger fish I could never understand. However it kept us entertained for an afternoon, we were fascinated.

We were relieved at six o'clock in the evening, the same time that the camp guard changed. It seems we had missed all the fun last night as there had been a shoot-up in the H.Q. Company canteen. The one doing the shooting was a Corporal. Mundrey the Quarter Masters. chief store man. Mundrey was a very old soldier over six feet tall and about eighteen stone in weight and tales of him abounded like he had once been the battalion Regimental Sergeant Major. He never did parades like the rest of us squaddies and seemed to have more sway than his rank of Corporal would suggest. The incident started with a visit of some Americans to the canteen. Although the war had been over for more that twelve months now the Americans still went about armed to the teeth. Corporal Mundrey had borrowed a pistol off one of the Americans on the excuse he would just like to look at it. No sooner had he got it, he started firing at the bottles at the back of the counter `Wild West` style. However they managed to get the pistol of him before he killed some one and he was taken to the guard room. The senior officers seemed to take a, `well who'd have thought it` view of the whole thing and I don't think he was ever charged. What did come out of it was anyone visiting the camp bearing weapons would have to leave them in the guard room before they entered the camp and another warning on the perils of drinking Lucky Seven Korean whiskey. It was made with industrial alcohol or so the M.O. claimed. Mundrey was kept in the jail for a while but just seemed to vanish after a while and no one seemed to know what happened to him. He had always seemed a bit strange and the poor old soul had probably lost his marbles altogether, another one to be kept out of the sun.

I was up on company orders one night to report sick the following morning. This was a surprise to me as I didn't know I was ill. I duly reported to the medical room the following morning to be told I was to go to the field hospital where I'd had my teeth out. I was sat in the chair and was expecting to lose some more teeth until a Sergeant of the Army Dental Corps said 'we are going to make you some false teeth Power'. They got me biting down on little trays of stuff to get the shape of my gums, given a mug of water to wash my mouth out and told to come back in a week's time. This I did and they had made a plate with two teeth on it for me. It didn't fit too well but after they had ground it here and there it wasn't too bad. They were obviously pleased with their handy work by the look on their kissers. For a while it was strange having them in your mouth but I got used to it.

I was now entitled to some more leave only this time it was called rest and recreation. This was at a town on the coast called Inchon where the U.N. forces had mounted an amphibious invasion in nineteen fifty. The leave or rest would be for six days Monday until Saturday. Ten of us squaddies were taken in a lorry on Monday morning as it was only a two hour drive away. The camp was in the grounds of what had been a Monastery wrecked during the invasion. The accommodation was in Nissen huts and there was a N.A.A.F.I. there but the beach was separated from the camp by a sea wall. This didn't matter as the beach was all black mud. There was a large deep fresh water pool at the far end of the camp and rods we could borrow to fish with. The emphasis here was on rest the only recreation was a dart board in the N.A.A.F.I. and a W.V.S. lady who held free bingo sessions with fags as prizes on Tuesdays and Fridays. The fishing was good in the evenings with some big fish in the old Monastery pool; it was the monks stock pool, so they told us. The only other excitement was on Wednesday morning watching an old Mitchell bomber towing a target over the sea while the Americans fired anti air craft shells at it. However it was better than being back up the Imjin doing parades. We had a good week lying on our chariots reading with a bit of fishing and the N.A.A.F.I. in the evening, it was a good skive. It all came to an end on Saturday morning when the lorry came and took us back to camp.

With there being some new chaps in the platoon we were now doing quite a lot of training. They had only done their basic training when they came out to Korea and needed to train to use the Vickers machine gun. The platoon hadn't done much gun training since coming to Korea as we'd had other things to do. As was usual we all did the gun training, driver and wireless operators every one except the R.E.M.E. fitter. As part of the training program a live firing exercise was arranged. This would be held on an area used as a firing range where the rivers Hatan and the Imjin met. This was the place that the Belgian battalion, which was part of the British twenty ninth brigade held during the battles of the Imjin. The afternoon before the exercise was spent loading the ammo into the canvas belts, sometimes it came already belted but this time it was loose ammo. The following morning after breakfast and first parade we set off for the exercise. I was cook for the day as usual and we had the British five man ration boxes for our food. When we got to the ranges it was first things first so that meant a brew-up. For the lunch I did a stew that always went down well and it was easy to do. This was finished with some tinned fruit and a few boiled sweets all topped off with a mug of tea of course.

Most of the day was used to give some experience to the new

squaddies but all the gun crew members had to shoot. It all ended with the guns firing at the trunk of a tree about four hundred yards away just to use up the ammo. The idea was to try and bring it down but they didn't manage it. I washed the dixie's up in the river while the guns were being packed up. It was all go when we arrived back at camp to get the guns and equipment cleaned and oiled before our evening meal.

Our next little caper was due to the peace talks being held at a place called Panmunjom. After arguing for over twelve months they had agreed to release some more Chinese and Korean prisoners of war. We only saw prisoners when they were employed cleaning out the ditches at the side of the roads. They had always been known to us as the 'Gooks' which I think was probably an American term for the Chinese army. The ones in our area were to be taken over the Imjin and up to the thirty eight parallel and released. This would give them the opportunity to go home or return to the 'free west' as the Americans put it. The Stafford's were to go down to the river and just wait but we never found out why. Some of the wags reckoned it was to welcome them all back but none came, the prisoners all went home.

It was while hanging about down there that Dave told me his father had retired from the army. Since his retirement he had started to take the Walsall Observer, he had been a Walsall man before joining the army and still had family there. Dave told me his mother had offered to send it out to me after his Dad had read it if I wanted it. Did I just, and his mother continued to sent it to me up until I was demobbed.

It was now posted on Battalion orders that our next posting would be Hong Kong and we would be moving at the end of October. There was now a scramble to get things up in the hills finished although I don't think most of it would ever be finished. It was while working on our defensive position up there that I acquired a watch. Sergeant. Jones had bought himself a fancy watch from the N.A.A.F.I. and was now short of cash and trying to flog it. He wanted twenty five quid for it, he said he had paid thirty two quid for it. I offered him five and after some bargaining we agreed to toss a coin. If I won I would pay five quid for it, if I lost twenty although I would have had to draw my credits to pay him. But no one had a coin with us all using B.A.F, however the Sergeant had a deck of cards in his jeep so we drew highest card and I won. It was a self winding watch made in Germany and it kept good time.

One morning while we were up there digging we got a visit from the General commanding the Commonwealth Division, a Major General West. He just mooched around asking questions as to what we were doing. The main interest was his jeep as he had one of the new Austin Champs. It was a monster thing compared to the American jeeps we had. According to the driver it would do five forward speeds in off road gear and five in normal gear. Due to some quirk of the design it also had five reverse gears. Our M.T. had been trying some new vehicles mainly a Humber fifteen hundred weight and a Bedford Q.L. The Humber was a much bigger vehicle than the old Morris but the Q.L. the same size as the old one, it just had a different shaped cab. The General usually drove around the divisional area with just his driver and adjutant unlike the American senior officers who always had two squaddies with sawn-off shot guns sitting in the back of their jeeps.

It was autumn now and the Elephant grass was tall and dry so there were a few fires breaking out. I think a lot of it was deliberate to explode all the abandoned ammo that was lying about.

Once it got going there were little explosions everywhere it was burning. The area around the camp had been cleared for just this eventuality because there was no way we could have put it out.

Things in general were just now starting to run down ready for our move. A few squaddies had received letters over the time we had been in Korea informing them their girlfriends were marrying some one else. These were known as `Dear John letters` after a Country and Weston song about American squaddies being jilted. The news was round the company like wildfire for any one who had received one. It was always a great giggle to everyone bar the poor sod who had got it; squaddies are a cruel lot. Another of the little games was asking the chaps who were married what they think their wives would be doing to night. Everyone seemed to get along and in spite of the jibes I never recall there being any punch-ups.

Battalion orders announced the advance party for Hong Kong would leave the first week in October. This would be some H.Q. company staff plus an officer and two N.C.O's from all the other company's to help prepare the ground for the arrival of the battalion in Hong Kong. Orders also stated that personnel with less than six weeks to serve before returning home would not be accompanying the Regiment. They would go to the Commonwealth transit camp at Kure in Japan and be shipped home from there when their time came. This only affected two squaddies in Support Company, Dave and the A.C.C. cook Wilf. Dave and I had been buddies ever since he had joined the South Stafford's when we were stationed in Ireland.

I don't remember any advance party from another regiment coming to our camp. Now the war had been over for more than twelve months I think we would be part of the reduction in the troop numbers in Korea. That's probably why the camp was still all tents except for the canteens. The day before we were due to leave a ceremonial parade was held with all the Korean squaddies there as well. After marching on to the parade ground the battalion formed up into a square with the Korean squaddies on one side. The C.O. now presented each Korean squaddie with a cigarette lighter with the Commonwealth divisions badge on it, as sold by our own P.R.I. The Padre then took over and it turned into a bit of a church parade with him reading a lesson and us singing hymns. I think this was a bit out of place as the Korean lads were mainly Shamanists and a few Buddhists.

There had been an incident earlier in the year between the Padre and a Korean squaddie we all called Milo. Milo was with the platoon attached to D company and could speak a little English. Although he held no rank he was obviously their religious leader. It had happened when the Padre was paying a visit to D company one day. It had always been the Padres practise to go round with a tin of cigarettes offering every one to every squaddie he met. He was offering the Korean lads one when Milo walked up to him and said, you f—k off you `poxy`. Apparently the Padre just walked away and to his credit didn't make a disciplinary issue of it. It's the sort of thing could have easily have blown up into an international incident.

On the morning of our parting we got haversack rations, the usual two rounds of bungy 'cheese' and two of prairie chicken 'corned beef' before being carted off to the railhead at Kaesong for the train. It was a day trip back to Pusan and the train passed through Seoul on the way. This was the first time most of us had seen the city centre, all be it from the train. It looked like there were some nice buildings there but anything would have been an improvement on the suburbs of Seoul. The journey back down to Pusan took a lot less time than it did coming and we were in Pusan for our evening meal. The battalion would embark for Hong Kong in the morning and although it had been an interesting year I don't think any of us wanted to spend another winter in Korea.

Chapter Thirty One

It was a bright sunny morning in early October and we were all lined up in companies on Pusan docks. There we stood with our weapons and kit bags waiting to board the troop ship.

My abiding memory is of an old biddy in a matron's hat and uniform gazing down at us from the ship. She looked a right miserable old sod, all old lace and vinegar. Songo turned and said to me 'I'm not going to get ill on this ship if she's in charge'. I think we all had the same sentiments. Each company was loaded onto the ship one squaddie at a time so the neutral arms commission could tick off on their clip board what weapons we were carrying. There was one weapon going on board that wouldn't be on their list and that was the old forty five pistol in Harold's kit bag.

Once on board we were divided up into groups of four, given a cabin number and a plastic token for our meal sitting. This was another ship that had been used for taking immigrants to Australia so it had been converted into family cabins. This arrangement was far better than the smelly old standees. It didn't take long for us to settle in and before night fall the ship was on its way out of Pusan harbour. I don't recall any one going up on board to wave Korea good bye. After spending the last twelve months living in tents and sleeping bags we were now living in the lap of luxury. That was until you arrived in the dining room and saw what got slapped on your plate. That brought us back to reality a bit quick. The boat had the usual facilities, duty free bar and a recreation room with the inevitable piano.

Battalion orders were posted and there would be no training under taken on boat during our journey to Hong Kong. Each company would have a muster parade after breakfast each morning for a roll call but this was probably just to check no one had jumped overboard during the night. Of course on our first one Jim had to weigh in his halfpenny worth didn't he? Jim had probably heard some squaddie calling the front of the ship the pointed end and was now going to put us right 'the front is the bow the back the stern, the left-hand side the port and the right hand starboard'. This prompted Corporal Martin, always one to wind Jim up to say 'is this looking from the pointed end or the blunt end of the ship'. This got the usual response off Jim of 'what are they doing for a village idiot while you're in the army Corporal?'

As we sailed south the weather got warmer and the East China Sea was calmer than when we had sailed up to Korea twelve moths ago. The ship got its daily visit by the American navy reconnaissance Neptune aircraft, although it was supposed to be watching China and not us. The ship was not full as it had only picked a few squaddies up at Kure before coming to Pusan but when we disembarked at Hong Kong it would pick the Welsh Regiment up. This was the regiment the Stafford's would be replacing in the New Territories. Apart from the morning parade and inspection, time was all our own and we made full use of it doing nothing.

It was on the sixth day that we got to Hong Kong and we had to find our boots out. The regiment disembarked company at a time and Support Company was the last. We loaded our kit bags on to a three ton lorry before being marched over to Kowloon railway station. Kowloon looked the same as when I left three years before, the only changes I could see was that the stuffed tiger advertising the Siberian Fur Store had gone, it must have escaped.

We had been told which camp we would be going to while we were on the boat; it would be the Birds Hill camp where I was stationed last time. The train ride up to Fanling was familiar and the only differences were the buildings by the station. They had now been turned into a bar called The Better Hole.

Bird's Hill camp was still surrounded by rice paddies but there had been a few improvements. All the barrack blocks had now been built and the corrugated tin latrines had been replaced with concrete ones. The toilets were still like the old earth ones with a trap door at the end so the Shit Bibby could get down to clean them out. It could put you off eating rice pudding for life.

Support company lines were just past the H.Q. offices at the entrance to the camp. Company office and stores were at the side of the road through the camp and our billets behind. Each platoon had two blocks each and even with that some of the beds were double bunks just to accommodate us all. Our block had a little garden in front with a flower bed and we looked down a hill to the carrier park and the paddies beyond. The company was given the rest of the day to settle in and sort our kit out, it would be all bull again now. The one good thing was we were keeping the new green webbing with the painted buckles so we would not need to Blanco it. We would be keeping the old belts and gaiters which needed blancoing for parades. The platoon soon got itself sorted out and settled in, the only surprise was on company orders that evening. Support Company had a new commanding officer a Major Simmons, Major Lowens our old C.O. was retiring. Old Lowens had been taken ill a few times while we were in Korea and he never looked very well at the best of times. He had been a prisoner of the Japanese during the last war and that had taken its toll on him.

On our morning parade we were introduced to our new C.O and he gave us the usual talk of what he expected of us. He then went on to tell us that all of us who had spent the last twelve months in Korea would get a payment of eighteen pounds. This was paid to us by the Korean government. This would be added to our credits and we should save it for our demob, and as he put it, not draw it out and take a flying f—k at the high spots in Nathan Road with it. After Major Simmons had finished the Sergeant Major took over to tell us he was going to smarten the company up a bit. Things had been a bit lack in Korea but from now on things were going to change. After we had fallen out we all went back to our billet where Captain Bow our platoon commander took over to explain what our training program would be. Before he got onto the training he explained that the young Chinese lads we had seen hanging about were house boys. These lads would make our beds and keep the barrack rooms tidy and for this service each of us would pay the lad one dollar a week. They would only do the house keeping and were not there to Blanco belts and gaiters. This was a big change from the usual army set up, something to do with employing local people according to Captain Bow.

The main change to the platoon would be the transport as we would now be back to using Bren gun carriers. Most of the drivers who had been with the platoon in Trieste were still in the platoon so there should be no problems. Training sessions on the M.M.G would be on going and we would shortly have some new squaddies joining the platoon as replacements. After this meeting the drivers would go down to the M.T with Sergeant. Bridge and Corporal. Stanley to sign out their vehicles. The rest of the platoon would draw the guns, check them over and do a bit of gun drill.

Within a week it was like we had been in the New Territories for months, the little barrack blocks were a site more comfortable than tents. The char wallah came nightly and first thing in the morning with his tea and bickies plus visits from the `sew-sew` woman to do our sewing, we were living in luxury.

One of our first priorities was to get our selves some civy shirts and trousers plus a pair of shoes to go out in. The shoes were the dearest part of it as you had to have leather lace ups in black or brown. Canvas, suede or `brothel creepers` (crepe soled shoes.) and they wouldn't let us out of the camp. You could get yourself togged up at the Contractors tent but he was a bit pricey. Best to wait until you could get down town. On Friday night Brownie and I had a stroll down to Fanling for a look around. The place was much the same as it was the last time I was there. The same couple of five dances for a dollar dance halls and the open air cinema and there was a new bar on the main street besides the one by the railway station. We called at the Better Hole, the new bar by the station, after touring Fanling. There was quite a crowd in and it looked a nice place, they did food as well as booze. It was run by a couple of middle aged English chaps and one of them was married to the Chinese lady serving at the bar. We slaked our thirst with a couple of bottles of San Miguel before making our way back to camp. It would be two or three weeks before we made it down to Kowloon.

The third week Support Company was Duty Company which meant we did the guard for that week. There were three guards, the camp, the ammo dump up Birds Hill and the Robins nest O.P on the hill overlooking Sha Tu Kok, spying on the Chinese army. I got picked for the Birds Hill detail. When we got up there on Monday morning there had been some changes since I was last there. The tents had been replaced with a couple of huts, one to sleep in and one for a cook house. The next surprise was there was a Chinese cook to do our meals. It was a good week up there and the woman with the bottles of Cola and chocky bars came up every day for those with the money to buy. Unlike the char wallah and the Watson's ice cream man she didn't run a strap book for obvious reasons. This would be the last time I would be on the ammo guard detail. Every time we were duty company in future I would be on the Robins Nest O.P detail. They had two huts up there plus the concrete bunker with binoculars to watch the Chinese. Unlike Birds Hill they didn't have a cook up there, well not until I got the job. I only did it three times before I was demobbed and being the cook you got your nights in bed, not the two hours on and four hours off in the bunker. I don't know why they bothered at night because you couldn't see anything. Like the old Low Wu O.P you had to write down in the book everything you saw so there were pages of useless information to read and keep us entertained.

The Regiment was soon back to normal with the parades on Saturday mornings.

The first one we did I had a job to get my self ready with me having to show half the platoon how to wind their putty's on their boots on hose tops. It was after this parade that a gang of us decided to go down Kowloon for the afternoon. After being checked we were smart enough to go out we walked down to Fanling station and caught the train to Kowloon. Me having been here before got the job of unofficial guide so we all splashed out ten cents and got the Star ferry over to Hong Kong and had a wander along the Victoria district. The old trams were still going backwards and forwards along the main road. We all called in the Cheery Ho club for a drink before catching the ferry back to Kowloon, they all wanted to see the delights of Nathan road. By now it was tea time but we were too busy to bother about that and as we walked up Salisbury Road past the Peninsular Hotel who should we run into but Dave and Wilf. They were on their way home for demob and the troop ship had stopped to take on some squaddies from Hong Kong so they were on shore leave. So we had to go in a bar for a drink. It was a Chinese run bar just in Middle Road but it was full of squaddies and navy chaps plus the usual working girls. They now all had little pink cards from some clinic to prove they were disease free or so they claimed, however it didn't seem to stop some the punters ending up with `blobby knobs`. Trade must have been a bit slow as they were offering a discount on a short timer. A happy half hour was spent with Dave and Wilf before we said our goodbyes and continued our tour of Nathan Road ending up in the Nine Dragons club. A good evening was had even if we had spent most of our money and we made it back to the station for the last train to Fanling. From now on if we were not on duty we would spend most of our Saturday afternoon and evenings down Hong Kong and Kowloon.

A few days before Christmas after our morning parade the Colour Sergeant announced that all squddies who had been in Korea last Christmas should report to the stores as we all had a parcel each. They should have reached us last Christmas but had been held up. All the parcels had mainly the same sort of thing in them, a knitted article like a scarf or a pair of socks and a paper back novel. I got a balaclava helmet with three feet of scarf attached to it and a guide to the best restaurants in the Swiss Alps. I still had the balaclava long after I got demobbed, I hadn't got the heart to throw it away. Some old dear somewhere had knitted it thinking it would help keep some poor squaddie warm.

The officer served us our Christmas dinner as was the tradition in the British army and I must have had some booze because I don't remember anything about the rest of the day. What I do remember was the news on Boxing Day that Corporal Stanley had been arrested by the Hong Kong police and was being held in the Kowloon jail. The word was that he had an altercation with one of the street girls. This was not unusual and he wasn't the first and certainly wouldn't be the last to get locked up over a punch up with one of the pros. The memorable part of this little incident happened. When Corporal Martin got Stanley's kit out to pack it he discovered Stanley's secret; there was a pile of women's knickers in the bottom of it, souvenirs of past exploits no doubt. Of course Corporal Martin fished them out and was waving them in the air shouting 'look what I've found!' Every one thought it hilarious and there were suggestions that Stanley probably wore them for special parades. Corporal Stanley was back the following day and he hadn't been charged. No one had the nerve to ask about the knickers as Stanley had always been a bit touchy. What ever happened down town couldn't have been much as Stanley remained Corporal. It was only a few weeks later that Harold Mayes got chucked in the Kowloon klink. He had taken the old forty five pistol we had in Korea down town with him and must have been flashing it around in the Y.M.C.A. Some one phoned the police and before Harold knew it he was surrounded by armed coppers. Harold wasn't as lucky as Corporal Stanley as we didn't see him again for a couple of weeks. When we did, Harold was a bit chastened; apparently Kowloon nick was not a great place to spend a holiday. He was put on company orders as soon as he got back and got seven days 'jankers' for his troubles.

The battalion had now settled down into usual regimental routine which we hadn't done since leaving Trieste. With the National Service squaddies who joined the platoon in the build up to the Korean trip now getting demobbed and new squddies joining us, gun training was going on for a period most days. Digging defensive positions in the hills was where we spent a lot of time. You could see it was a bit further forward from when I was last there in nineteen fifty one. The battalion did the grading tests in the spring, I hadn't done any since Germany but it was just the same; assault course, marching two miles in eighteen minutes then nine miles in two hours. It was up to the border at Sha Tau Kok and back for that one and then the rifle ranges to do our shooting. What ever I did I wasn't going to get any more pay as I was a five star private already. All the tests had been completed just before the monsoons came. It was back to the ponchos and soggy bush hats, mozzies, leeches, ringworm and the locals planting rice wearing their bamboo rain capes.

Chapter Thirty Two

In spite of the monsoons we carried on as normal although we didn't spend as much time digging in the hills. The battalion did manoeuvres to practice defending the colony which always seemed to me to be wishful thinking as there were the North Stafford's, The Argyle and Sutherland Islanders, the Kings Shropshire Light Infantry and a Battalion of Gurkers probably about three thousand men in all. A couple of miles up the road the Chinese had an army on the other side of the border, however things had quietened down a bit since the last time I was here and there was now a fence along the border. If the Chinese were coming they would have done it by now. It was on one such defending the colony scheme that I was detailed to drive a Brengun Carrier. I tried to talk myself out of it as I hadn't driven one since Trieste, but as Captain Bow pointed out I was down as being a licensed driver and anyway I wouldn't get locked up if I ran one of the locals over, I would just have to pay for their funeral. However once I'd driven it for an hour or so I was alright with it or so I thought. I was never asked to drive one again though.

As we got into the month of April extra battalion parades were the order of the day practising for the Queens Birthday parade. The North Staffordshire Regiment was the one chosen to fire the salute. When we came to practice firing the C.O called it a `wer des swar` or something like that. To do it you came to the high port position and loaded your rifle with a blank cartridge; then on the next word of command placed the butt of the rifle on your right shoulder with the muzzle pointing in the air, all in time with each other of course. When the order to fire came the first man on the left of the front rank fired his rifle. As soon as he had fired the next man fired and so on along the front rank down the middle rank and back up the rear rank.

Our normal uniforms of olive green with hose tops and putty's would be replaced by white ones which fastened up to the neck for this parade. All we wore of our usual uniform was our boots, belts and berets, we looked more like ice cream salesmen than soldiers. The battalion had several parades to practice on beforehand and the main concern was that we all had the rifles at the same angle when in the firing position.

On the great day we were taken down to Kowloon in our smart

white uniforms and lined up on Boundary Road. At the head of the line was the Navy, being the senior service, the Army was in the middle and the R.A.F detachment at the rear. The parade was called to attention slope arms left turn, the band strikes up with the regimental march (the days we went a gypsying) and off down Boundary Road we marched. We were halted in front of the dais and right turned and there was the Governor General and all the bigwigs; the governor, a one Sir Alexander Grantham resplendent in his cocked hat the plumes waving in the breeze and a macramé sample dangling off his shoulder. We did a present arms before firing the salute. The salute went off without a hitch except for a shot about two seconds after the rest had fired. With everyone facing the Governor and his gang only they would know who it was and they were too polite tell on him.. It was three cheers for her majesty next, the C.O. shouting hip-hip and the regiment holding our hats in the air shouting hooray before marching off with the band and drums going full blast. It seemed to have been a great success and by early afternoon we were back in camp handing in our ice-cream suits to the stores.

Now the Queens birthday parade was over it was back to playing soldiers again and a scheme was thought up by the bigwigs. It assumed that a Chinese warlord was attempting to take over the colony. They must have thought Chairman Mao was going to come mob handed. C company would act as the insurgents with their C.O Major Penrose known as Tusky to all and sundry, the war lord. The battalion did a few schemes but I think this one sticks in my mind due to the shear daftness of it. The M.M.G platoon would not be using our machine guns, for this exercise we would be lightening commandos, what ever they are. Togged in our battle order we were marched down to a place known as canopy corner, infamous for army lorry drivers losing the canopies of the backs off their Lorries on the overhanging trees down there. The platoon set up camp in a little wood by the village there and awaited further instructions. Sergeant Jones worked out a guard roster for the night and a meal was sent down for us from the main camp and we settled down for the night. At four thirty the next morning there was a stand-to called and Sergeant Jones tells us the platoon was to climb Tai Mo Shan and occupy the summit. This must be achieved as soon as possible to deny Penrose Pong the high ground. The mountain was about a mile to the south of us, three thousand feet high and we would be climbing the steep side so it would take us two or three hours. Breakfast would be brought to us at the top of the mountain. It was damp and misty as we set off and by the time we were about half way up Tai Mo Shan we had lost radio contact with our company. It was after eight o'clock when we finally made the summit and we were in the clouds. It was bitter cold and wet and with us squaddies sweating getting up here it's a wonder we didn't get pneumonia. Luckily there were a couple of tank scraps up there so we crouched in them out of the wind. Just before half eight Capt Bow along with our company Sergeant Major arrived in a jeep. There was a jeep track up to the summit from Lead Mine pass. Captai Bow was not a happy bunny as we were supposed to be in defensive positions, not hiding out of the wind. He did however have a couple of insulated gallon dixes with him, one of porridge and the other tea. Radio contact was established and there had been a change of plan. The platoon was to move down to Tai Po railway station and meet a mule convoy. This was only about five miles to the east of us and down hill all the way. Half way down we meet D Company and having drunk most of our water bottles dry tried to get them filled up again. The Colour Sergeant said as we were not on his ration strength we couldn't have any water and we had to wait until we got to Tai Po station and fill them out of their tap. The mules were already there waiting with a large Service Corps Staff Sergeant in charge although most of the muleteers were local recruits. C Company who was supposed to be the insurgents had set up a cook house there and our Colour Sergeant was with them. Our job was now to escort the mules back into the hills carrying C Companies lunch and ours as well. Why they needed so many mules I could never figure out, two would have been enough for what they had to carry. When they came to load one of the mules he started to buck and play-up. The Staff Sergeant gave it a right punch to the side of its head and the poor old mule buckled at the knees but he didn't play up anymore after that. Just as we about to set off our Colour Sergeant came over to us with two of the oblong tapered seven pound tins. The corned beef usually came in tins like that. There were never any labels on them but the stores new what was in them by the numbers printed on the tin. 'Take these with you and give them to me when we get back to camp' so, off we all went and after an hour reached our destination which was the remains of an old volcano. It had left a bowl of about fifty yards wide with a little hillock in the centre.

There perched on the hillock was Tusky himself. The food was dished out with Tusky's batman being first in line to collect Tusky's lunch. It was the usual stew and the batman had to pick all the bits of carrot out of it before taking it to him. Apparently he couldn't stand to eat anything that was red in colour. Each of the company platoons who had taken up positions round about were brought in one at a time to collect their lunch.

After lunch there was nothing to do only wait about until three o'clock when a radio message came. The platoon was to move south and take up a position overlooking Clear Water Bay and covering to the road to Kowloon. We ambled down there stopping for a couple of breaks on the way to have a smoke and watch the ducks. There was a duck farm or duck ranch as the sign called it from where they drove the ducks down to Clear Water bay for swim and it was amusing to watch. There were thousands of ducks and they would have two men in charge of a herd of a couple of hundred ducks. The ducks were controlled by the herders using long bamboo canes with a feather stuck in the end.

By the time we got to our destination it was six o'clockish. A Company were in the area but not being on their ration strength we wouldn't be getting any food off them. Although their Colour Sergeant not being a miserable old sod like D Company's did let us fill our water bottles. By eight o'clock there was no sign of any food for us and it seemed we didn't belong to any group so the two Sgts, Jones and Hardcastle who were in charge reckoned we should open one of the tins the Colour Sergeant had dumped on us. Every one thought it a good idea particularly as we could blame them if there was any come back. A tin was duly opened and it was salmon, so now we knew why the Colour Sergeant wanted it, probably destined for the Sergeant's mess. Sergeant Jones shared it out but between thirty of us and we got about a quarter of a pound each. Sergeant Jones had almost finished doling it out when an officer from A company appeared. He was a young fresh faced National Service Second Lieutenant and when he saw what we were doing he put his hand on his hips and shouted `you little piggy beasts' at us, he repeated his piggy beasts` rant before storming off. It was not long after the piggy beasts' incident that we got a radio call to pack up and move down to the Kowloon Road and wait by the Pagoda. A couple of three ton lorries came and took us back to camp. What the object of it all was we were never to find out and to cap it all I left my watch in the showers and when I went back for it, `there it was gone` No more was heard of the tin of salmon we ate, mind you the Colour sergeant couldn't do a lot about it could he as he was pinching it out of our rations! I asked at the company office the following morning if anyone had handed my watch in. They hadn't but the company clerk said he would get it put on the battalion orders. This he did but I didn't get it back.

A lot of the lads who had made up the platoon to go to Korea had now been demobbed so we were getting new lads joining the platoon. Every one got along well, I never remember much falling out. The only two I recall not getting on with each other was Pete and Skelding one of the carrier drivers. All this was about Pete's mother who would send him a parcel with a cake in occasionally and Skelding thought he should get some of the cake. However it didn't add up to much, Pete and Skelding just didn't like one another and that was that.

As the monsoon season passed, life was easy going and I was now in the last few months of my army service. Most Saturday afternoons were spent down in Kowloon. Saturday mornings would be Regimental Sergeant Major's parade and as soon as it was over you got your civvies on and went down to Fanling railway station. With me not having long to do I started looking at suits in the tailors shops in Kowloon. I had a made to measure single breasted woollen suit in a blue dog tooth material. I got measured up one week had a fitting the next week and collected it on the third week. It cost me one hundred dollars, (six pounds twelve and six pence). I was chuffed with it so much I went back and had a Frankie Lane suit made as well. This was a double breasted drape suit in dark blue gabardine. Before I was allowed out of camp wearing either of them I had to get the Company Commanders approval. I was marched before Major Simmons all done up in collar and tie. I got the O.K 'very smart Power, see if you can turn out like that when you are on parade in future'.

Things had quietened down along the border with China since I was there in nineteen fifty one. The battalion didn't do the border patrols any more but we still did what were called penetration patrols. It was now our platoons turn to do one. At the briefing given before we set off Captain Bow said it was a 'show the flag' exercise to remote villages out on the east side of the colony. The following morning we were taken down to Tai Po where we were joined by two officers from the Hong Kong police force. Sergeant Bridge got the map out and showed us where we were going, it was out beyond Plover Cove. It was not that far as it was only about ten miles to the east coast. An officer from the Intelligent Corps joined us and pointed out the people out there had more contact with people from main land China than they did with the colony. Before we set off a Corporal from the Medical

Corps with his bag of cures and bandages joined our merry band. The patrol managed to visit four villages during the day and each visit followed the same pattern. The village headman was main target he would be questioned by the Intelligence Officer with one of the policemen acting as interpreters. The other copper did the interpreting for the medical man dispensing Aspirins and advice. Each village had been issued with an old three-o-three army rifle and fifty rounds of ammo to defend themselves against pirates. Our job was to clean and oil them to keep them in working order. The ammo wasn't checked but if it was in a state like the rifle it wouldn't be a lot of good.

Then it was back to Tai Po to get a swim in before our evening meal arrived from camp. The Intelligent Corps bloke, the coppers and the medical man all vanished for the night and the platoon set up camp on the beach. Why we didn't go back to camp for the night I could never work out as it was only five miles away. The next two days followed the same patten, out in the morning and back to Tai Po for the evening. It had been interesting, as although it was only a few miles away it was another world, China as it had been for hundreds of years. I returned to camp minus my false teeth; I'd got a mouth full of water while swimming in deep water and had spit them out and they had sunk. I reported sick back at camp and the medical officer said if I wanted to replace them I would have to attend an inquiry as to how I lost them. This could well result in disciplinary action being taken against me. His advice to me was go to the Chinese dentist down Fanling since they would probably make me some new teeth for twenty bucks or so. This I did and they cost me twenty four bucks.

Chapter Thirty Three

It was now May and the battalion moved to the summer schedule which meant first parade would be at six o'clock in the morning and we would finish for the day at one o'clock unless you were on duty. With the warmer weather a lot of the chaps started to get the old Tinea rash between the legs and to avoid the trouble of reporting sick some squaddies had tried to cure themselves. They usually ended up in a worse state and had to go sick in the end. To stop this happening in the future the whole company would have their crotch inspected every week. This would take place at the Thursday pay parade and a drill was devised that took account of the army's usual concern for personal dignity. Pay parade was always held on the veranda of the first block overlooking the road. The drill was you marched up to the pay desk when your name was called, halted two paces before you reached the table saluted, pulled your shorts down then lifted up your scrotum with your right had so the officer could see between your legs. You then did an about turn and bent over (so he could view your behind) before standing up and pulling your shorts up. About turn, two paces forward and hand the officer your pay book with your left hand, draw your pay, salute, and fall-out. This little pantomime would go on all summer.

Towards the end of July a charity field day was held on the sports ground by the Kings Shropshire Light Infantry camp. This would be in aid of the Fanling Orphanage. An old English woman named Gladys Aylward was in charge of it. She seemed more concerned about breaking up the liaisons between the local girls and some of the squaddies than she was about the orphanage. I must say she didn't have a lot of success; Joe Brow in our platoon married one of them. What I could never figure out was who she was protecting, the girls or the squaddies. She had spent most of her life on missionary work in China until the Commies chucked her out in the late nineteen forties. A film was made about it called the `Inn of The Sixth Happiness`. The field day went off alright with a boxing contest and mule racing but I don't remember how much cash was raised.

The day following the field day we were all stretched out on our beds at about four in the afternoon when the bugler started blowing battle order on. My heart sank as I thought the Chinkie army was making a move and I only had a month to do. We all got togged up in battle order and went to draw our rifles. The Sergeant Major was there and told us we only needed our rifles, we wouldn't need to draw the M.M.Gs. The company was formed up and marched over to the parade ground on the other side of the Sha Tu Kok Road. No one had told us what was happening we were just formed up in our normal ranks. The battalion had been there a few minutes when a Rolls Royce car comes and out pops Field Marshall Harding, the army chief of staff. Everyone had to look twice as generals and the like were usually six feet tall or more but he was only just over five foot tall. He could walk in and out of his Roller without ducking his head. He gave the battalion a quick inspection then told us how well we all looked, got back in his Roller and vanished. So that was it and we got back to camp just in time for our evening meal.

I now only had another three weeks before I was due to go back for demob. I would spend a week of it down on the ranges at Sai Kung. The M.M.G platoon together with the mortar platoon would do some live firing exercises. It was a nice camp there and right by the sea so we were swimming at every opportunity. It was on the road just out side of the camp gate that I saw something that I'd seen a few times when I was here in fifty one - a woman at the roadside breaking stones to repair the roads with. She held the stone with her toes and cracked them using a two pound engineer's ball pain hammer on a bamboo cane. It was always women who did it. I don't know if it was some kind of punishment but it certainly wasn't much of a career.

The platoon had an easy week training but the show was going to be on Saturday. On the Thursday both the M.M.G platoon together with the Mortar platoon had a training session on the three point five rocket launcher. The last time we ever did any training on this weapon was over two years ago. Tomorrow we are going to actually fire it as the Yanks must have given us some free rockets. On the day we would be firing one rocket each at a rock about two hundred yards distance. It was all a bit informal as we were only in our shorts and bush hats. Sgt Jones was the first to have a go and when he fired it the connecting wires whipped back as the rocket launched and cut his back. It was 'all get your jackets on before you fire' after that. Every one had a shot including our company C.O Major Simmons. It was all a bit of an anti climax really. Gun crews for Saturday were selected and I hit the big time I was a number one in three section. I'd done every other job in the M.M.G platoon on many occasions but this was my first time in charge of the gun. On the day the Brigade Commander came to watch us perform, and he must have known I would be firing, the platoon had to move forward and set up the guns as though it was battle conditions. We crawled forward and set up the guns then it started to pour down with rain. It came down in rods and that's how it was all morning. The guns were firing across a valley at targets on a hill just above a Chinese village. It all seemed to go to plan and as we finished firing and pulled back, the Mortar platoon moved forward and took over our old positions to do their firing. The rest of the day was spent cleaning the guns and packing up ready to move back to Bird's Hill tomorrow.

On the Monday night when I was having a drink in the N.A.A.F.I Nipper Horton our company pay clerk came over and said he was sure the wristwatch the battalion Adjutant was wearing was the one I'd lost. Captain Pyke was our present Adjutant; he had been the Mortar platoon officer while we were in Korea and was an easy going sort of a chap. The following day after we finished for the day I went round to the H.Q offices and knocked on the Adjutants door. 'What do you want Power?' he asked, "has anyone handed a wrist watch in Sir?" I replied. "What's the watch like Power?" I said "a lot like the one you are wearing Sir!" "How do I know it's your watch?" he asked, I replied "because there is a number on the back".

Now after I had acquired the watch off Sgt. Jones I'd made note of the number in the back of my pay book. I told Captain Pyke the number and he took the watch off and gave it me back. I thanked him, saluted and gave a sigh of relief; it was easier than I thought it would be.

The day before we were due to catch the boat home I was down the H.Q offices again along with sixteen others. Four of us were from Support Company; Nipper Horton, Pete Boulter, a lad named Heath from the anti tank platoon and me. Heath had his left forearm in plaster, he should have gone sick but he was making good his escape while the going was good. All had to sign the official secret's act before we left Hong Kong. I couldn't imagine what secrets we were supposed to be party to. After we all signed, the second in command of the battalion, a brusque little major, came and told us that we should just go and not consider signing on again; there was nothing in this army for the likes of us! None of us had any intention of signing on again. John Rudd wasn't among us so he must have signed on again.

After breakfast the following morning we packed our kit and

handed our bedding into the stores. All of us had a case stuffed with clothes and presents that we had acquired while in Hong Kong for the family but I didn't have anything for friends and family, only my suits, shirts and fishing tackle.

The sixteen of us paraded in front of the guard room as instructed and were picked up in a three ton lorry and taken to Kowloon docks. The troop ship waiting was the Empire Asturias the ship that we had come out to Korea on two years ago. The ship wasn't due to sail until the following day so after our lunch a few of us went for our last walk around Kowloon and Hong Kong. Along with a couple of the lads from a rifle company, I went up the peak tramway. The legend is if you go up the peak before you leave Hong Kong someday you will return. The ship got underway next morning and as there were not many families on board we only got a few fire crackers to ward off the evil spirits. The Asturias was still a nice ship but the food was the usual swill, the only decent thing was that after the Singapore stop we got some watermelon.

Jobs were found for all us squaddies sailing home I think just to keep us out of mischief. I along with three others was to report to the Master of Arms. He was a nice old stick and said he didn't need us but had to follow orders so we would help with the baggage. It was only a nine until twelve job and all we did was every time the ship docked was sort the baggage to be unloaded and stack the baggage being loaded. Luggage not wanted on voyage was stored at the back and the wanted on voyage luggage was put where we could get at it. It was a great job as there was always a mug of tea for us at ten thirty and we spent most of our time sitting on the boxes smoking.

The Master of Arms did find us one afternoon job while we were crossing the Indian Ocean. Someone had been stuck down with appendicitis and they were going to operate on him. This was going to take place in a little room on deck; I think it may have been the officers' sitting room. We were placed on guard to stop anyone going near the room while the operation took place. It was over four hours before they came and told us to stand down. With no morning parades and no one in charge of us we were to have a nice trip. I only got off for shore leave twice - Singapore and Colombo. I didn't bother at Aden or Port Said so I was never going to see the women and the Donkey now was I?

Being September it was a nice cruise down the Mediterranean and we made the most of it. By the time we had reached Liverpool I was already late for my demob. The twenty seventh of September was my release date and it was the twenty eighth now. Customs gave us the customary going over and I had to show them all my fishing tackle before I could pass.

A lorry took us all over to Lime Street Station and we caught the train to Lichfield Trent Valley. A couple of the lads lived in the Lichfield district and had welcoming mothers waiting; Carl Arblasters mother was in tears when she saw him. 'Oh my son what have they done to you?' she cried. In spite of a month on the boat doing nothing we were still like whippets, well suntanned and fit as butcher's dogs.

It was gone four o'clock by the time we were taken back to Whittington barracks - too late to get demobbed today. I was told to go and draw some bedding for the night and report to the stores to hand the kit in at Ten o'clock tomorrow morning. All of us who lived within fifty miles or so of Lichfield didn't bother, we just went home.

When I got to Alice's she was surprised to see me although I had written and told her I was coming home. Our Bill was now lodging with Alice and he only had a single bed so I would spend the night on the settee. I paid Jeff Slater a visit later and he was pleased to see me - well he looked like he was. The next hour was spent yapping to Jeff and his wife Minnie and I told them I was getting demobbed tomorrow morning. Jeff asked me how I was getting back to camp and I told him on the bus. Jeff said 'don't worry about that I've got a car now and I will take you back'. He came and picked me up from Alice's in an old Lanchester car at seven thirty the next morning and ran me back to Whittington barracks.

I joined the chaps who had stayed the night at the barracks and had a bit of breakfast with them. Everyone had made it back in time to hand in their kit and we were all at the main stores by ten. The Q.M.S told us we would keep our second best battle dress uniform plus one pair of boots, two shirts, some underwear, a towel and a beret. Everything else we would hand in to the store and it would be checked off as we handed it in. Any missing items would have to be paid for. It was all going smoothly until I tried to hand in the long johns we had been issued with in Northern Ireland. The store men called the Q.M.S over 'these are not army issue' he said, so I explained when and where we got them.

"I've been in this man's army man and boy" he said "but I've never seen anything like them before, they're not on my list, so I don't want them" so I just left them on the counter.

Once the hand in was completed the Q.M.S called both Nipper and I to his office to explain that having served five years we were entitled to a demob suit. This couldn't be issued at Whittington and we would have to go to the depot in Surrey to be fitted with it. Alternately we could have a payment of twenty eight quid instead. Both Nipper and I chose the money and signed for it there and then. A Major showed up while we were still in the stores and wished us luck in Civy Street and said all moneys owing to us would be posted to us and that was that. We were now free to go.

With it being demob day Nipper and I together with a lad from Bloxwich splashed out and we got a taxi back to Walsall. We couldn't escape fast enough but forty years later we would all have given our right arms to do it all again.

Did I ever go back to Hong Kong? Yes - on October the first two thousand I was up the Peak watching the firework display over the harbour for China's National Day.

Lightning Source UK Ltd.
Milton Keynes UK
UKOW040627260213

206823UK00001B/17/P